Moire O'Sullivan is an accomplished mountain runner and adventure racer. In 2009, she became the first person to complete the Wicklow Round, a 100km circuit of Ireland's Wicklow Mountains run within twenty-four hours. She is married to Pete and is the proud mother of their two young sons, Aran and Cahal. While busy adapting to and learning about motherhood, Moire won Ireland's National Adventure Race Series in 2014 and 2016. *Bump, Bike and Baby* is about this personal journey.

BUMP, BIKE & BABY

MUMMY'S GONE ADVENTURE RACING

Moire O'Sullivan

First published in Great Britain by
Sandstone Press Ltd
Dochcarty Road
Dingwall
Ross-shire
IV15 9UG
Scotland

www.sandstonepress.com

The publisher acknowledges subsidy from Creative Scotland towards
publication of this volume.

ISBN: 978-1-912240-06-7
ISBNe: 978-1-912240-07-4

Cover design by Mark Ecob
Typeset by Iolaire Typography Ltd, Newtonmore
Printed and bound by Totem, Poland

To the two crazies, Aran and Cahal

Contents

1

Resistance

'Oh, look! Isn't she gorgeous?'

My friend has completely lost interest in what I am trying to say. Her attention is now solely on Niamh, who has just walked into the room.

Niamh used to be a kick-ass mountain runner, but lately she's been missing from the racing scene. One day she was competing, and the next, she was gone. Everyone assumed it was injury that had forced her untimely departure. We thought it must have been a serious muscle tear to make her disappear for so long. Back then, she was a formidable force. She used to bound up steep hills like a spring-loaded gazelle. She would stride down slopes no matter how treacherous the terrain. Now Niamh has barely the strength to carry the large plastic monstrosity anchored in the cradle of her arm.

Niamh disappeared around nine months ago. Now I know *exactly* what happened to her.

A fluffy pink blanket is wedged inside the industrial black crate Niamh is trying to transport. She manages to lug the contraption as far as ourselves, then drops it unceremoniously at our feet with obvious relief.

Mountain running is thirsty work. All that huffing and

puffing up and down hills can make a mountain runner crave liquid refreshment. After a particularly hard race on a warm summer's day, we mountain runners have congregated in the local village pub in the heart of Ireland's Wicklow Mountains. Under the auspice of prize-giving, we have descended on this fine establishment to cure our dehydration. And while we are busy knocking back our pints of beer and cups of tea, Niamh has come to pay a visit, but she has not come alone. Inside the car seat that Niamh was shouldering is the root cause of her being missing in action.

'A little girl,' my friend coos. 'Isn't she so lovely!' She bends down and gently pulls the blanket back a fraction. She reveals a tiny, reddened, scrunched-up face beneath a woolly baby bonnet. Its features begin to quiver as the warm pub air and stark neon lights flood its crash test carrier.

Oh God, it's going to start crying.

I look up in distress, hoping Niamh will do something to put the child at ease. But she looks far too tired to comfort her baby right now. Her eyes are bleary from lack of sleep. She has never looked this drained before, even after finishing long, arduous mountain races. Before, she stood tall and straight at starting lines, dressed head to toe in tight Lycra. Now her body hangs limp under baggy clothing.

What has this child done to her? And why has she chosen to give birth to a baby just when she was doing so well at our sport?

More mountain runners spot Niamh and start to congregate. They oh and ah at the little baby, who has now thankfully fallen back asleep. They hug and kiss Niamh, who has finally returned to the mountain running fold.

The arrival of these supporters and well-wishers give me a perfect excuse to escape.

I have no interest in babies, and I can't understand why someone would want one of their own. They can't talk, can't walk, can't feed or clothe themselves. It all seems like a lot of milk and shite to me. So the idea of standing around, congratulating Niamh and marvelling at her baby totally confounds me.

I also fail to comprehend why Niamh would agree to subject her body to pregnancy. Not only did she miss a full season of racing while her baby grew, but she also jeopardised her own return to peak performance post-pregnancy. I have heard too many stories of dodgy hips, caved-in cores, and wonky pelvises that render mummy running impossible. How could someone agree to risk all this, just to have a baby?

My query goes unanswered, because I dare not pose it to a soul.

My reluctance to ask such a basic question is not without reason. I am a thirty-six-year-old female. All around me, my friends are breeding. Society dictates that this is what I should also do, what I should explicitly want. My biological clock should be ticking. But when I see babies like Niamh's, I feel zero maternal pulse.

I have another problem: I am married. And my husband, Pete, wants to start a family. We've had a few months of trying to get pregnant, without success. So when I arrive home from my mountain race, I tell him all about the course and the conditions but purposely avoid mentioning Niamh and her infant. I know where such talk of bumps and babies will inevitably lead.

I cannot, however, avoid the subject forever. Only days later, it comes up, as if on cue.

'My sister's pregnant,' Pete says, as he coolly puts down his mobile phone. He has just finished his weekly catch-up call with his family. I am sitting on the couch, watching TV. I have no interest in what's on, but keep my eyes fixed firmly on the flickering screen.

'That's nice,' I say. 'How long's she gone?'

'Don't know. But she is due sometime in March.' He crosses the room and stands beside me. I freeze in anticipation of what is about to come.

'You know she's younger than me?' Pete says.

I nod, waiting for the tirade that has become the norm.

'For God's sake, Moire. I'm forty-three.'

Here it comes.

'I can't wait forever to have children,' Pete says. And just for good measure, he adds, 'Sure, you're not getting any younger yourself.'

I look up to feign offence. We've heard that a woman's fertility falls off a cliff after thirty-five. Mine has been free-falling for a whole year already. Our time is running out fast.

'It will happen, Pete,' I say, trying to calm the situation.

'But when? You promised me before we got married that we'd have children. You knew this was a deal breaker for me.'

It is a promise that I have lived to regret. It is amazing what you agree to when you are in love and having tonnes of fun as a couple. Getting married, being pregnant, and having children seemed a whole lifetime away. My promise to have children was based on the hope that I would see lots of babies born around me, and start wanting them eventually. But with that possibility fading fast, my faith is now with female friends who had declared themselves

4

distinctly un-maternal. 'It is different when they are your own,' is what they have all promised me.

Now more than ever, I need them to be right.

'Maybe we can't have kids,' I say. 'There are plenty of people who have fertility issues these days,' I hasten to point out.

Pete sits down. 'Then we'll get tested. We need to do whatever it takes to start this family.'

It takes all my powers of restraint to stop myself saying that we already have a family. There is Pete and I, and our dog Tom. And judging by the way Pete hugs Tom these days, the dog might as well be his little baby.

'Okay, okay,' I say. 'We'll work it out. I promise, we'll try harder from now on.'

Pete gets up from the sofa, patting my knee as he rises. We both force out a smile. He has been successfully pacified.

Little does he know that, despite the promise I have just made, I have ulterior plans. My friend, Paul Mahon, has just asked me to be part of his four-person team for the upcoming Cooley Raid Adventure Race. The route traverses several hundred kilometres of Northern Ireland's Sperrin Mountains and lasts for twenty-four hours. Teams need to be mixed sex in composition. Paul has already gathered together three lads: Peter Cromie, Adrian Hennessy, and himself. He needs a female member to complete his line-up.

Paul introduced me to the world of mountain running and adventure racing six years ago. He told me which races were worth doing and invited me on training runs and spins. I quickly grew to love mountain running. However, after a few unfortunate experiences, I concluded that adventure racing was not for me. But out of sheer loyalty to Paul, this time I agreed.

Training for an adventure race is not conducive to starting a family. It involves mountain biking for miles, mountain running for long hours, and kayaking in between. Such physical exertion leaves you with very little energy to do much else once you land back home. And as adventure racing is a team sport, you are expected to put in sufficient training and to turn up fit on race day.

So when I tell my husband Pete about my race plan, he is obviously miffed.

'When are you going to stop doing all this crazy sport,' he asks, 'and just settle down and have babies?'

But Pete knew exactly what I was like before we even started dating. I was training for the Wicklow Round when we met, a one-hundred-kilometre circuit of Ireland's Wicklow Mountains to be completed within twenty-four hours. He saw me training diligently every morning and racing every weekend. If he expects me to change now that we are married, he has another think coming.

'What about you?' I say, swivelling around to defend myself. 'Are you going to change once we've got this elusive family you keep going on about?'

Both Pete and I have day jobs as consultants for the international charity sector. It is how we originally met. Our work involves frequent overseas travel from our base in Ireland to developing countries in Africa and Asia.

'I know I'm going to be left here at home, holding the baby, while you're off on your foreign trips!' I exclaim.

Pete says nothing. He knows we haven't really considered what happens after any potential birth.

Since we got together, Pete and I have lived and worked in places as far-flung as Vietnam, Cambodia and Nepal. We enjoy eating out, drinking fine wines, and absconding on weekends away. Many of our friends and family have noted our lack of forward planning, and they know what our lifestyles are like. They are well aware how much I love my mountain running and adventure sports. They've heard I have just come back from running the Camino de Santiago across northern Spain in seventeen days, when most people walk it in five weeks. Very little in our current lives seems conducive to minding young children.

'We'll work it out,' Pete says, patting the dog, who has appeared out of nowhere. Tom knows he needs to be close by when Pete and I are arguing, which seems to be increasingly frequent these days.

Just as I set off for my adventure race, par for the course, Pete heads off to Cambodia for a week's work. So as he jets off to the humid climes of South East Asia, I drive to the race start in drizzling, autumnal rain along narrow rural roads crisscrossing the Sperrin Mountains.

'We have to go out fast,' our team leader Paul declares. All four of us agree. Looking around the start line, there is some serious competition. Not only have some of the best Irish teams turned up, but there is a group of foreigners in our midst. They have to be good if they are sponsored by Salomon and have travelled all the way from Denmark just to participate.

Other teams have similar plans to set a brutal pace. As soon as we start, everyone charges up the first mountain on foot towards the first checkpoint. We reach it first, but are quickly followed by the Danes.

'I thought that living in a flat country, they'd be useless on the hills,' Paul says. I pant back in agreement. The lads are all running so fast, I can barely match their speed.

I'll never keep up with this pace.

'Here, give us your bag,' Cromie says to me as we pelt

back down the hill. Cromie may be long and lanky, but he is as strong as a pack mule. My rucksack contains all the food and water I need for the next couple of hours. Its heavy load is surely the reason I'm struggling.

With the Danes now ahead of us, our race strategy has to change. 'Going out fast' changes to 'Follow those Danes'. It is a cunning plan: it means we can stop poring over maps and religiously following compasses, activities that expend endless amounts of mental energy, and let the Danes do all this hard cerebral work for us instead. We stay behind them for the next few hours while we trek up and over the trackless, barren mountains, watching and waiting for the Danes to make their move.

It is dark, cold and raining when our teams arrive at the bike transition. We are vying for the lead. My hands are too swollen to fit into my bike gloves. My shoes and socks are wringing wet from being immersed in cold bog water and mountain streams. But despite all these minor discomforts, our team manages to edge away from the elusive Danes.

Our lead is not to last. First, we take a wrong turn, then Paul's bike gets a puncture that needs repairing. Within a few hours, we have lost all sight of the Danes.

We cycle on through the night, along mountain tracks and country roads. After six hours in the saddle, we are all pretty tired and scruffy. Finally, we arrive at a checkpoint based at the Shepherd's Rest Inn near Draperstown. This checkpoint also contains a mystery task as part of the race: a spot of rifle shooting.

I have no idea how to fire a rifle, so I ask the owner of the shooting gallery to give me a quick lesson. It soon becomes apparent that my fellow teammates also have no clue. But being male, they dare not ask the man in charge. They fire pellets randomly at the discs in front of us. A potent mix of exhaustion and ignorance mean they register poor scores.

I, on the other hand, score five out of five. 'Sure what do ye expect?' says my teammate Cromie. 'She's from Northern Ireland.' Apparently growing up in the Troubles somehow imbued me with superior shooting skills.

I take the opportunity to nip to the Inn's loo once we are done with the rifles. Peeing on trails and behind trees is the norm in adventure racing, but I can't resist the allure of a proper indoor toilet while the guys work out where we're headed next. The pub is wonderfully cosy and dry compared to the wet, wintery weather I have left outside.

I find the Ladies, and scoot inside for a wee. It should just be a quick stop, but I hesitate, as I notice a smudge of blood on the toilet paper. It is not my time of the month. I shouldn't be bleeding like this.

I am visibly distracted when I return to my teammates, trying to work out what's wrong with me. Everyone is always out of sorts in the dead of night when adventure racing, so I totally blend back in.

We continue on, running and biking through the dark, arriving at Lough Neagh for the kayak section just as dawn appears. The Danes arrived at the kayaks an hour earlier and are the firm favourites to win. Our aim now is to claim the runner-up prize.

I sit in the boat and paddle away without speaking, summoning up all my energy to work out what's up with me. The boat floats on, but my stomach sinks when I recall reading recently about spotting between periods. It was on a pregnancy website. Something about when a fertilised egg fixes itself in the uterus, it can cause implantation bleeding.

The lake waters churn beneath me.

We get out of our boats and on to our bikes, and cycle to a mucky mountain. The driving rain and howling winds batter us as we climb towards its summit. From there we battle our way home and cross the finish line before twenty-four hours is up. We secure second place behind the dynamic Danes.

Though the race is over, I sprint back home to work out what's happening to my body.

A few days later, I call Pete. He is still on assignment in Cambodia.

'I think I'm pregnant,' I say to him across the crackling phone line.

'What? What did you say?' Pete shouts at me from the other side of the world. 'Wait a minute. Wait until I step outside and get a better signal.'

I wait for what seems like an eternity until I hear Pete's voice on the line again.

'I think I'm pregnant.' I try again, hating to have to repeat these horrid words.

'You think, or you know?'

'I know. I did a test.'

'Oh, that's great!' Pete says. He laughs to himself. 'That's so great.'

Oh God, I think I need a drink.

2

Denial

I reach for the bottle of red wine on the kitchen counter. I am well aware that drinking while pregnant is bad. But I am making an exception this time.

Because I am one of the few women who doesn't want to be pregnant.

I can't really be pregnant.

Oh God, I'm pregnant.

I slump down on the sofa, and pour myself a large glass. The alcohol slides down my throat with remarkable ease. It soon burns all talk of pregnancy from my brain. It anaesthetises me from the thoughts of what is about to come.

I know there are women who would love to be me right now. There are so many who desperately want a baby, but for whom it never comes. Am I a bad person for being unhappily pregnant, when others would do anything to be in my shoes?

Pete isn't even here to talk this thing over with. Typical husband, off on a business trip just when I need him most. Instead I am home, alone.

I don't even feel like picking up the phone and calling a select friend or family member. I am just not ready to talk to outsiders. They might do something terrible like congratulate me, with me unable to share in their unfettered excitement.

I am too numb to feel what I'm meant to feel about this awful news. All I want to do now is get drunk. I reach for the bottle to pour another glass.

But then I stop myself.

Even if I despise the idea of being pregnant, I have to be responsible. Getting drunk might do untold harm to the baby growing inside of me. I would never forgive myself if I did something now that would hurt this other person.

I pick up my phone and start to do some research. '*Drinking alcohol,* especially in the first three months of *pregnancy,* increases the risk of miscarriage, premature birth and your baby having a low birth weight.' Well, that's pretty conclusive.

I put the bottle and glass away.

Instead, I dial the number for my local doctor and make an appointment to see her. Then I resolve to do the right thing, and be a responsible patient.

Two days later, I am at the surgery waiting to see the doctor. I feel like a fraud. I am not sick, like all the other patients who are lining the waiting room walls. But apparently I should seek medical attention, given my current situation.

'I think I'm pregnant,' I tell the doctor as soon as I sit down. She is only the second person I've told thus far.

'Congratulations.'

'Thanks,' I mumble, hoping I sound convincing.

'You will need to book an appointment with the midwife when you are twelve weeks along.' Our calculations put me at five weeks, so I have still a way to go.

'So, how much exercise can I do now that I am

12

pregnant?' I ask, cutting straight to the chase. I have no idea what I can or cannot do. This whole pregnancy thing is totally new to me.

'Well, if you haven't run a marathon before, you probably shouldn't start now.' She swivels around to her computer and types some details on to the screen. I want to stop her.

'But,' I say, needing more info, 'I was doing slightly more than marathons before I got pregnant.'

'Walking and swimming are great for expectant mothers,' she replies. 'And stop if you are ever feeling tired.'

I want to ask another question about fitness, but a huge lump has appeared in my throat. The doctor interprets my silence as acceptance, while I fight back the tears welling up.

'What about my work?' I say, miraculously finding my voice. It has an added tremor to it now. I don't think I can cope. 'I have a couple of weeks in Ethiopia already scheduled. I am meant to leave in a fortnight.'

The doctor's fingers stop typing. She spins her seat around and stops dead in front of me.

'Can't you cancel?'

'No,' I say. 'No, it's not possible. I've signed the contract and everything.' I am stunned that she would even make such a suggestion. I have lived and worked in developing countries for over fifteen years. Colleagues of mine have conceived and given birth while entirely living abroad.

And sure, African women have babies all the time. How else would the continent be populated?

'I assume you know there are obvious risks.'

If this doctor could wrap me up in cotton wool for the next nine months, I swear to God she would. First she puts a downer on my sport, and now she wants me to stay put.

'First, there is malaria to consider. If you catch that during the early months of pregnancy, there is a significant risk of miscarriage.'

She pauses for effect, but I refuse to react. I have always wanted to go to Ethiopia. How could she dare threaten my travel plans?

'Then there is the question of hygiene and food poisoning,' she continues. 'You need to be really careful to avoid parasites, as they can also affect the pregnancy.'

I am so used to getting food poisoning on my travels that I am probably immune by now, and I have never caught malaria despite years of working in remote African and Asian mosquito-ridden climates. How likely is it really that I will be infected at this stage?

'I am sure it will be fine,' I say.

She turns away slowly, and starts to tap again on her keyboard. 'You'll need to take malarone if you are travelling to malaria-prone areas,' she says, handing me a prescription. 'And you will have to increase your daily folic acid intake from four hundred milligrams to five micrograms when you are taking it. Malarone blocks its absorption.'

I win. I am going to Ethiopia.

I am convinced, however, that Pete is colluding with my doctor.

'Do you think it's wise to still travel?' Pete says, just back himself from Cambodia.

'So you're allowed to travel for work, and I'm not?'

'Well, I'm not the one who's pregnant.'

'Yeah, well, fine,' I say, annoyed by this discrimination. 'Listen, it will be okay. I will take the malarone, be careful with what I eat and drink, look both ways

14

crossing the road, won't talk to strange men, etcetera'.

Pete folds his arms. My attempt at humour has failed to lighten his mood.

'Look, Pete, I am taking this thing seriously. Sure haven't I stopped drinking alcohol?'

'I think drinking wine and contracting malaria are on slightly different scales, Moire.'

But there is no talking sense into me now. I need to find myself an ally.

'Okay, if it helps resolve this issue, I'll ask Linda what she thinks,' I say.

Linda is the Country Director in Ethiopia for the charity that I will work for. She was the one who hired me before all this pregnancy mess. Linda and her husband, Phil, have both lived abroad and worked for charities for many years. They also have two young children.

'All right,' says Pete. 'If Linda thinks it is safe enough for you to go, then I'm okay with it.'

I email Linda within seconds of our conversation and give her my pregnancy update. She is wonderfully pragmatic. 'So long as you are happy with the medical advice and the doctors are happy for you to travel, then it is all fine with us,' Linda writes me back. She also informs me that I will be primarily working in Addis Ababa during my stay; because the capital is above two thousand metres in altitude, it is recognised as malaria-free.

My conversation with Linda puts both Pete and I at ease. It also makes me realise that, if I am to survive these next nine months, I need to find like-minded women who I can talk to, and who lead similar lives to myself.

Eight days later, I take an early morning flight out of Dublin, and with a quick transit through Amsterdam, I arrive in Addis Ababa. It is dark when I step out of the airport and I struggle to find my prearranged ride. My mobile phone doesn't work and the taxi drivers don't speak English. God, it's good to be back in Africa, with all its idiosyncrasies.

I eventually find my driver and arrive at the charity's guesthouse late that night. I am shattered from the travel and quickly hit the sack.

Linda is bright and bubbly when I meet her at the charity's office the next morning.

'Hi there,' she says. 'Great to see you! Did you have a good trip?' Linda and I worked together in Nepal four years ago. I am looking forward to catching up.

'Good, thanks,' I reply. 'All things considered.'

'It's great that you were able to make it,' Linda says. 'And don't worry about anything. If you're not feeling well or need a break, just say and we'll arrange it.'

I flush with embarrassment. I can't believe people have to make allowances for me already, at this early stage.

'Thanks, but I'm grand. Six weeks in and I'm feeling totally fine. No morning sickness or tiredness or anything.'

Years of running and biking have made me very aware of my body. I am certain that being fit for so long will make this pregnancy a doddle.

'Good for you!' Linda says. 'I was going to bars, drinking beer and eating peanuts for weeks before I realised I was pregnant with number two.'

I settle in quickly and set to work, reviewing documents and conducting interviews. Though most of this assignment will be carried out in Addis Ababa, I also need to travel outside of the capital to do rural field visits. The charity works in Wollo Province in northern Ethiopia and

Wolayita Zone in the south. I must visit both locations to successfully complete the mission.

We set off bright and early the next morning to travel the long distance to the northern city of Dessie in Wollo. I am accompanied by one of the programme managers, Zehara, and a local driver.

I watch the countryside unfurl outside the car window as we drive for several hours. We pass cultivated fields of green and brown, dotted with grass-roofed farmers' mud huts.

It is past midday when we stop at a local café on the roadside.

'Coffee?' Zehara asks.

'Absolutely!' I reply. I am totally addicted to the drink.

Ethiopia is considered to be coffee's birthplace. Its highlands cultivate some of the best-quality Arabica beans in the world, and even in the remotest rural area, you can still find an excellent cup.

'Macchiato?' Zehara asks. I nearly choke with excitement. Ask for a macchiato in Ireland anywhere outside Dublin or Belfast, and all you'll get is a blank look. Now I discover that in the middle of nowhere in rural Ethiopia, a macchiato is the norm. I salivate, as they serve up a small cup of potent coffee, ready to blow my mind.

'Another?' Zehara says, as she sees me downing its contents in one. Much as I want to order not just another, but several, I know I am not allowed.

Before leaving for Ethiopia, I had researched what I am allowed to eat and drink as a pregnant lady. The list was long, and most of it not applicable to me; I don't like liver, and I despise mouldy cheese. But what stood out most were the limits set on coffee. Apparently I am now meant to restrict the amount of caffeine I consume. The recommended amount for pregnant women is two hundred milligrams a day, the equivalent of two mugs of instant coffee.

I don't drink instant coffee. I drink proper coffee. Proper *strong* coffee, to be precise. I think I have just blown my weekly limit with this single macchiato.

I get back into the four-wheel drive, buzzing with caffeine. It makes the day-long journey to our destination all the more pleasant. Deeper and deeper we drive, into the Ethiopian countryside. Soon I see women bent double in empty fields, digging the dry earth into furrows. Babies are strapped to their backs with coloured cloth. These infant loads shudder with every hoe strike their mothers make. I watch as older children herd gaunt cows and sheep along the roadside. I wonder if I could ever cope being a woman and a mother in Ethiopia.

I am relieved when we finally arrive in Dessie after a dusty day's travel. I am looking forward to getting out into the field and finding out more for my assignment. But when I wake up the next morning, I am not feeling the best. I figure the car ride must have taken it out of me, as long journeys sometimes do.

It is only when I meet my colleague Zehara for breakfast that I know that something's up. We are grabbing some food in a local restaurant before we head to the charity's regional office. Zehara has already placed her order by the time I arrive. The waiter soon appears with Zehara's breakfast and sets it down on the table.

'What's that?' I ask, trying to sound polite.

'Avocado shake,' she replies. 'Want to try some?'

The green gloop in the glass makes me feel distinctly queasy. I am normally up for sampling local cuisine and I

18

am huge fan of avocados. But for some reason, today my stomach is pleading for leniency.

'Do they have plain bread?' I ask. 'And maybe some coffee?'

Zehara passes no comment as she orders my bland meal. I just hope she is not offended by my rejection of her own breakfast selection.

We spend the day in the countryside, visiting women's groups and co-operatives, inspecting farmland and watershed management schemes. The hot sun and pot-holed roads tire me slightly, but the interesting work distracts me from this fatigue.

We return to Dessie, and I agree to meet with Zehara later to share an evening meal. I am starving after the day's excursion, and am looking forward to some proper food. Again she brings me to a local eatery, to sample authentic Ethiopian fare. After Zehara speaks at length to the waiter in Amharic, I wait to see what she's ordered.

He soon returns with a large flat dish covered by a white spongy pancake, topped with pastes of different sorts. On one side, there is some raw meat that I assume will be cooked at a later stage.

Dinner is served.

'There's a basin in the corner,' Zehara says. 'We can wash our hands over there.' I get up and scrub my hands, then dry them meticulously. I don't want dirt or water to infect me, or the baby, while I eat my dinner.

I return to discover this meal has no cutlery. The food is instead shared off this communal plate, via a free-for-all. I hope Zehara has been as fastidious as I when washing her hands and nails.

'This is called *injera*,' Zehara explains, pointing to the white flatbread on the plate. 'And these are different types

19

of meat and vegetable stews,' she says, gesturing to the brown and red blobs dotted on top of it.

Taking her right hand, she tucks in, and indicates that I should do the same. I snatch a corner of *injera*, scoop up some stew, and pop it in my mouth. The sour and fiery tastes overwhelm me. Delicious! I tear off more and more, until the plate is nearly drained. Zehara gestures to the waiter and he brings us an entire refill.

'When will they cook the meat?' I ask, referring to the plate of flesh on the table.

'Cook?' Zehara says. 'Oh no,' she says, realising my error. 'You eat it just like this.'

My thoughts catapult back to the day at the doctor's, when she warned me against food poisoning and parasites. If I wanted to infect myself, and my foetus, this would be the perfect way to do it.

'Try some,' she says. 'It is a traditional delicacy.'

'Thanks, but no thanks,' I reply, hoping not to offend. I am willing to take certain risks while pregnant, but contracting salmonella isn't one of them.

I wake the next morning, with avocado shakes on my mind. But this time the thought of green gloop for breakfast makes me want to puke. Even the idea of coffee and plain bread is making me feel unwell. It must have been all the *injera* and spicy stews last night that is making my stomach churn.

I feel particularly sorry for myself. I am hungry, yet the thought of food revolts me. There is no way this can be morning sickness though, as I feel this way for the whole day. I am also tired, but I'm certain this is due to the long travel days as opposed to anything pregnancy related.

I am feeling especially wretched at one point when we call into one of the charity's rural compounds. Outside, the land is brown and barren, parched from the scorching sun. Inside, local women are queuing around the compound walls.

'There are food shortages at the moment,' Zehara explains to me. 'They are here to collect flour and cooking oil donations from our emergency supplies.'

I notice a young woman standing in the queue, holding a toddler by the hand. I look again and see her swollen belly. She is also with child.

My cheeks flush with shame, thinking how I've wallowed in self-pity all day. I don't have to worry about feeding another child. I don't have to walk for miles under the hot sun just to feed my family. I have all the food and drink I want. I have all the medical help I need now that I am pregnant. How lucky am I, how spoiled I have become.

I return to Addis Ababa, chastened by what I have seen. I resolve to get on with having this baby, to do the best I can for it.

It's the weekend, so I decide to take some time off and treat myself after roughing it all week in the bush. I find out there's a spa in downtown Addis Ababa.

Over the last couple of days I have noticed some unexpected growth. In particular, my nails have begun to sprout. Before, they were short and brittle, but now they resemble creepy monster claws. Oestrogen is coursing through my body, causing everything it finds to grow. I book myself into the spa to sort out this hormonal inconvenience.

I ease back in the comfy recliner that the kind spa lady has given me. She hits a switch, and suddenly it jumps into relaxing massage action.

'Manicure and pedicure, please,' I say, pitying her

21

already. She practically needs a bolt cutter to tame my unruly nails into submission.

As I sit there receiving all this soothing care and attention, I feel emotions beginning to well. For the last few weeks, I have tried so hard to continue on as normal, as if this pregnancy won't change a thing. But now I have to admit that I was lying to myself. There is still no sign of the slightest bump, but already my body is no longer my own. My body is lethargic. My stomach is rebelling. My hair and nails are going through a growing frenzy. I can't believe I'm in such a mess when I'm less than a quarter through this pregnancy.

I wonder to myself how Pete is coping with the impending stress of fatherhood. I find out soon enough, when I get a call from him at midnight a few nights before I'm scheduled to return home.

'Moire, Moire!' he shouts down the phone, as if I can't hear him calling all the way from Ireland. But I also know he shouts out loud when he is very drunk. It's a trick he taught himself in his youth when he used to frequent rowdy pubs.

'Pete, I hear you!' I say, shaking myself awake. 'Why are you calling at this hour? Is something up?'

'It's your father!' he shouts.

Oh God, what's happened? What's wrong?

'He made me go drinking,' Pete stammers. 'Oh God, I'm so drunk.'

My dad is in his seventies. He is still strong and fit for his age, and can be very persuasive when he wants.

'Pete, go home,' I say.

'I can't,' he says, holding back a sob. 'I'm going to be a father!'

'Oh no, you didn't tell them, did you?' I was going

22

to wait for the first trimester to finish before giving my parents the news.

'No, no, I—'

The phone goes dead.

'Pete, PETE! Where are you?' It is now my turn to shout down the phone line.

'Moire? Moire, is that you?' This time it's a female voice.

'Mum, is that you? Why have you got Pete's phone?'

'Oh, hello, dear. How is Ethiopia?' My mother hasn't understood I am about to freak out with the sudden disappearance of my husband.

'Mum, where's Pete?'

'Oh, he's just fallen over,' my mum says, as if this was totally normal. 'He dropped his phone and I was going to give it back, but then I heard your voice. Is it true that he's going to be a father?'

This was not how I planned to convey the news of their impending grandchild.

'Mum, can you pick Pete up and bring him home? I'll be back in Ireland in a couple of days.'

She puts Pete back on the phone.

'I love you, Moire,' Pete slurs. 'I miss you,' he says, before abruptly hanging up.

Well, at least I know he cares.

I start to feel a bit better before I'm due to leave Ethiopia. So I join a weekend running club to go for a little canter. We meet up in town and travel to the outskirts of Addis Ababa. There we jog along meandering trails, through hilly forests and brush-filled fields. Though the pace is quite sedate, I struggle to keep up. I find my lungs unable to deal with the city's high altitude. Or perhaps my breathlessness is yet another random symptom of being bloody pregnant.

When the runners invite me to join them for beer and raw beef afterwards, I reluctantly yet politely decline, without revealing my real reason. It seems that pregnancy is curtailing every aspect of my life, even before having this damn baby.

I think it's time I go back home and deal with this situation.

3

Acceptance

I arrive home in Ireland, trying hard to accept my pregnancy predicament.

Running in Ethiopia was hard. I felt tired and sick and breathless. How will I cope when I actually have a bump to lug around with me as well?

I am very aware, however, that keeping fit is paramount. Pregnancy, labour and birth are apparently so much easier if the mother-to-be keeps active. But in terms of what to do, how much and when, I still absolutely have no clue.

I start searching for information, eventually finding some online articles that give me clearance to run. But when I look to see how hard and how far I can push myself, the authors refuse to provide specifics.

It depends how fit you were before.

It depends on how hot the weather is.

It depends on how pregnant you are.

It depends on how you're feeling that day.

I am so frustrated by this dearth of concrete guidance. Though I always strive to be self-reliant, I need to reach out to someone, anyone, who has lived through and survived this pregnancy ordeal.

I decide to contact fellow adventure racer and brand-new

mother, Susie Mitchell. A mutual friend had introduced us via email just before I got pregnant. As soon as I tell Susie that I am now expecting, she kindly offers assistance. I am sure she will understand what I am going through, and provide me with some solid, prescriptive advice.

'Oh God, it's so frustrating, isn't it?' Susie says when I meet her for the first time. Susie is tall and athletic, with long blonde hair tied back in a ponytail. Despite her steely appearance, she sports a warm smile and a friendly manner that puts me right at ease. We are meeting in the national library in the heart of Dublin City. Our location forces us to speak with hushed, secretive words.

'When I got pregnant, I looked everywhere for some practical tips on how to stay fit,' Susie says. 'I am a vet by profession, so I needed any advice to be backed by scientific proof.'

'Any luck?' I ask. I don't have the energy or brainpower to engage in any extensive research like Susie did. I just want to be told what to do and what to avoid, and to just get on with it.

'I suppose you could call it luck,' Susie says, leaning a little closer. I feel like she is about to divulge the where-abouts of the Holy Grail. Could it be lying on these dusty bookshelves around us, waiting to be found?

'I finally tracked down a Dutch researcher who did a study on the benefits of exercise during pregnancy,' Susie says, revealing the extent of her mission. 'He gave me two bits of decent advice.'

I grip the wooden table tightly.

'Number one: listen to your body.'

I nod slowly. I think I understand.

'Number two: avoid sports with a risk of blunt abdominal trauma.'

Susie searches for my second nod. Instead I am staring blankly back at her.

'Don't take up kick-boxing.'

I have found the Holy Grail. 'So, that's it?'

'Pretty much,' Susie replies.

'Makes sense,' I say, once I've had time to digest her palatable suggestions. 'I suppose I've been listening to my body for ages, what with all the training I've done over the years.'

'I am sure you're finding that your body is doing strange things at the moment,' Susie says. 'You're just not too sure how to react to them.'

'Exactly!' I scream. I feel like lunging across the table and giving Susie a big bear hug. Suddenly I remember that we're in a library and I don't know Susie well enough for close physical contact. 'Like I can normally jog along quite easily at ten kilometres an hour, at a heart of rate of around one hundred and fifty,' I say, finding it hard to contain my excitement. 'Now if I attempt that pace or heart rate, my lungs feel like caving in.'

'That will be the progesterone,' Susie says, delving swiftly into her medical compendium. 'That hormone increases your breathing. It's to make sure your baby has a good supply of oxygen and that you don't overheat yourself.'

'So how hard can I go?' I ask, not sure if I want to know the answer. From out of nowhere, I feel real fear; fear that I may have already damaged my baby from the running and adventure racing I've recently done.

'Probably best to just use the "perceived effort" scale,' Susie says, without batting an eyelid. 'Think about a continuum of one to twenty, where one is easy and twenty is really hard. Fifteen is about as hard as you should go.'

'Thanks, Susie,' I say with some relief. In the space of a few minutes, she has helped me more than all those endless hours of Internet searches.

'The problem I had was that I discovered I was pretty good at track cycling just before I got pregnant,' Susie says. 'I spent the whole nine months worrying that I wouldn't be competitive once the baby was born.'

'I know what you mean,' I say. 'I have seen a fair few girls from mountain running who simply disappear once they have children. Or if they do return, their results just aren't the same.'

I dare not tell Susie that my deepest fear is that I will become one of them.

'To be honest, I shouldn't have worried,' Susie says, flashing a wide, triumphant grin. 'Just six weeks after the birth, I won an Irish National track medal.'

'No way!'

'I'm serious,' Susie says. 'I managed to win a World Masters title four months after Tori was born.'

'But how?'

Her claims are at odds with everything I know about pregnancy thus far.

'I think I benefited from a bit of a post-partum boost!' Susie says, shining with pride. I bask in her glow for a moment. 'There are a number of physiological changes that happen during pregnancy,' Susie starts to explain. 'Your ribcage expands to help with breathing. And your heart's chamber capacity increases, so it can hold much more blood. This means your muscles can be supplied with oxygen much more efficiently.'

'So you are effectively blood doping,' I say, before quickly clarifying, 'but in a legal way?'

'Well, if you consider all the negatives, like weight gain

28

and loss in fitness while pregnant, a little physiological boost probably can't hurt, can it?' Susie says.

For the first time in a long time, I find myself smiling. At last, I have found a silver lining.

'But remember, it won't last forever,' Susie says, as she pops my party balloon. 'You'll have the gains for about a year before your system returns to normal.'

Twelve months of natural doping? Have I found an advantage to this whole pregnancy thing at last?

'So what type of exercise did you do when you were expecting?' I ask, as I start to formulate my plan. I'm going to get fit, really fit, after this baby is born.

'I actually spent a lot of time in the gym, weight training if you can believe it.'

'That must have been a sight,' I say. 'A pregnant woman squat lifting!'

'Totally! Especially when I was overdue by two weeks and was still pumping iron,' she explains. 'I actually lifted a personal best of one hundred and seven kilograms when I was seven months pregnant, thanks to all the extra testosterone. I've not got even close to squatting that weight since.'

Susie is a slim, slight lady, not exactly what I would term a bodybuilder. But if she's a track cyclist, she is probably hiding a pair of rock-hard thighs underneath the library desk we're sitting at.

'The only reason I kept going to the gym up to the delivery was that I was afraid of going into labour while out on my road bike.'

'Road biking?' I say. Now there's an idea. My doctor had already informed me that walking and swimming up to my delivery date was okay. But she never prohibited me from exercising on two wheels.

'Sure I biked right up to my due date,' Susie says proudly. I am so jealous of Susie. She is totally amazing.

'But was it . . . safe?' I ask, surprising myself with my caution.

'As long as you're careful, you should be fine,' Susie says. 'Like no riding on the roads if there's frost or rain.' I figure Ireland's cold and wet weather might hamper my spins, but I'm sure I'll find a workaround.

'Probably best not to ride in groups in case of any crashes,' Susie continues. 'If you avoid groups, you can also choose your own pace and route, so you can avoid serious hill climbs and scary descents.'

It all sounds logical, but still pretty conservative. But given that Susie has gone through all of this herself just lately, I am willing to give her the benefit of the doubt.

I thank Susie profusely for all her help, and leave her in peace to do her library work. Anyhow, I've got stuff to do, like find myself a road bike.

I decide to go and buy one before there's the remotest sign of a bump. I don't want to have to waddle into a bike shop and have a salesman stare at my midriff while I ask about chain-rings, pedals, and cranks. I'm also afraid he'd refuse to sell me one on health and safety grounds.

I search out my adventure-racing teammate, Peter Cromie, who just happens to own a bike shop.

'I need some new wheels,' I tell Cromie. 'A road bike, to be precise.'

'Not a bother,' he says, leading me into a room packed with bikes of different shapes, sizes and weights. They all look so tantalising, but I have no idea which one to choose.

'I've got two grand to spend,' I say, deciding to be pragmatic. 'Which one do you recommend?'

Cromie leads me over to the ladies' bikes, which already limits my selection.

'This one will do the job,' Cromie says, getting straight to the point. 'Carbon fibre, women-specific size, and Shimano Ultegra group-set.'

'Perfect,' I say. 'Does it come in pink?'

Cromie decides to ignore my question, and suggests I take it for a spin instead.

I wobble slightly as I balance on the saddle and try to change its gears. But once I get it going, I marvel at its speed. I race down the high street, blowing the pedestrian lights. I swoosh around the roundabouts as if on a merry-go-round.

'I love it,' I exclaim as I pull up outside the bike shop. Cromie knows he has a sale. 'Just please don't tell my husband how much I've spent on it,' I say.

It is still winter when I take my bike home and decide to go for a proper ride. It is cold out, but no frost, so I'm at least following Susie's advice. The only problem is that I don't know anybody to go biking with, so I have to go on my own.

'Will you be all right?' Pete asks, as I give my tyres a quick pump. He is standing over me, all concerned, as I do my final checks before heading out.

'Of course I will,' I reply, though I'm a little sick with nerves. I've got brand-new clip-in pedals and I'm still not used to the strange brakes or gears. 'I'm just going towards Carndonagh and back. Should be home within two hours.'

I give him a quick peck on the cheek and wheel my bike out the door.

I am less than five kilometres down the road when I feel the rear wheel slowly deflate.

Feck, that's embarrassing. Good job I brought a spare inner tube.

I stop the bike on the roadside and flip it over on its handlebars and saddle. That's how mountain bikers usually repair their wheels. I get out three levers, and try to claw off the tyre.

Oh my God, this thing is on tight. My mountain bike tyres are wide and spacious, and I can pull them off the rim with my bare hands. But now I've discovered that road bike tyres are thin and skinny, sticking like limpets on to the wheel rim.

Eventually I manage to remove one side of the tyre and extract the tube from inside. There's no visible damage to the tyre itself, so I quickly set about replacing the tube. I have to work fast as my fingers are now freezing, the cold winter weather trying to foil my biking plan.

Replacing the tyre with its new inner tube inside is easier said than done. I try to push it on with both my thumbs, until blisters form on both pads. Then I use the levers with brute force, until I come close to snapping all three. Eventually, the tyre agrees to comply, and everything is back in place.

All I need to do is fill the tube with air, and I'm on my way. I press the pump and the air goes in ... then it comes out again.

No, no, no, air that's pumped in stays in. I push more in, but there it is again, that bloody hissing sound.

I am standing there, totally bereft, when two male cyclists breeze past. I must look like a damsel in distress, for they halt their trusty steeds, and come and have a look.

'I've just put a new tube in,' I say, trying to appear somewhat competent.

'You must have got a pinch flat,' one says. 'Often

happens when you force a tube in and it nips itself against the rim.'

I don't have another spare. Damn it. I didn't want it to come to this. 'I suppose I better call my husband.'

At the mention of another male, they quickly remount their rides.

'Next time you need to change a tyre, best if you don't flip over the bike,' the other says before leaving. 'You'll damage your bike computer on the handlebars.'

Having bestowed their wisdom upon me, they cruelly cycle off.

I am mortified when Pete pulls up in our car less than five minutes later, yet ridiculously happy to see him. I need rescuing as my sweaty clothes and my oil-stained hands have frozen solid from standing still on the roadside.

'Sorry,' I say, throwing my bike into the boot. 'Got a puncture I couldn't repair.'

'It's all right,' he says as he drives us away. 'Let's go home and have a cup of tea.'

I am so glad when he says nothing more about the incident.

My disastrous solo outing makes me reconsider some of Susie's wise advice. After much consideration, I join a cycling club.

I turn up on a cold Saturday morning in January at Foyle Cycling Club's meeting place, in the car park of Templemore Sports Complex on the outskirts of Derry City. No one knows me, or my current disposition. I resolve to keep it that way for as long as possible.

Though I know I shouldn't be riding with them, it does me the world of good. Together we cycle along the banks of Lough Swilly and up through the Donegal hills.

We stick together in intimate formation, closing ranks if anyone punctures or falls behind. As the bell rings, and we all change places, I get to chat to everyone in the group. Not that I get to know any of them that well; without their bikes or Lycra uniforms, I would never recognise them on the high street in civilian clothes.

I do see on occasion what Susie sternly warned me about. I see a lady fall from her bike, and the pile-up of bodies that ensues. I am glad I wasn't in that pack, but know I could have easily been one of those who landed slap bang on the hard tarmac. At the start of another spin, I am following a rider, only for her water bottle to fall out of its cage and land right in front of my wheel. I am lucky enough to swerve out of its way and still stay vertical. If I had hit the bottle head-on, it would have been a different tale.

Despite these hazards, I decide to keep on riding with the club. I need to be with other athletes to maintain my mental health. These are the risks I have to take to preserve my sanity.

4

Reconciliation

The end of my first trimester can't come soon enough. I'm tired of the nausea. I'm sick of the lethargy. And I'm bored with all the secrecy.

The risk of miscarriage drops dramatically after twelve weeks, so Pete and I agree to keep the pregnancy under wraps until those three months have passed. I'm glad I have reached the mark now, with the baby still on board. My lack of alcohol consumption was starting to look awfully suspicious to my Irish friends and I'd run out of excuses for why I couldn't enter key events on next year's racing calendar.

So, now that the first trimester is over, it's time to announce the good news.

First up are my parents. But seeing that Pete spilled the beans to my mother while he was emotionally wrecked, and totally pissed, there is only my father left to tell.

'Sure I knew already,' my father claims, as soon as I tell him I'm pregnant. I'm not surprised by his reaction. He likes to think he is always one step ahead of the game.

'Weren't you sick for most of your Ethiopia trip?' Dad says, when I ask him how he had deduced this one. If sickness is the measure he uses to figure out I'm pregnant, he must have presumed I was knocked up a few times already during my overseas career.

'Your first grandchild!' Pete shouts, changing the tone.

'That deserves a drink,' my parents declare in return.

Oh good God, here we go again.

Now that parents have been duly informed, it is time to make it official with the medical establishment. I book an appointment to see the midwife for my twelve-week antenatal check-up.

I sit down beside the uniformed lady all neatly dressed in blue. She has a large green file on her desk, with my name emblazoned right across it. It looks like this pregnancy thing is going to involve a lot of admin.

'So is this your first baby?' she asks, opening proceedings. Despite the formal setting, her manner is still friendly.

'Ah, yes,' I say, my voice quivering, not realising how nervous I feel.

'And how are you doing in general?'

'Ah, fine. I think.' I wonder if this is a trick question. Doesn't she know I've been through hell and back with nausea and tiredness? Is she trying to uncover if I was foolish enough to go to Ethiopia, despite the doctor's explicit warning?

'Good,' she says, opening up the file. She takes a pen off her desk, and prepares to take my history.

'Do you smoke?'

'No.'

'Do you drink?'

'Not any more.'

I am wondering if these are the expected answers; if I will get a perfect score. But it's not until she takes my blood pressure that I really start to excel.

'One hundred and twenty over sixty. My goodness!' she exclaims. 'Do you run marathons?'

I try to conceal my frown. 'No. Not any more.'

She registers my disappointment and quickly moves on. The midwife brings me through other lifestyle questions, areas like diet over which I have complete control. It is only when she starts asking about family history that I realise that I cannot influence everything.

'Does anyone in your family have inherited diseases, like sickle cell anaemia or cystic fibrosis?'

'I don't think so,' I say, trying to wrack my brain.

'Or has anyone in your family had a baby with an abnormality, such as spina bifida?'

'Not that I know of,' I say, slightly unsure of my reply. My mother and grandmother were of a generation where birth defects or babies born out of wedlock were strictly not talked about.

Then she asks about Pete. Fortunately he has a clean bill of health. It makes me think about other pregnant women who have not inherited such good luck from their partners or parents.

Up until now, I have always had full control of my body. I could attribute any illnesses I've had to choices I've deliberately made. But now for the first time ever, somebody else could influence the health of this foetus growing inside of me.

Our conversation also reminds me of all the things that can go very wrong during pregnancy. I understand now the doctor's resistance and stern warnings about going to Ethiopia.

'You'll need to have a blood test today as well,' the midwife tells me. 'Just to check for things like HIV, syphilis, and hepatitis B, as well to find out your blood group.'

'Blood group? I know I am O negative,' I say. 'Now that I think of it, my mum is as well. I remember her saying something about being lucky that all her children were O negative too.'

'Do you have any idea what blood group your husband is?' the midwife asks as a follow-up.

'I am pretty sure that Pete has a different blood type to me, something like O positive,' I say. 'Why? Is there a problem?' I ask, unsure if I want to unearth one right now.

'No, not at all,' the midwife says. 'It is just that you'll probably need an Anti-D injection when you're twenty-eight weeks.' And with that swift reassurance, she returns to my file.

'Now, what type of birth would you like?' the midwife asks, turning over the page. We have completed my history in under an hour, and now we have reached the planning stage.

'A normal one would be fine, I guess.'

'How does a water birth sound?' she replies, beaming with enthusiasm. I do a double take. I took this middle-aged midwife to be a traditional health worker. But now she has suddenly transformed into Mother Earth. 'They are wonderful! No doctors are there. It's all midwifery-led. They have just opened a brand-new unit in Altnagelvin hospital where you'll deliver.'

I am no hippy-chick, but the idea of dimmed lights and soft sounds and warm water does sort of appeal.

'The only thing is, the birthing pool limits your options for pain control. For example, you can't have an epidural or pethidine if you're delivering in water.'

That does it. If it means I can showcase my exceptionally high pain tolerance levels, then I am all on for it. 'Sign me up!' I say.

With the midwife meeting successfully complete, my first trimester is now well and truly over. As this significant milestone passes, I thankfully regain some of my old energy.

I eventually tell my cycling club that I am pregnant, now that they're used to having me around. My admission comes from my growing paranoia that something might actually happen when on the road. I also don't want them accusing me of slacking when I refuse to head up the group. Working hard so that others can slipstream me would cause me to shoot off the end of Susie's 'perceived effort' scale.

When the biking lads find out my status, some of them become intent on beating me. The slightest hill, and they accelerate, lest the pregnant lady overtakes them. But in the end, these male instincts allow me to dander along at the back of the pack, keeping well out of collision trouble. However, they won't know what hits them when I deliver the baby, then crush them with my secret weapon: my post-partum boost of speed.

As soon as Pete sees that I'm back to semi-normality, he suggests that we go for a weekend away. 'I hear it's hard to travel once you've got kids,' he says, 'so let's go somewhere before the baby arrives.'

After my Ethiopia experience, I'm not sure I want to venture too far afield.

'What about the Lake District?' I say, expecting the idea to get shot down immediately.

'Why? What race do you want to do there?' Pete asks, assuming a hidden motive when I suggest visiting a mountain range.

'No, there's no race,' I say, telling the truth for once. 'It's just a lovely area, with nice cafes and restaurants. And we could do some hillwalking.'

'Hillwalking?' Pete says, trying to suppress his laughter. 'You?'

Pete and I tried to hillwalk once. It was a total disaster. I bit my tongue as we climbed super slowly, taking forever to reach the summit. When we got to the top, the mountain runner in me wanted to turn around straight away and scamper quickly downhill. All Pete wanted to do was stop forever and look at all the spectacular views.

'We can bring Tom,' I say, clutching at straws. 'I hear Lake District pubs are dog-friendly.'

'Tom can come?' Pete says, perking up immediately. Tom's ears prick up too, with the mere mention of his name. Pete picks him up and swings him round. 'Tom, Tom, do you want to go the Lake District for walkies?'

We book into a cosy guesthouse in a town called Ambleside. Tom is even allowed to sleep in the room with us, something that Pete appreciates immensely.

'I wonder how Tom is going to react when the baby arrives?' I say, when Pete has tucked the dog in for the night.

'I am sure he'll be fine,' Pete says. 'He's such a good dog.' Pete always takes Tom's side.

'Yeah, but I've read that some dogs can feel abandoned when the focus shifts away from them,' I say, as I lie down in our comfy guestroom bed.

'Things will be just fine,' Pete says, kissing me goodnight. 'I'm sure we'll work it out.'

Pete and I haven't talked much about what happens once we have a baby. One or both of us seems to be always away for work these days. That, or when we're at home, we are just too busy or tired to think about babies. We now have a weekend of close confinement ahead, with little else on the agenda.

The next day, we decide to resolve our hillwalking deadlock, and go for a hike up Helm Crag. Though only four hundred metres in height, this peak towers gracefully above the Cumbrian village of Grasmere. The distinctive boulders on Helm Crag's summit means we'll easily be able to find it.

'Now, no sprinting off,' Pete warns me before we start our hike.

'Pete, I'm four months pregnant,' I say in disgust. 'Of course I'll take things easy.' We bring Tom along for the walk, hoping his little doggie legs will carry him the full distance. Soon the rhythmic step of our feet and the lull of nature ease us to speak our minds.

'I don't think I'll be a good mother,' I say from out of nowhere.

Pete doesn't try to contradict me. 'What makes you think that?' he says.

'It's just, I see all the other mothers. And I just don't think I'll be like them.' I'm not sure what I'm trying to say. 'Like they hold their babies and cuddle them and speak to them in baby talk and they genuinely love them. What if I don't feel that way?'

Pete says nothing. I turn to see if his silence is due to what I've said, or because of the steep slope we're scaling.

'I'm scared too, you know,' Pete says, after a moment's thought. 'But then again, I never thought I could love another pet after my childhood dog, Reggie, died. Now look at how close Tom and I are.'

As daft as it sounds, if Pete loves the baby as much as he loves Tom, things will work out just fine.

'But don't think we'll be on our own,' Pete continues. 'We can always get some help.'

I stop for a moment to consider his suggestion, but also to catch my breath. As we pause, I actually have time to take in the magnificent views. Snow-capped mountains surround us; High Raise rises to our west and Fairfield dominates the east.

Damn it. I hate it when Pete is right.

'We could always move abroad again for work, and maybe hire a nanny,' Pete says. It may sound contrived, but it's what a lot of our fellow colleagues end up doing. 'Or we could move closer to our parents, and they could help us out.'

I raise an eyebrow. Our parents are in their sixties and seventies. I wouldn't subject them to such a workload.

'And I am sure we could use crèches or childminders,' Pete says, laying out all the options.

'Well, whatever you think best, Pete,' I say. 'I'll make the baby, and you can work out how's it looked after.'

We have never formally agreed to this division of labour. But given that I'm the one being waylaid for nine months, I think it's important that Pete has some responsibilities lined up as well.

We reach the top of Helm Crag, its rocky cliffs looming large over the landscape. With all three of us feeling fine, we decide to continue on. We head north to Gibson Knott, then on to Calf Crag at the end of the narrow ridge we're following.

'Look, it will be grand,' Pete says, as he carefully picks his way through the boulders, showing me the way. 'We always seem to work things out in the end. Like when we wanted to bring Tom back to the UK from Cambodia, and the civil servant responsible for his documents wouldn't sign them without a bribe.'

I remember it well. We came within hours of missing

42

our flight and having to leave Tom in Cambodia forever. It was a stressful day.

'Or what about when Tom got attacked by six street dogs and I had to pull him out of the fight with my bare hands,' Pete says. 'Tom and I both had to get rabies shots because of all the bites we got.'

A litany of doggy traumas comes flooding back to me now.

'What about the time I brought you and Tom for a forest run in Nepal, in the middle of rainy season?' I add. 'I didn't know that the forest was full of leeches, and Tom got one up his arse.'

'The blood pouring from poor Tom's bum was something else!' Pete says, before we both can't help ourselves, and burst into nervous laughter.

'God, if our parenting skills are anywhere like our canine ones, this baby is doomed!' I say, looking down at poor Tom. Tom, however, is unaware of our guilt, as he happily dashes off along the ridge.

Maybe it will all work out in the end. Tom is happy and healthy. Neither social services nor animal welfare have had to intervene on his behalf at any stage.

We make it safely back to Grasmere via Far Easedale Gill valley, a respectable eight-mile hike. Tom's white fur is grubby from galloping through miles of soggy bog. Pete's feet are wet from crossing rivers, something he detests, but this time has refused to complain about. As promised, I refrained from mountain running for the whole of the day's walk. Everyone has made some sort of compromise, and we have successfully managed to stick together.

We decide to decamp to a café in the village for some much-needed, post-walk refreshment. As we sit down to our food, I notice two ladies in their mid-thirties at an adjoining table. They are both happily chatting to each other, oblivious to all around them. I see that one has a small baby on her lap, who seems to be fast asleep. But when I take a second look, I realise its mother is breastfeeding.

'Look at that,' I say to Pete. 'Oh no. Actually, don't look,' I add quickly. 'That would be very rude.'

'What? What's up?' Pete says, his eyes darting everywhere, confused by what he's banned from seeing.

'It's just, that woman is breastfeeding over there, like it's totally normal.'

Of course breastfeeding is normal. It's just not normally done in public, at least not where I am from.

'The midwife spoke to me about breastfeeding,' I start to explain to Pete. 'She said it was good for mums and babies, but I thought it might be hassle.'

'Doesn't look like too much hassle for her,' Pete says, articulating what I am thinking. 'Of course, it's up to you what you want to do. But it might be worth a try?'

I watch the mother for a moment, before looking away again. I am truly intrigued by how this baby is just hanging out, simply part of the mum's daily routine.

'It's nice that lady can just meet with her friend and bring her baby along with her,' I say. I'm so distracted I've forgotten my lunch, even though I was ravenous before we arrived.

'But you do know that's what I want as well?' Pete says, tucking into his sausage rolls. 'I don't want this baby to radically change the way we live either. I still want to go out to restaurants, travel, go to rugby matches. I want to keep doing fun things too.'

Though I think Pete is unrealistic about how much

disruption this baby will cause, it is good to hear that he shares my hopes for a relaxed parenting approach.

We head back to the guesthouse to rest our weary heads. The last few months have been stressful. First there was the pressure I felt from Pete to get pregnant, then the realisation that I was indeed expecting. There were the woes of first trimester sickness, and the fears that I may never be fit again.

This weekend's time and space has allowed me to put some of these stresses away. Talking through these issues with Pete has not only helped resolve them, but has made me realise that I have a partner and parent in crime. Neither of us knows what's going to happen, but we will work through it together, come what may.

I lie back in bed and lay my hands on my stomach. Then I feel it. A little bump, just below my belly button. It's as hard as a stone, barely noticeable, but it's definitely there. I take Pete's hand and lay his gently where mine was before. 'Hello, Bump,' Pete says softly. It has a new name.

One month later, Pete accompanies me as I attend my twenty-week scan. By now Bump has grown bigger and I am beginning to show. I lie on the narrow, padded couch and make visible my growing tummy. The sonographer squirts the cold gel on my stomach and starts the ultrasound.

Pete and I glare anxiously at the screen.

'Here's the back, and there's the heart,' the sonographer starts to explains.

'And there's the arms, hands, legs, and feet,' she says, Pete and I listening intently to every one of her words. All has outwardly gone well thus far and I am looking fine. But we know all too well that the inside story can be a very different one.

She slides the sensor across and takes a series of measurements.

'It's all looking good,' she says as she finishes her work, and hands us a series of printouts.

'Do you want to know the sex?'

Pete and I nod ferociously.

'Congratulations. You're having a baby boy.'

5
Big

Pete leaves the hospital, floating on cloud nine.

'A boy? A baby boy?' he says. 'How cool is that?'

He has always dreamed of breeding his own rugby squad, and now he has his first male team-member. They'll be able to pass the ball to each other, go drinking in the pub together, and travel around Europe supporting Pete's rugby club. I suspect in Pete's mind he has already fast-forwarded several years, conveniently ignoring any stages involving dirty nappies or tearful tantrums.

I scrunch the ultrasound printouts into my back pocket, without the slightest thought.

'Aren't you meant to frame those things?' says he who has a photo of Tom our dog on his office desk.

'Are you? Really?' I say, genuinely surprised by his question. 'But sure you can't really see much apart from an outline. Like it doesn't really show what he'll look like.'

I gain from Pete's silence that these black-and-white blurred pictures should take pride of place on our mantelpiece. I extract them from my jeans pocket, smooth them out as best as I can, and place them carefully in the maternity file I'm carrying, earmarking them for future mounting.

I don't think of these pictures as keepsakes, however. For me, the photos serve as concrete evidence that the baby is okay. Since Bump started to show himself back in the Lake District, I've been wracked with guilt and worry. What if I severely damaged the baby by taking malarone in Ethiopia? Did I push myself too hard on the bike, and deprive him of his oxygen supply? And what about that glass of red wine I drank after taking the pregnancy test? Did it adversely affect the development of his brain and spine?

I realise now how reckless I was during my first trimester. But now that I have a bump, and an actual photo of what's inside, I decide to sober up and be more responsible from now on.

But it's not just my belly that is increasing in size. My boobs have expanded exponentially.

'I need to get some new clothes,' I tell Pete. 'I'm going to Mothercare.'

'I'll come too,' Pete says. Even though it's a maternity store, he can't resist the prospect of a shopping expedition. I sometimes think Pete represents our relationship's feminine side.

Our initial enthusiasm for this shopping trip is quickly tempered. We both recoil when we enter the store and see all the crap we could buy. There are cots and baskets; bibs and car bottles; baby monitors and highchairs. I feel distinctly overwhelmed.

'Why don't you have a look around while I try and find the maternity section?' I say to Pete, trying to regain my composure. Pete still looks bewildered.

'If you don't move,' I say, shoving him past the sliding doors, 'I'll make you look for bras with me.' With that threat, Pete scampers off, in the direction of baby clothes.

A young lady approaches me, sporting a Mothercare name badge.

'Need any help?' she says with a chirpy smile.

'Ah, yeah. Sure,' I say. Where the hell do I start? 'I need a new bra. A bigger one.'

'Of course,' she says. 'We can easily measure you.'

She leads me inside a changing room. There I receive the devastating news that I am no longer a 34A. The attendant seems to derive great pleasure in announcing, that in the space of five months, I have become a 38D. Thanks to my pregnancy, my cup size and chest circumference have spiralled out of control.

'You might want to also buy some larger ones later,' the attendant says. 'When you're in your third trimester.'

The changing room starts to seem very small. I think I'm about to faint.

'And if you decide to breastfeed, you can get specially designed bras for that.'

Faint? No, I'm literally about to suffocate.

I run out of the cubicle with a fistful of random brassieres. I need to find the checkout as quick as I can, and get out of this store immediately.

Pete. I forgot Pete. Oh God, I've got to rescue him.

I search the aisles for my lost husband, fearing the worst. I eventually track him down in the pram section. I can tell by the way he is standing that he too needs to abort this shopping mission.

'Have you seen how much this thing costs?' he says, pointing to a multi-digit price tag. It is attached to what I can only describe a souped-up, Formula One stroller. Pete's face has gone distinctly white.

'But what is it?' I ask.

'A "travel system".'

49

'A what?'

'I don't know,' Pete says. 'But apparently we're meant to spend a thousand pounds on one. We bought our whole car for less!'

We are lucky to get out of Mothercare with just some underwear.

'I can't cope,' I say, as we get into the car and do a high-speed getaway.

'Don't worry,' he says, looking nervously in the rear-view mirror. 'I'll talk to my sister. She'll know what to do.'

So while Pete finds out what purchases we really need to raise a healthy, normal child, I get on with the business of making us a baby.

I keep on going out for daily runs whenever I feel up for it. Each time, I come home a little later as it takes me longer and longer to complete my ten-kilometre circuit. My slower times are due initially to Bump weighing me down. But when I finally get used to the extra weight, I develop frequent urges to stop and urinate. My uterus is pressing down on my bladder, expelling whatever liquid is in there. The literature suggests planning runs with toilets available on the route. I opt instead to run off-trail, and pee behind bushes and trees.

My ten-kilometre times start to depress me so much that I have to take evasive action. I need some sort of distraction, to stop this manic clock-watching. I decide to go back orienteering, a sport I gave up five years ago. I figure that having to read a map and compass on the run will force me to momentarily forget all about my pace and current shape.

'You know there's some rough terrain out there,' the race organiser tells me when I line up to register. I look at him blankly. Orienteering often takes place in forests and on mountains. Today's race takes in some small, trackless hills. It looks wet and slippery up there, with a scattering of boulders and cliffs, but it is nothing I haven't navigated before. Why is he warning me today of all days, when the course is nothing different from the norm?

I quickly catch myself when I realise he's referring to my bump.

'Don't worry,' I say, 'I'll be careful.'

He doesn't seem convinced.

I bite down hard on my tongue to stop myself from yelling, 'Are you discriminating against me for being pregnant?'

Pete has come along with me to my event in Fermanagh, a two-hour drive from home. Pete has never beaten me at orienteering, but today he has high hopes that this is about to change.

The orienteering does wonders for me. Within a few minutes, I am totally lost on a steep, grassy hillside. My mind doesn't have time to think about my breathing or my belly. It just wants to get me out of there. I line my compass up with my map, and take a direct bearing. If I am where I think I am, the control should be right over there.

I try to run across the boggy hill, but clumps of heather seem intent on tripping me. My balance is a little off, what with the frontal load I'm carrying. I'm also aware that I'm being bombarded with relaxin in preparation for childbirth. This hormone is making my ligaments and tendons more elastic, causing my joints to loosen up. This is all great when preparing for baby's arrival, but inconvenient for runners like me. A knee or an ankle can easily pop, when normally they are solid and injury-free.

51

Running over rough terrain like this, with bog holes and hidden rocks underfoot, is akin to me attempting to jog through a minefield.

I think it's best if I walk.

Though I reduce my speed considerably, my orienteering times improve. This sedate pace means I actually take time to look at my map and figure out the right direction to go. Normally I would sprint around like a headless chicken and take ages to complete the race. But this time, I actually plan my routes and take the terrible terrain in my stride.

I reach the finish and wait to see how Pete has done. I wait. And wait, until finally he limps across the line.

'How did you get on out there?' I say, feigning total ignorance.

'Got lost,' he says, peeling off his wet, muddy shoes, and flinging them into the car.

'Oh no,' I say, confirming my suspicions while trying not to appear too smug.

'Couldn't find the fifth control, so gave up and came home,' he says. 'Disgusted with myself.'

I totally kicked his ass. 'Ah well, maybe you'll beat me next time, when I'm in my third trimester.'

'Whatever,' he mutters, as he throws himself into the passenger seat and slams shut the car door. Conversation over.

The orienteering makes me realise I am still able to compete, so when I find out there's a multi-sport event close to home, I'm sorely tempted to sign up.

'There's a race across Inishowen Peninsula next weekend,' I say to Pete when I'm nearly five months gone. I take a deep breath. 'Is it okay if I go?'

I have no idea why I am asking for his approval. I know

wives are allowed to do whatever they like these days, without their spouse's express consent.

'Ah, sure,' Pete says, searching for his words. 'If you want. Like, if you feel up to it.'

Normally I inform Pete of my pre-ordained race schedule and it's up to him to work around my plans. This is the first time I am specifically seeking his consent to race. Pregnancy is making me do very strange things.

The race itself involves road biking; running on roads, trails, and mountains; and kayaking, but no navigation is required. Unlike normal adventure races where co-ed teams of four are required, these adventure races are for individuals. However, to make them sound sexy and exciting, this type of race is also called an adventure race, albeit of a slightly different format. They are basically a type of triathlon, with kayaking instead of swimming, and a few lakes and mountains thrown in.

I have to ask for Pete's permission, as I need his help to get me to the start. The race begins on the eastern side of the peninsula, in a village called Redcastle. It starts with a thirteen-kilometre run up and over Puckan Hill to the bike transition near the town of Carndonagh. The race route continues over mountain roads for eighteen kilometres, where it brings you and your bike to the base of Slieve Snaght, Inishowen's highest peak at six hundred and fifteen metres. From there, it's a question of summiting the mountain, and returning to the bottom again. It's downhill then on your bike until you reach Lough Fad, where kayaks wait for you to complete a short paddle. Next, it's a pedal up and over twenty more kilometres of hills, with a last two-kilometre sprint to the finish in the town of Buncrana, on the other side of the coastal head. I need Pete to drop me on one side of the peninsula, and to pick me up on the other.

Thirty-seven of us turn up to the starting line on Saturday morning, on a surprisingly dry and sunny day in March. I immediately see Peter Cromie, my adventure-racing team-mate who carried my bag in the Sperrin Mountains, and the man who sold me my bike.

'Howaya, Cromie,' I say. 'Grand day for a race.'

'How ye keeping yerself?' he says, without stating the obvious. My bike jacket is tightly stretched over my bump. It makes me look enormous.

'Good, good,' I say, with two hands on my belly. 'Hope this thing won't slow me down. It isn't too aerodynamic.'

Cromie has his own weird contraptions to improve his race performance. He has lightweight bike gear on, and a strangely shaped plaster stuck right across his nose.

'What's that for?' I ask, pointing right between his eyes.

'This? It's a nasal strip,' Cromie says, without a hint of shame. 'Keeps the airways open. Supposed to make me faster.'

Maybe I should get one of them too to help me with my pregnancy breathing issues.

'So when are you due?' Cromie asks. I tell him in July.

'Just the one I hope,' he says.

I nod.

'Good,' he says. 'One's enough. I've a four-year-old boy. He's great craic altogether, but wouldn't want another.'

I refrain from telling Cromie my husband's intentions to keep adding to the brood. I don't want to even think about it myself until I'm done with the one I'm currently bearing.

There's no more time for small talk as we're soon under starters orders. I place myself firmly at the back of the pack, to keep Bump and I out of trouble.

Cromie rushes off from the beginning. I, on the other

hand, just aim to make it to the finish. I've had to lower my racing goals considerably since getting pregnant.

I trot along the first tarmac section, trying to keep a steady pace. I find it hard not to speed up when everyone starts disappearing out of sight. We soon hit undulating roads, and I finally find my advantage. Though the other racers power up the hills, my greater weight, with the help of gravity, allows me to overtake them on the downhills.

Soon, though, this downhill running becomes too much for my bladder and I have to pull over for a pee. The other competitors run past, eyes fixed straight ahead, pretending not to notice. But it must be hard not to stare at the race's only pregnant lady, squatting behind some long roadside grass, having a quick leak.

I finish the first run section and arrive at the bike drop. I am convinced I am in last place. It is only when I take a quick glance up the rack that I see some competitors have still to collect their bikes. I bounce on to my bicycle and start to pedal ferociously, stopping briefly for a moment to readjust Bump's position. What with Bump's growing girth, he is forcing me to sit more and more upright on the bike every week. I need to put my hands on the bars in just the right place so he doesn't get too squished.

Though this race is for individuals, Bump, Bike, and I are now an adventure-racing team. We career down the bog-lined, rolling road, pedalling fast on the descents to give us some momentum to get back up the other side. Sheep on the roadside watch us as they lazily graze on the marsh reeds and tough grass. I swerve nervously to avoid hitting one. I don't want to do irreparable damage to Bump, Bike and me. I take a swig of water from my bike bottle when I get a chance; I've got to make sure we are all well hydrated for the remainder of the race.

We soon leave the rolling boglands that heated so many Irish homes in centuries past, leaving Bike all alone at the transition while Bump and I climb Slieve Snaght. The going is tough, with glacial marshland freezing my feet as I begin the ascent. The climb takes forever; time enough to watch Peter Cromie bounding down the hill with ease and back to his bike in first place.

'Not far to go now,' he says, as he passes me on my ascent. I look up and see a wall of rocks that Bump and I must clamber over to reach the top. I have been racing for nearly three hours. I am feeling really tired.

It is only when I touch the cairn that I realise I am in trouble. I spin around to start the return, only to be stabbed in the side by a sharp, piercing pain.

Oh God, was that the baby?

Or did I just turn around too fast?

Am I about to miscarry?

Or did I just drink that water too quickly, and now have a stitch?

There's nothing I can do but descend the mountain and get help. If I am in trouble, the race marshals can call an ambulance. But if the pain is a mere figment of my imagination, I'll just continue on with the race.

It takes forever to get back to Bike, as I stagger down Slieve Snacht's steep slopes. But once Bump, Bike and I are all successfully reunited, all thoughts of the stitch dissipate.

I tell myself not to worry. We are officially back in the race.

Within fifteen minutes, Bike brings Bump and I safely to the next race section, a kayak leg on Lake Fad.

'I'm pregnant,' I shout out to the marshals above my screech of brakes. The kayak officials stare at me blankly, not sure if they've heard me right. I don't have time, however, to repeat myself.

'Is it okay if I don't kayak?'

I have difficulty getting out of the sofa these days. Heaven knows how I'll get in and out of a floating boat.

'Ah, sure,' one says. And, just to be fair to my opponents, I tell the marshals I'm happy to take a time penalty.

Bike, Bump and I cycle away before the officials can stop me. I don't want them pulling me out of the race out of concerns for my safety.

We complete the race without further incident, and gladly cross the finish. I discover I am so far behind my friend, and overall race winner, Peter Cromie, that he has already gone home long ago.

I sit down in the finish-line marquee to bask in my successful race completion. Everyone who congratulations me politely ignores the fact that mine was a team effort.

But Bump doesn't like to be ignored.

From out of nowhere, an almighty kick reverberates around my core. It is delivered with such force that I can't stop myself from roaring.

I don't think Bump is happy. I promise him I'll race no more.

However, I am not long recovered from the weekend's event when the racing bug hits again.

'Once this baby is born, I want to race,' I say to Pete.

We are in our kitchen at home, where it is much easier to corner him. He slurps his tea, then hugs his mug close. 'Why am I not surprised?'

'I want you to promise me that, whatever happens, I'll have the time to train and compete again after I deliver.'

'Of course you will,' Pete says, putting his cup down. 'I know how important it is to you.'

I lean against the counter top, wondering if I should get him to put this down in writing.

'Stop stressing,' Pete says. 'Have the baby, then we'll make sure you have a couple of hours each day to do the training you need. Trust me, I won't leave you holding the baby on your own.'

This is probably a promise that Pete will live to regret. But, now that he has given it, there is no way I will let him break it. Training is far too important to me.

When I was in my twenties, I let exercise slide. I ended up gaining weight and feeling horribly round. Maternity wear and my currently ever-extending belly are giving me vivid flashbacks of that plump stage in my life. All I want is to fit back in my size eight clothes, and to be slim and strong once more.

But training isn't all about how it makes me look. It also challenges me to better myself. It allows me to set small daily goals, to run a certain distance or clock a given speed. If I achieve it, I beam with pride for the rest of the day. And if I don't make it, although disappointed, it gives me a clear goal to work towards next time.

With Pete agreeing to daily training slots, and racing shelved until after Bump's birth, I resolve to try and keep fit for the time being. I return to my training schedule and go out for simple jogs. Knowing my running days are numbered, I peruse online forums to see how long I've got.

The pinnacle of pregnancy running seems to be getting past twenty-eight weeks of gestation, or past your second trimester. Beyond that pale, the baby grows rapidly. I just wonder how big Bump will get before I must hang up my own trainers?

I manage to keep my daily runs going until I reach week thirty. I have resorted to wearing oversized T-shirts and baggy pants; the only gear that still fits me. I feel fat and unfashionable, yet ecstatic to still be able to exercise with an obvious baby in my belly. All good things always come, however, to an eventual end.

I am on my usual route, a one-hour slow jog on quiet rural roads. It is now two months since the Inishowen adventure race, when the downhill mountain section gave me a fleeting stitch. I have not had such pain since. I had put it down to a racing thing.

I am thirty minutes into my run as I start down a small incline. When the stitch comes this time, I am totally paralysed. I double over in pain as it pierces my side. Even when I start the long walk home, the stitch refuses to go away.

I have left my mobile phone at home, as my temporary running gear does not have a proper pocket. I had figured trouble would never come my way, but when I find myself barely able to walk, I go into a blind panic.

I will never reach home.

Pete will never find me.

If only a car would drive past and help me.

But I am so deep into rural Ireland that I see not even a single soul. I stretch and take deep breaths; the pain slowly subsides.

After ten minutes of shuffling, I finally reach the main road and civilisation. I climb on to the pavement with my right arm raised high and thrown limply over my head. I wrap my left arm across my belly to hold on to my screaming right side. I must look a proper sight. Stabs of pain arrive without warning, making me stop and grit my teeth. Though I would gladly take a lift from a passing motorist, no one stops to offer this crazy, contorted, pregnant lady a free ride.

It takes me another twenty minutes to finally reach our house. As soon as I get through our front door and see Pete in the sitting room, I burst into floods of tears.

'What?' Pete says, jumping out of his seat to catch me. 'Oh God, what happened?'

I am so distraught that I can barely speak. The shock of my run has just hit me.

Pete does what he does best, and just gives me a huge hug.

Susie told me to listen to my body, and now it's screaming at me. It's time for me to stop running, to stop trying to be a super-fit expectant mum. My body is telling me that I've had a good stint for the last thirty weeks. But now it's time to curtail my running habit for the final ten weeks of this pregnancy.

6
Birth

'Does anyone have any questions?' the midwife asks, addressing our antenatal class. The mild-mannered woman is pointing to some photos pinned to a large whiteboard. I look down at Bump and back at the lady. How could Bump even contemplate doing such a thing to me?

The midwife has just brought us through, in graphic detail, the process by which a baby is born. I still can't work out how a baby so big can get out of a hole so small. Words from the presentation, like *tearing* and *stitching*, stand out in particular in my mind.

Pete is leaning forward in his seat, avoiding all eye contact. I can't wait to get him out of this classroom, and berate him for what he's done to me.

'And birthing partners, what kind of things can you do to help during labour?'

More silence. I think this midwife might need to give us a couple of hints.

'Well, you can hold their hand, wipe their face, maybe give them sips of water,' she says.

'What about massaging their back and shoulders?' one man says, searching for brownie points.

Pete nudges me. 'That sounds like a great idea,' he says, looking all pleased with himself.

'Are you kidding me?' I say. 'If you dare massage me when I'm having contractions, I will seriously punch you between screams.'

'Oh, come on, Moire,' Pete says, retracting his smile. 'You know I like to participate in things.'

Whereas I am happy to do individual sports, Pete is the ultimate team player. I need to remind my husband that giving birth is definitely a solo game.

'Okay, so does everyone know how to put nappies on?' the midwife asks, quickly changing the topic.

Pete and I stare at the ceiling. We are nappy-fitting virgins.

The midwife passes around baby-sized plastic dolls and a set of Pampers each. It brings back vivid memories of how, when I was small, I dealt with my Tiny Tears doll. My Tiny Tears came with a baby's bottle and a soother, and had a pee hole to wee water out. With no nappies to hand, I found the soother not only fitted in the doll's mouth but also sat perfectly snug in the orifice located between its legs. I was able to feed her the contents of several baby bottles before she started to leak. I think though it's probably best not to relate this childhood experience to the midwife, and just to listen quietly to her commands.

The nappy-fitting exercise proves a lot less taxing than initially thought. There are no safety pins or complex folds to do. Just two sticky tabs, and a quick check to make sure it's not on back to front.

'So does anyone have any other questions?' the midwife says, wrapping up the day's session.

Pete raises his hand. I look over at it, desperately wishing it back down.

'I just wanted to ask,' he says, keeping us all in suspense. 'Do we need to buy something called a travel system?'

I feel Bump deliver a warning kick. I think he wants his daddy to stop embarrassing him in front of the other expectant parents.

'Well, not if you don't want to,' the midwife says, encouraged by the question. 'Of course, you'll need a car seat for the baby, as that's a legal requirement. But as for all the other stuff, it's really up to you.'

The midwife diverts her attention away from Pete to the other members of the class. But Pete is on a roll, and has more questions to ask.

'And, just to clarify,' he says, 'do we also need to buy a new car?'

I bite my lip. I'm going to have to sack my birthing partner once we're out of here.

'It's just that someone told me our car's too old and small,' Pete says, trying to clarify. True enough, we had bought our second-hand Citroen Xsara hatchback off a narrow country roadside a couple of years back, for less than five hundred pounds.

'Parents are often told they need to buy loads of things,' the midwife says, taking a few small steps towards us. 'But between you and me, you will probably work out what you need and don't need once the baby is born.'

Pete and I are currently feeling pressure to buy lots of baby things before the birth. Some have interpreted our reticence to spend hard cash as a distinct lack of interest in the child. But, having lived in developing countries and witnessed parenting there, we know that children can be brought up fine without major expenditure. Anyhow, we don't like being hassled into spending money unnecessarily.

We eventually mention our lack of baby items to our friends and family. 'Don't be ridiculous,' they all say. 'Sure we can give you some of ours.' They happily donate to us a mountain of toys and baby books. Pete's sister kindly gives us tons of barely used baby clothes. We also receive a cot, a steriliser, and a car seat, all free of charge.

We welcome all these donations, amazed by their generosity. It takes a while for us to realise that they are simply glad to rid their garages of all their old baby junk.

While we stock our own house with baby-related stuff, I start to dream of the day when the baby finally makes his exit, and I get my body back. A friend tells me of the benefits of camomile tea to induce early labour. I drown myself in the beverage, hoping the baby will hate the taste as much as I do, and take an early flight.

I also haven't forgotten the promise I made myself to get fit again after the birth. I want to be like Susie and to get back in the saddle as soon as I possibly can. I am aware though of the array of difficulties women can experience post-pregnancy. Our bodies are flooded with the hormone relaxin, which relaxes the body's muscles, joints, and ligaments. It's great for making the pelvis stretchy enough for birth, but it can also cause post-partum problems with ankles, knees, and hips. The Olympic runner Jo Pavey suffered a stress fracture in her foot after having children, all because relaxin extended her foot size and changed her foot mechanics. Then there are the issues associated with a growing belly. A baby can make abdominal muscles separate, effectively ripping the core apart.

I am so worried about these repercussions that I decide to seek out help. I need someone to guide me methodically through this period, someone with the right knowledge and experience.

I decide to find myself a coach.

I ask my mountain runner buddies if there is anyone they can suggest. But before I can select the right instructor, I have to figure out what I want to train for. I think back to the adventure race I did across Inishowen peninsula when I was five months pregnant. Despite the obvious discomforts, I really enjoyed the event. I liked the mix of biking, running, and kayaking that it delivered up.

In addition, this single day adventure-racing format is becoming increasingly popular in Ireland. There are races springing up all around the country, as far south as Killarney and as far north as Donegal. There are also a few dotted along the country's wild Atlantic coastline in places like Dingle, Westport, and Achill. Doing such races might motivate Bike and I to get out and about, and not get stuck permanently at home with husband, baby and dog.

After making a few enquiries, I contact Eamonn Tilley, a triathlon coach based in Dublin. We arrange to have a Skype call to see if we can work together.

Eamonn pops up on my screen as soon as I answer the phone. He is sitting down at his home office desk, tapping in some details on a hidden keyboard. Friends have told me Eamonn is a towering figure of a man. My Skype connection shows him from the shoulders up, so I feel a little less overwhelmed.

I am still nervous though. I'm not even sure if he'll agree to coach me or not. I'm close to giving birth, will soon have a baby to nurse, and I'm asking him to train me in a discipline I've never really competed in.

'Ah, sure I have two kids myself,' Eamonn says, trying to put me at ease. They are all grown-up now, he tells me, but he knows what it's like to raise them. Eamonn

65

also tells me he used to mountain run for Ireland back in the 1980s. He knows the race routes I've done and some of the athletes against whom I've competed. It is good to know that we at least share some common ground.

I give him a rundown of my athletic history, as well as my preference for long-distance mountain running and multi-day races. I tell him I doubt I'll have the time or energy to do such pursuits once the baby comes and instead ask if it's possible to train for the one-day adventure races that I am hoping to contest.

'Not a problem,' he says. 'Happy to support you with your goals.'

With that reassurance, I ask him when we can get started.

'Just wait to have your baby and get your six-week check-up,' Eamonn says. 'Once the doctor gives you the all-clear, we can definitely start from there.'

I was kind of hoping we could start training with immediate effect. It feels like it will be forever before I can get fit again. Sure there are days when I can barely get off the couch from pregnancy tiredness. But there are also days when I am full of energy and gung-ho to get back exercising again.

'Just keep active in the meantime,' Eamonn says on a positive note. 'Swimming and walking are great during the final stages of pregnancy.'

It all sounds so sedate, yet realistic for the shape I'm in. I promise to do as he suggests, and we agree to touch base again in a couple of months' time.

His swimming and walking suggestions come at an apt time. Bump, Bike, and I are not getting along as well as we had before. Bump is taking up far too much room when I lean forward in the saddle and try to hold the handlebars.

I feel like I'm balancing a basketball between Bike's crossbar and my bulging boobs. But Bump is not content with just this latest acquisition. He is busy pushing my internal organs out of the way, and has recently commandeered the place where my lungs are meant to be. My lungs now only have a fraction of the space they normally would have to function. Each breath is now smaller and more laboured. Thanks to Bump, by week thirty-five, Bike and I must tearfully part company.

I am resigned to exercising in the local swimming pool. I swim up and down the lanes for an hour each day, feeling the drag from Bump's bulge. Being the frugal person that I am, I refuse, however, to fork out for a maternity swimming costume. I resurrect an old bikini that is stretched from overuse. It fits perfectly over my bum and breasts, with Bump fully exposed now in the flesh.

Not that I really care what I look like by now, because I am living in denial. In my head, I still have a flat stomach and tiny bottom. I refuse to use any mirror that shows anything to the contrary. I shun full-length looking glasses, sticking to ones that only show me from my shoulders up. Much to Pete's disappointment, I even outlaw him from taking any photos of the pregnancy. I have no desire to be reminded at a later date of the sorry state my body is presently in.

I also take over our household's dog-walking duties during my final months. It means that, for half an hour each morning, I have a leisurely stroll with Tom. Tom seems chuffed with this consistent routine now in place. He is also ecstatic when he can romp off to sniff out other dogs, while I am too slow to catch up and pull him away from his new-found friends.

Out of sheer curiosity, I head one day to a local studio

for a bit of pregnancy yoga. I have done yoga before, so am looking forward to a proper stretch. However, the session turns out to be sedentary to the extreme. When we are told to lie on our backs for ten minutes and think about how much we love our unborn babies, I resist the temptation to leave mid-session, but resolve never to go back again. I wish I could feel all this mushy love stuff that the other mums-to-be seem to feel.

It's at times like this that I wonder if there is something profoundly wrong with me.

The forty weeks are not up soon enough. My due date arrives, then passes without baby coming out.

'It's pretty normal, I hear,' I tell Pete, when he wonders if there's a problem. 'First-time babies rarely arrive on schedule.'

The next day comes, D-Day plus one, and Pete is starting to lose the plot. It seems as if he is following my every move and won't let me out of his sight. I decide to go to the supermarket just to get away from him.

'I'll come too,' Pete says, grabbing his coat. Pete never comes grocery shopping with me.

'No, you're grand,' I say. 'I've only got a few things to get.'

'Sure I'll help you with the bags.'

We arrive back home with food for the entire week. Pete has spent the whole trip glued to my side. I just can't shake him off my tail.

'I'm going for a walk,' I say, when I see he's busy putting the groceries away. I run out the door before he can object, and in my haste, forget my mobile phone.

I take a long stroll via a deserted beach, delaying my return. I'm so tired of being pregnant. And now my husband won't feckin' leave me alone.

Pete is worried sick by the time I reach home.

'You didn't answer my calls,' he says.

'Sure we've spent all day together,' I retort. 'I'm sure you had nothing additional to say.'

Two hours later, my waters break. I am very lucky they didn't go when I was on my extended walk.

If I thought Pete was losing it this morning, he is now totally freaking out.

'Calm down, Pete,' I say. 'Just drive me to the hospital, and the midwives can take it from there.'

'Oh my God, oh my God,' he says, as he nearly takes several wrong turns in the car. It is only when we arrive at Altnagelvin Hospital around 9 pm that he finally stops hyperventilating. I wheel my bags up to the maternity ward while Pete parks the car, badly.

I am less than thirty minutes in the door when the contractions start to come. I am whisked away to the birthing suite, where a large jacuzzi lies in wait. The lights are low as two midwives gently help me up the steps and down into its warm waters. Pete looks a little jealous as he arrives in and sits down outside the huge tub. He loves a good spa weekend.

I was told first-time mums can take ages to deliver. Bump, however, is in a hurry. The contractions come thick and fast. I feel like I'm having the worst period ever. I had heard water births are a great way to manage labour pain. But all I know now is that this hurts like hell. God only knows how bad childbirth is if it's all done back on dry land.

'Have some gas and air,' the midwife says. I suck on the tube as if my very life depends on it. So much for my high pain tolerance levels! Who exactly was I kidding? But I am too proud to exit the waters and try a different pain method. I am in the water now, and that's where I intend on staying.

I lose all track of time as the waves of pain come and go. It is only when I see my skin all wrinkled that I realise several hours have passed. I look up to see Pete leaning on the bath's edge, stifling a yawn. It must be well past midnight by now, way past his bedtime. I take his hand and try to tell him it will be okay. I want to thank him for not massaging my shoulders between my terrifying screams. It is only then I realise how exhausted I am, when I can barely say a thing. Pete grips my hand tightly. It is ridiculous how we are both in this together, but only I can do this alone.

The midwives have a good look between my legs now and then to see if there's any sign of baby. If I had any dignity before this moment, it has totally evaporated. I am sprawled out in the bath, naked from the waist down. I don't have the energy to cover up or adopt a more attractive, seductive pose. All I want is this pain to go away. All my thoughts and energy are devoted to this single, solitary cause.

I push down when I'm told to, and stop when given the sign. I'm so focused on getting Bump out that I don't even question the midwife when she whips out a sieve from out of nowhere. She skims the water's surface and scurries away its contents. I glance down, and see no blood or baby. Just some brown-floating stuff. Here I am, trying to push a baby out, and all I've succeeded in doing is emptying out my bowels.

The midwives keep a close eye on me, advising me on what to do and when. When the time comes for the penultimate push, I feel like I'm shitting a gigantic watermelon.

'Do you want to see your baby crowning?' I hear the

midwife say between my screams. I look down, and see her angling a mirror right between my legs.

I shake my head ferociously, and divert my eyes away. The last thing I want to see is the total mess of blood and hair that is wriggling away down there.

'Oh my God. Oh my God,' Pete cries, when I give my final push. 'It just slithered out.'

Our water baby is born at 2.30 am.

The midwives scoop him up out of the water and place him in my arms. He is small, red, and naked. I can't believe he has just come out of me. 'You poor thing,' is all I can manage to say as I hold him to my skin.

The midwives leave him with me for a few moments before taking him away for some paperwork. Once my placenta is delivered, the other midwife is charged with hauling me out of the bath. I stand up and shuffle towards the exit steps. I look like a wrinkled prune from five hours underwater. But just as I start to emerge from the bath, I begin to shake uncontrollably.

It's a lovely feeling. I've shaken violently like this after multi-day long-distance runs. It is my body's unique way of dealing with exhaustion and sleep deprivation. After the strange, unknown sensation of childbirth, it is good that my body is doing something I finally recognise.

The midwife is not as appreciative of my body's reaction.

'Call the doctor,' she shouts. 'I think she's going into shock.'

I hear her words, but am so absorbed by recent events that I forget to intervene.

Pete immediately steps in instead. 'Oh, don't worry,' I hear him say. 'She always does that when she's really tired.'

It's nice when your husband knows your idiosyncrasies.

71

Somehow Pete manages to convince the midwives that all I need is a little lie-down. Within a couple of minutes, I'm right as rain again.

We name our baby Aran after the Aran Islands, a stunning yet bleak set of rocks anchored off Ireland's west coast. Such a combination of beauty and desolation perfectly depicts my experience of pregnancy and childbirth.

I pity the boy already.

Pete stays with me for an hour before making the short journey home. I catch snatches of sleep, but wake often, despite how exhausted I feel.

I open my eyes the next morning to see Aran in a cot by my bed. He is fast asleep, the rigours of childbirth having exhausted him the previous night. I watch him breathe in and out, trying to make sense of it all.

Is this love at first sight?

Am I totally elated?

Have I achieved my purpose in life?

No. I don't think or feel any of these things.

What I do feel is guilt that I am not awash with endearing, warm emotions. I wish I loved babies and dreamed of smothering him in cuddles for hours. Whether I like it or not, that is unfortunately not who I am.

What I do feel is fiercely protective. This child beside me looks so small, and so terribly helpless. I want to hold him when he cries, feed him when he's hungry, pick him up when he falls. I want to make sure he comes to no harm. I am the one who has brought him into the world. I am responsible for him.

Aran starts to move his chubby legs, and lets out a tiny whine. I look over at him, not entirely sure what I should do now. I've never been around a newborn child before. I take a wild guess and pick him up. My hand slides under his fragile neck, with my other hand cupped under his tiny nappy. I lift his eight pound five ounce body and do what comes most naturally to me: I cradle him like a doll.

He lets out the briefest of yawns, then falls asleep on my bosom. I stare down at him, amazed that he trusts me enough to sleep in my arms, especially when we only made our acquaintance in the early hours of this morning.

My friends were right. Maybe it is different when they are your own. Maybe I will be able to figure out this maternal thing after all.

7

Trapped

I slide Aran out of my arms and place him back in his bedside cot. I then get out of my hospital bed and tiptoe to the bathroom. I'm unsure of how much noise wakes a sleeping infant, but I don't want to find out right now by disturbing baby Aran. I close the door quietly behind me and make my way over to the toilet. It takes a while for the pee to come, and it stings like hell when it finally does.

I was extremely fortunate that Aran came out without tearing me, and no stitches were required. I can't imagine the screams I'd hurl now if I had been torn apart last night.

A large mirror is stuck on the wall above the washbasin. I suppose I should have a look at myself now that the baby is out. I start at the top and work my gaze slowly down. My hair looks bedraggled, after a crazy late night of childbirth. But it still looks beautiful, thick, and shiny thanks to a rich hormonal supply of oestrogen. I know my mane will slowly but surely fall out over the coming months as the oestrogen levels subside. Equally numbered are the days I will behold these long, strong fingernails and perfect cuticles that adorn my ageing hands.

Next, my billowing, stripy, cotton nightgown comes

into view. I bought it especially for my hospital stay, and it is so not my style. But it manages to cover up nicely my post-natal torso, which I dread to look at even now. I see the outline of my oversized breasts, which are all ready to swing into feeding action if and when required. And there it is, my wobbly belly, still swollen after months of growing a child. Before, it felt like a basketball, pumped up hard with air. Now, it feels slightly deflated, but still very much bloated and round.

How will I ever get my body back in race shape again?

I don't have time to work out the answer to this burning question. Instead I open the bathroom door to hear a faint whimper of a baby looking for his mother.

The midwives had shown me last night, just after his birth, how to breastfeed my new baby. Both Aran and I were full of first-time fumbles. Him, opening his mouth like a goldfish, trying to work out what he is meant to suck. Then there was me, moving his head back and forth across my upper body, directing him towards the nearest nipple. Finally, we made contact, and he took his first proper drink of milk.

Now, with the midwives busy elsewhere, I have to attempt this feeding process on my own. I pick Aran up from his cot, holding his head gently, petrified that I might break this tiny creature at any moment. I carefully put him in the position the midwives suggested and, after a few near misses, he manages to latch on successfully. This breastfeeding malarkey might just out work in the end.

'Look at you!' a voice coos from around the bedroom door. I have lost all track of time, but it must be visiting hours. My mum has come to the hospital to see her first-ever grandchild.

'Oh, isn't he the cutest?' Mum says, coming over to the

bed and beaming at the breastfeeding baby. I look down at Aran. Cute? He looks just like every other baby I've seen before.

'Aren't you so lucky you can feed him yourself,' Mum says. 'I remember when I was in hospital after giving birth and the midwives told me I didn't have enough milk to feed you.'

I am surprised by this revelation. Mum is much more endowed than me in that department. But I suppose, back in the day, the benefits of breastfeeding weren't fully appreciated. Formula feeding was the preferred maternity policy.

'Do you want to hold him?' I say, expecting Mum to snatch Aran straight right out of my arms.

'Are you sure?' she says, aghast. 'I might break him.'

'Sure didn't you bring up a whole pile of children yourself?' I say. 'I thought you'd be a dab hand at it.'

'That was a long time ago, my dear,' Mum says. 'I don't remember much about child-rearing.'

'But I thought you were meant to give me loads of parenting advice?' I say. I heard some mothers can be quite interfering when their daughters reproduce.

Mine shakes her head. 'I'm certain the midwives will give you much better guidance that I can, my dear,' she says. 'They are surely more up-to-date on all the new-fangled baby stuff.'

I force Mum to take a seat as I deposit Aran on her lap. She slowly melts as she rocks him back and forth. Watching the two of them happily swaying away, I realise that as long as Mum's there to be his granny, that will be ample enough.

Though everything goes well with the birth, Aran is not immediately discharged from hospital. The doctors find he has a touch of jaundice caused by a build-up of bilirubin in his blood.

Bilirubin is a yellow substance produced when red blood cells are broken down. It is a common enough condition with newborns, especially those who are breastfed. Aran needs to undergo phototherapy to help his liver break down this intrusive blood by-product.

Most new mums would be distressed by their baby's unforeseen illness. But I come from a medical family, where sickness is dealt with stoically. My grandfather was a doctor who delivered thousands of babies across Derry city throughout the Second World War and during the Troubles. His two sons, my father and uncle, both studied medicine at university. I am therefore used to medical male relatives intervening with their expertise and knowledge, restoring calm as soon as sickness hits my family. So when I see a doctor taking charge and ordering Aran's immediate treatment, I promptly place my confidence in this professional, never doubting that my son is in anything but perfectly safe hands.

Aran is stripped down to his nappy, given some eyeshades, and placed on a blue florescent sunbed. Despite the seriousness of this illness, I can't help but see the lighter side of his treatment. All Aran needs now is a piña colada and some calypso background music and he's on his first sunshine holiday.

I stay with him during this time, allowing me to grow gradually accustomed to motherhood. I change his nappies. I practise breastfeeding, waking every few hours to feed him. The midwives give me lanolin ointment to soothe a cracked nipple or two; but apart from this minor discomfort, breastfeeding comes pretty naturally.

Aran makes a slow and steady recovery. Every day the

nurses draw his blood to check his bilirubin levels and to ensure that they are dropping.

I had originally hoped Aran and I could go home straight after his birth. Admittedly, I had an ulterior motive. I wanted to go to the first-ever Wicklow Round prize-giving ceremony that week, where I was to receive a commemorative plaque. But with Aran's unexpected illness, I am unable to attend. Before, I would have been devastated at missing such an event. Now, with Aran around, I know that it is more important to stay with him until he gets better rather than receive prizes and adulation for some long run I once did.

After seven days in hospital, Aran is given the all-clear. Pete and I hastily pack up his things, and prepare to bring him home. We still haven't acquired a stroller, let alone a travel system. Instead, we spent thirty pounds on a strip of fabric that wraps itself into an African-style sling. I carefully tie all the knots and place Aran inside the cloth's folds. He is snug within the wrap, held tightly against my chest.

Pete and I carry our brand-new baby down to our old, faithful car. Pete has managed to install the second-hand car seat we were given, after a few frustrating attempts in our home's driveway. We lower Aran into its arms.

'I'm amazed that the hospital has allowed us to take him away,' I say. 'We needed far more paperwork to bring Tom back home.'

Pete starts the car and inches us on to the main road. Every couple of seconds, he glances into the rear-view mirror.

'Is he okay?' Pete says, throwing looks over his shoulder. 'Is he still breathing?'

I am nervous too. It was fine when Aran and I were in

the hospital, with medical staff close at hand. Now we are out in the wide open, with just Pete and I completely responsible for Aran's well-being. Fortunately, help is at hand from the community midwife service. Just as Pete and I are leaving the hospital with Aran, I am informed that a community midwife will visit us in our home the next day.

I really appreciate the offer of help. However, being confined to a hospital for a whole week has made me a little stir-crazy. I was really looking forward to getting out and about with baby Aran. But now this midwife visit, at an unspecified time tomorrow, means I have to stay at home the whole day.

The next morning, I get up with Aran bright and early and make ourselves ready for our visitor. I feed us both, get washed and changed. 9 am comes and goes, but no sign of the midwife. 10 am soon arrives, and I'm wondering what to do with myself. I can't leave the house, so I instead start cleaning the place from top to bottom. I dust the shelves, the mantelpiece, then the picture frames. By 1 pm, I start to polish the silver that hasn't been touched in decades.

Where is this midwife? If she leaves it any longer, she might find me stripping the wallpaper and repainting the walls.

Finally she arrives at 3 pm, and immediately apologises. 'There were a few urgent cases I had to attend to this morning,' she explains.

'No worries,' I say, hoping we can now just get this over and done with so that we can both be on our merry way.

'So how has everything been going?' the midwife asks, when we finally sit down in my sparklingly clean living room.

'Fine,' I reply, trying not to look at the time on the watch dangling from her lapel. I wonder how long this will take.

'And your stitches?'

'No, no stitches.'

'Okay,' she replies, noting that down in my file. 'And how's the breastfeeding going?'

'Grand,' I reply. I figure the less I say, the sooner I can get out of here.

The midwife puts the file to one side. 'And how are you feeling in general?'

I open my mouth to give another curt response, but all that comes out is a muffled whine. Then I burst into desperate sobs.

'I'm sorry, I'm so sorry,' I say. Emotions have secretly pooled somewhere, unknown to me, and now they are exploding all over this poor midwife. 'It's just ... It's just ... I want to go out for coffee,' I blurt out. I try in vain to stop the tears streaming from my eyes. I am blubbering from my very core. All because I need a cup of coffee, from a real coffee shop in town.

'That's all right, love,' the midwife says, resting a hand on my knee. 'Are you feeling a little down?'

Oh God, please let this not be post-natal depression. When I was expecting, several friends had told me how they suffered from this condition after giving birth. And after hearing about their dreadful experiences, I have prayed night and day that I will not suffer a similar plight.

'I'm sorry,' I say, fiercely wiping my nose and face. 'It's just all been a bit much. Aran got sick, you see, and we had to spend a whole week in hospital, and I wasn't sure if or when he would be all right.'

I had managed to hold myself together for the whole

time in the hospital. But now that I am back in my own home, and I've a kind, listening ear, I have totally fallen apart.

'Don't worry,' she says. 'Many women get baby blues a couple of days after their baby is born.'

She assures me it is totally normal. But if I continue to feel emotional or anxious, I should contact her or my local doctor.

We conclude our home-based meeting, but it's not long before I have to call the midwife again. I know next to nothing about babies and their health, and my total ignorance in this department becomes apparent very soon.

I accidentally cover up his umbilical cord wound with his nappy, and it becomes oozy, red and sore. Aran's left eye starts to weep pus, as he develops conjunctivitis. His scalp becomes horribly flaky when he contracts cradle cap. Then he doesn't poo for days, as we anxiously wait for his first stool deposited outside of the hospital environment to arrive. Thankfully, the midwife's threat of a suppository soon gets Aran's bowels moving once more.

Soon, ten days have passed since Aran has appeared on the scene. And I've barely left the house.

'Why don't we go for a walk with Tom?' Pete says. 'I think we'd all appreciate some fresh air.' The mere mention of the word 'walk' sends Tom into a mad frenzy. It looks like we're going out, whether we like it or not.

We opt to visit the deserted beach I walked on just before my waters broke. I enclose Aran in his wrap on the excursion, and despite being buffeted by strong coastal winds and swirling sands, he soon nods off to sleep. The beach walk is the remedy I needed. Every step I take makes me realise that my lung space has finally returned.

I don't feel too breathless from the gentle steps I take on the shore.

Pete runs after Tom, who has spotted another dog frolicking in the waves. However, I am very aware that even a gentle jog towards the sea would be a very bad idea. Aran's abrupt exit has caused my pelvic floor to collapse. In addition, I have suffered a urinary prolapse. I am so stretched down there that I fear running might cause all my internal organs to slump out between my legs.

I am disappointed with myself. Irish Olympian Sonia O'Sullivan was back running ten days after giving birth. I am nowhere near that stage. So if I ever had the notion I was even close to Olympic material, I now know I was terribly mistaken.

When I get back to the house, I email my biking and pregnancy guru, Susie Mitchell, to see how soon she started exercising. Though she had a C-section, so had different issues to deal with, she suggests that once I can sit on a bike saddle, I should be able to go for a spin.

I am not convinced by Susie's suggestion. Sitting on a bike sounds really sore. But there is ultimately only one way to find out how bad the pain will be. I wheel out Bike, who has undergone solitary confinement in the garage for nearly two months. I slowly slip myself on to the saddle.

Much to my surprise, it is not sore at all. Within seconds I shout, 'Pete, can I go for a bike ride?'

Back in the day, I could hop on my bike and inform Pete when I'd be back from my spin. But now, with baby Aran about and me breastfeeding him, we need military-precise coordination for when I can and can't leave the house.

'So, if I give Aran a feed now, he probably won't need one for another hour,' I say to Pete, trying to work out when and for how long I can abscond.

'But what if he looks for a feed while you're away?'

'I don't know,' I say, trying to escape the house with Bike. 'Can't you figure that out yourself?'

Pete looks at me blankly.

'Look, I'll be back in sixty minutes,' I say to Pete, begging him to let me go. 'If he cries, I don't know, sing to him or something.' I cycle off before Pete can lodge a formal protest.

Riding Bike is sheer heaven. I had forgotten how fast you can go, how the wind whips your hair and catches your breath, how the rhythm of the pedals soothes away all your cares. It is also wonderful to be back cycling without a baby inside me. My lungs feel as large as life, no longer squashed against my ribs. I can push myself a little harder on the hills, and not worry about raised heart rates or overheating myself. Gone too are the fears I had of falling off Bike and doing Bump permanent harm.

It is not only the joy of being outdoors and doing some exercise that thrills me so much. It is the fact that I am getting a brief break from motherhood. Since giving birth two weeks ago, I have felt so fat and unfit. With Aran waking up every couple of hours at night, sleep deprivation is hitting me hard. Now, for this single hour, I am doing something I love that could reverse all these afflictions. I tell myself to cling to this time that it is solely mine.

I arrive back home, on a high from my ride. It's great to have different chemicals coursing through my veins instead of pregnancy hormones. I bounce through the front door, full of serotonin and dopamine. I feel like a completely new woman.

Aran is starting to stir from his slumber on Pete's shoulder.

'Perfect timing!' I shout to Pete with a smile.

I take Aran off him and carefully slide Aran under my biking top. Though my breast milk is now laced with lactic acid from my exercise, Aran doesn't seem to mind a bit. He drinks greedily from the supply, then falls back fast asleep.

Though I have been away from Aran for a relatively short period, I am so happy to see my son again. Not that he has much of a personality or provides much entertainment. It's just that I'm so full of the love hormone, oxytocin, that I can't help but attach to him. He's been in my life for a mere two weeks, but already I kind of like him.

8
Training

Getting out on Bike gives me a new lease of life. And though Aran is less than a month old, I reckon he needs to get into the habit of regular exercise too.

I do some research and discover there are water babies' sessions in the local pool. Aran and I are going to start swimming together. I need to register at the local Sure Start centre before turning up for classes. Pete comes along to Sure Start out of curiosity. He also wants to see if there are activities he can do with Aran to bond with him as well.

'I want to sign up for water babies,' I tell the lady-in-charge at Sure Start. We are in her office, perched on a soft, spacious sofa. Aran is sitting snuggly on my knee. I don't want to lean back though and get too comfortable. All I want to do is register and get out of there.

'That's wonderful!' she says, patting her floral skirt. 'Swimming is brilliant for mums and babies. And is Dad going to go as well?'

Pete opens his mouth, but nothing comes out.

'No, just me, thanks,' I say.

'Marvellous!' the lady says, shuffling through some random papers before handing me a registration form.

'While you're here, would you like to join the breast-feeding support group?' she says. 'They are actually just meeting in the room down the corridor at the moment.'

I had already bumped into the support group by accident when we were looking for the lady's office. I had opened the door and seen all the mummies and infants spread out on the carpeted floor. I didn't mean to, but my instinctive reaction was to recoil.

'No, thanks,' I say. 'My breastfeeding is going fine. No support needed here.' I force a strained smile.

I'm just not interested in talking to strangers about lactation, or anything else baby-related for that matter. Now if they wanted to chat about power outputs and cadence, electrolytes and heart rates, then I just might reconsider attending.

'Well then, baby massage?'

'No,' I say adamantly.

This woman will not give up.

My knee has started shaking. Pete reaches over to calm down my leg.

'I'll go,' he says. The lady and I spin round in our seats. 'I'll go to baby massage.'

'Are you for real?' I say to Pete once we've escaped Sure Start offices. 'Or is this how you plan to bond with Aran?'

'God, no!' Pete says. 'I have zero interest in baby massage. I was just afraid you'd get put on a child welfare watch list for not participating in mother and baby stuff.'

'Ah, come on now, Pete, you're just exaggerating.'

'Listen, you said no to everything she suggested. And the tone in that room was starting to go south,' he says. 'I figured I should take one for the team.'

I mope back to the car, feeling guilty that I am not an

enthusiast mother who wants to participate in everything baby-related. And I thought I was doing so well wanting to sign up for baby swimming.

A couple of days later, I am at home with Aran when I receive a visit from a community health worker. I'm petrified she's going to take Aran away and haul me in to social services for refusing to engage with the support network.

'Oh goodness, I wouldn't worry about that,' Bridgeen, the health worker, says when I bring up the issue. 'Not everyone wants to go to those support things.'

I am relieved. At last someone who understands that bump and baby classes are not everyone's cup of tea.

Bridgeen is a health worker pro. She is about the same age as me, but already has two teenagers at home. She's been there before. Bridgeen is also the person who will guide me through the next two years while Aran grows and develops.

'So how are Mum and baby doing?' Bridgeen asks in her broad Northern Irish accent. I think hard and long about the question. I'm stuck in such a sleep-deprived haze that I can't really recall much of what's happened over the last couple of weeks.

'Okay, I think,' I say. I try to do a quick test and recollect what I had for breakfast. Actually, did I have breakfast today? Oh dear. I'm really struggling to remember pretty much anything.

'Well, why don't we have a quick look at Aran and see how well he's growing?' Bridgeen asks me to strip him down to his nappy so that we can weigh and measure him.

'Oh my goodness,' she says. 'What's that?' She is pointing straight at Aran's groin.

'It's a nappy,' I reply. 'A cloth one.' I think the water

birth experience has really affected me. Not only have I given birth like Mother Earth, but I have also become ridiculously eco-friendly. Having read about the landfills crammed with disposable nappies that refuse to decompose, I have opted to use cloth nappies.

'When I lived in Kenya,' I tell Bridgeen, 'they used to tie old jumpers around their babies' bums to catch the pee and poo.' At least I have a washing machine that I can throw Aran's soiled nappies straight into. The poor Kenyan mums I knew had no option but to hand-wash theirs.

Bridgeen places Aran carefully on the large scales she has brought along and records his current weight. She then lays him on a plastic mat marked out with lines, stretches his legs as far as they will go, and works out how tall he is. She then informs me that he is all wonderfully average in height and size.

As he lies on the floor, Aran starts to cry, protesting at all this poking and prodding of his nakedness. Without thinking, I pick him up, cover him up with a blanket, and give him a quick feed. I've found that mammy's milk seems to cure all his afflictions instantaneously.

'It looks like he's taking well to the breast milk,' Bridgeen says.

'It seems to work for me.'

'Absolutely. Whatever works for Mum. The recommendation is that, if you can, to exclusively breastfeed Aran for his first six months. Then you can introduce him to solids.'

I hadn't really thought about what happens that far down the road with his feeding regime. Thus far I've taken each day as it comes, pleased if Aran and I are in still in one piece by bedtime. But there's still one thing I've yet to figure out when it comes to feeding Aran. How can I breastfeed exclusively and still disappear for a couple of hours each day to do a bit of training? Wouldn't Aran get hungry while I'm gone?

'What type of training do you do?' Bridgeen enquires, her curiosity taking me by surprise.

'A bit of biking, a bit of running,' I tell her, convinced she's not interested in the details.

'I'm a runner too,' she says. 'I do road races in the summer, and cross-country during the winter.'

Cross-country at our age? Now that's well hardcore. I'm surprised that I hadn't already deduced her athletic prowess. Bridgeen is tall and muscular from years of hill sprints, with a taut, tanned face that's used to going at speed.

'I run with Sparta AC,' she says.

'Oh my God, that's my old athletic club!'

Maybe I can become Bridgeen's running bosom-buddy.

'It's best you wait until Aran is around eight weeks before you introduce him to a bottle,' Bridgeen goes on to explain. 'If you give him a bottle too early on, he can get confused between the breast and bottle-feeding.'

I look down at Aran on my lap. He has overdosed on milk and is busy sleeping it off. The poor thing has so much to learn in life, even when it just comes down to the subject of eating.

'But once the eight-week mark has passed,' she says, 'you can express your milk out of your breast, either with a pump or using your hand. And then you can put that milk in a bottle, and leave it with whoever is taking care of Aran.'

Whenever I see Pete next, I tell him this update on the breastfeeding news front. I then inform him with my latest plan: to give him the baby and a bottle, and for me to quietly disappear and go training.

'But you know I can't look after Aran every time you want to go for a bike or run?'

I look at Pete blankly.

'I have to go back to work sometime soon.'

I had forgotten that we need an income. With both of us working as self-employed consultants, we have the luxury of working when and where we please. But Pete has already neglected his clients for nearly a month, and he is going to lose contracts if he doesn't get back to the grindstone soon.

'But you can't leave me all alone with him,' I say. I hear desperation in my tone as I stare over at Aran.

'I know, I know,' Pete says. 'Sure didn't we discuss this already? The last thing I want is to come home to a crazy wife.'

I know I am meant to protest the suggestion that I could potentially go crazy, but I know it's a distinct possibility if I have to constantly mind the baby.

'Let's find somewhere you can leave Aran for an hour or two a couple of days a week,' Pete says. I like the idea. Not only will it give me a break, but it will also allow Aran to get used to other people. With just Pete and I around, I am worried that he might become a clingy child.

I ask around and find a crèche in the centre of Derry city that has flexible operating hours. Pete, Aran, and I arrange to visit it together before Pete heads back to work.

'Och, will you look at the wee love?' the woman in charge says as she opens the crèche door. She takes Aran's tiny fist and gives it a friendly shake. 'How old is he?' Her gaze is firmly fixed on Aran, but I think the question is directed at me.

'Four weeks tomorrow,' I say.

She beckons us inside the crèche doors. It is full of brightly coloured walls and various plastic toys. There are children running riot around the place. They are all much older than Aran. I wonder if this will be an issue.

'As long as he has his six-week vaccinations, we're happy to take this wee dote.' She seems totally besotted with Aran. I think he'll like it here.

We agree to leave Aran initially at the crèche three times a week for two hours. I feel guilty about leaving Aran there, but know we have few other options. Aran is not like Tom, who we can easily leave at home unattended for half a day. Pete and I are slowly coming around to the realisation that baby Aran needs constant, twenty-four-hour supervision.

With Aran's daytime schedule sorted, it is time to get myself checked out. I make an appointment to see my doctor six weeks after the birth.

'So how are things going?' the doctor asks me. I am asked this question with amazing regularity these days. Its consistent posing has allowed me to refine my answer to perfection.

'Fine,' I say, surprised by how convincing I sound. Contrary to my own expectations, the last six weeks have gone amazingly quickly. Time flies when you're ridiculously sleep-deprived. I try to recall what I've done for the last month and a half. All I can remember are feeds, nappy changes, and frequent nap interruptions. The occasional hour-long walks or cycles have served well to break the monotony of it all. The baby blues were a minor hiccup on what has been, in general, a well-managed upheaval in my life.

The doctor who does my check is the same one who

came close to scuppering my Ethiopia trip when I was pregnant. We don't mention that incident, and mutually decide to move on. All's well that ends well, apparently.

The six-week check takes a lot less time to complete than expected. I have healed up pretty well. And I appear somewhat emotionally stable and generally happy enough. So, in less than fifteen minutes, I am given the all-clear.

I pick up the phone as soon as I get home and call Eamonn, my new coach.

'All good to go,' I tell him.

'Great stuff,' he says. 'So let's get started and set ourselves a few ground rules.'

Eamonn tells me that, from now, I'll keep a training diary that's accessible online.

'I'll work out what you need to do each day,' he says. 'Your job is to get the sessions done.'

I am relieved. My brain has become a little fuzzy since childbirth and I struggle to make decisions. When I get a chance to train, it takes me forever to work out if I want to bike or run. Then I can't decide how far or for how long I will go. When it comes to training, Eamonn will do all this taxing thinking for me.

'You'll need to use a GPS and heart rate monitor during all of your workouts,' Eamonn continues. 'If you upload the data, I can then review it, and give you feedback every couple of days.'

'So you'll be checking up on me to see if I've done the session or not?' I say, unsure if I like this new level of scrutiny.

'Listen, it's up to you if you want to do the training or not,' Eamonn says. 'I know what it's like when you've young children.'

'Don't get me wrong,' I say. 'I *want* to do all the sessions. I'm just not sure how feasible it will be.'

I'm still not convinced my childminding strategy at the crèche will pan out, that I'll be free to do all of Eamonn's proposed sessions. And I'm wondering if I'll be physically able to train, what with the surprises post-natal bodies can unexpectedly spring.

But even with all these doubts buzzing through my mind, there is part of me that knows that I have no choice but to prepare to race again. Racing is something I enjoy, and was once good at before all this baby stuff. This reality I cling to more than ever, especially now that I'm faced with dealing with parenthood, an activity I'm a total novice at. Racing is an identity that I am proud of. I cannot abandon it right now.

Eamonn and I agree to take it slow, see how it goes, and revise the training plan when required.

The first week of training with Eamonn is mild-mannered enough. He gives me a paltry twenty-minute run to do at barely jogging speed, with instructions not to exceed a heart rate of one hundred and thirty. Although painfully slow, it is nevertheless marvellous to run without carting around a bump.

Eamonn then gives me an hour's bike session to do, but it is still at a snail's pace. And though the biking and running training is easy, he kills me with strength and conditioning. Not once, not twice, but three times a week I am now doing squats, lunges, press-ups, skips, and planks. My poor body doesn't know what's hit it. My core muscles that drifted apart during pregnancy are now being forcibly reunited. My glutes, quads, and hamstrings scream when I even look at a flight of stairs. I do a bit of yoga to try and relieve the pain. Everything just about folds and stretches like before, but it is a very creaky affair.

Painful though the training is, it gives me something very definite to look forward to each day. I now have a clear break marked into my daily schedule when I can totally forget about crying, feeding, and nappy changing.

Pete is now back at work and I leave Aran at the crèche for my bike sessions. It takes me a while, but I eventually figure out the most efficient sequencing. I rock up to the crèche's front door all kitted out in helmet, clip-in shoes, and padded shorts. Aran is strapped to my body, while I wheel Bike inside with my free hand. I then stash Bike in the corridor beside the other baby strollers that belong to the other kids.

I bring Aran into the crèche, and undo my top. I push Aran under my sports bra that is holding my udders in place. It is a bit of a squeeze, as the bras I have to wear these days have to be super tight; if not, there could be trouble with my boobs jiggling about while I exercise. Aran is still less than eight weeks old, so a bottle is not yet an option. So I have to fill him up as much as possible, directly from the source. I don't want him crying with hunger and bothering the crèche staff while I'm away. All he needs is ninety minutes' worth of breast milk so that I can do my session in peace.

I come back from my bike ride, buzzing with adrenaline.

'How was he?' I ask.

'Great,' the crèche staff tell me. Aran is bouncing about on one of their laps. I am genuinely happy to see him.

I take him into my arms and give him a quick top-up. This training and motherhood combination might just work out all right.

Pete sees how hard I'm working to get this combo going.

'Can I get you a birthing present?' he says. I look at him, slightly bewildered.

'Aren't husbands meant to buy their wives something,' he asks, 'to thank them for giving birth to their kid?'

'Buy me something? Like what?'

'I don't know. Diamonds?'

Diamonds are so not me. I don't even wear my engagement ring, as it just tends to get in the way. No, I've got a way better idea.

'Why don't you buy me a set of bike rollers as a thank-you present?'

'Bike what?' Pete says. 'What are they?'

'Don't you worry,' I say. 'I'll buy them online and send you the bill.' And so, to thank me for enduring all those months of pregnancy, my husband pays for a set of rollers that let me ride Bike inside the house. It is a genuinely romantic gesture.

But even when the rollers arrive, Pete is still confused. 'How exactly are you meant to use those things?' He is examining the three long metallic cylinders that are connected together by industrial rods. He spins them around with a push of his hand. They don't look safe at all.

'Well, you put your bike on top of the rollers, then pedal your bike,' I say, as if I know it all.

'All right then,' Pete says. 'Show me.'

I've never used rollers before but I am determined not to lose face in front of Pete. I balance my back wheel on the two rear cylinders, and my front wheel on the remaining one. Holding on to Pete's shoulder, I hoist myself on to the saddle, and press my foot down. My bike rolls one way, I roll the other, and Pete catches me as I fall.

'Think I need a little practice,' I say, trying to hide my shame.

I soon discover that the way to use rollers initially is to park them in a doorway. Then if you lurch to the left or right, there's a wooden beam on either side to break your immediate fall. I spend weeks practising on my rollers. At the start, I cling for dear life to both sides of the doorway. Eventually, one hand moves to the handlebars, then the other. It takes me nearly a month to perfect the balancing act.

In my mind, Bike and I are ploughing up highways together, careering down hills at breakneck speeds. But to all around us, I am pedalling frantically in my living room, going absolutely nowhere.

Roller sessions are perfect for minding Aran. I put him in his chair in front of me so I can watch his every move. I put Bike on the rollers, and I spin away, doing my session without leaving my front door.

Buoyed by the success of my indoor cycling, I try different ways to solve the 'training with Aran' conundrum. One day I have no crèche arranged and Pete is away for work. I have a thirty-minute run to do, so decide to hit the treadmill. I bring Aran to a local gym that I know will be quiet and welcoming. I lie Aran down inside a Moses basket, and place it right beside me. I start the treadmill and slowly quicken my stride. But Aran is unsettled.

He might need a little drink. I stop the treadmill abruptly and pick baby Aran up. Squatting on the stationary running belt, I give him a quick feed. It seems to do the trick, and he slowly closes his eyes. But as soon as I place him back in the basket, he starts to grimace and whine.

The sound of the treadmill. Does that lull a baby to sleep?

I ignore the growing sounds of his cries as I increase the pace of the track. With the surge in speed, the whirring noises rise, but so do Aran's squeals.

There is nothing more distressing for a parent than hearing their baby endlessly scream. After less than a minute, I can't take it any more and hit the emergency stop button. I dismount the belt and pick Aran up to calm his angry tears. But as his tears are soothed, mine begin to torrent down my cheeks out of sheer frustration. I am forced to give up on the treadmill idea for the foreseeable future.

It's becoming painfully obvious that, though I may have given birth to Aran, when it comes to child-rearing I know about as much as Pete.

Finally, Aran passes the eight-week mark, and I extract my milk with glee. I hand a milk-filled bottle and the baby to Pete, and go for my scheduled hour-long run. I come back home, refreshed by my brief break. Aran is fast asleep on Pete's shoulder. But Pete is not looking happy at all.

'How did it go?' I ask, unsure if I really want to know.

'He cried for the full hour and literally just fell asleep,' Pete says. 'He totally refused the bottle.'

'Oh no, you're not serious.' The happiness I felt coming in the door rapidly dissipates. 'Did you warm the milk?'

'Yes.'

'And did you try another teat?' I heard that could make a difference.

'YEEESSS,' Pete says. I am lucky Pete is busy holding Aran, or else he would get up and throttle me.

Before I had children, I could disappear for hours, even days on end, and run through the mountains without a care. Now even leaving the house for sixty minutes causes immense stress and upheaval. I had no idea how much I would have to sacrifice when a baby arrived on the scene. I am sure I was told, but could never fully understand, the time and effort required to look after one.

I am so close to promising Pete that I won't leave him alone ever again with Aran. That I'll stop all this silly training, that I'll make sure I'm around all the time to look after our child. It would be so easy for me to just give up right now. The problem is, I always finish what I start. It is something my parents ingrained in me from an early age. And I've just started this road back to fitness. If I give in now, not only will I lose all the benefits that exercise promises, but I will also consider myself an abject failure for forsaking something that is so fundamental to my identity.

Desperate for some respite, I too try to get Aran to drink from a bottle. Pete tries. The crèche staff all try to get Aran to drink breast milk from this receptacle. In the end, all of us fail spectacularly. Aran is a breast man through and through, and he's determined to stay that way.

9

Race

'I want to race,' I tell Eamonn during our weekly catch-up call. I'm sure he'll tell me it's far too soon. I've only done six weeks of proper training, and I'm struggling to get back into any sort of form.

'Great idea!' he says, making me do a double take. 'Nothing like a goal to keep you motivated. Which one are you hoping to do?'

I had already secretly researched some adventure races and found one in Donegal. Just like the one I did when five months pregnant, this one also takes place on the Inishowen Peninsula. The Rugged Peaks Race is a sixty-five-kilometre course across one of Ireland's remotest parts, full of rolling hills, rugged coastline, and stunning, unspoilt scenery. And it is literally just down the road. It means I can do the race and be back home in the afternoon without upsetting too much Aran or Pete's routine.

Days before the event, however, I am horrified to hear it won't go ahead due to insufficient entries. It is October, and it seems that everyone is either injured or penniless from competing in events throughout the summer. I am incredibly disappointed. Ever since I met Susie, I've set myself the mental target of competing at the four-month post-natal mark. Susie won her Masters Track title four months after giving birth; I want to do something like that.

I start to look around for something else that can take the place of the Rugged Peaks Race. There is barely anything left on the 2013 race calendar. After hours of clicking through websites, I happen upon the Sea to Summit adventure race. It takes place on the cusp of Ireland's winter, slap bang in mid-November. There are two race routes, a thirty-kilometre short course called Spirit, and the fifty-six-kilometre long course, aptly named Supreme.

The only problem is that Sea to Summit takes place in Westport, a three-and-a-half-hour drive from where we live. Aran will have to accompany me, what with his on-going refusal to be separated from my breasts for more than a couple of hours. And Pete will have to come along too, so that he can look after Aran while I'm on the course.

It seems like a logistical nightmare. I hope we'll be able to work it out.

I figure that if I'm going to travel this far for a race, I might as well do the longer course. I click on the route details and take a deep breath. The race starts with a four-kilometre run out of Westport towards the quays via the town's purpose-built greenway. From there, it is an eight-kilometre cycle along the Atlantic coastline towards the foot of Croagh Patrick Mountain. The peak is a paltry five kilometres up and down distance-wise. But the mountain's height of seven hundred and sixty-four metres knocks the wind out of competitors' sails. Having summited the mountain and returned to the base, the course returns racers to their bikes. It is then a thirty-five-kilometre cycle up and over the Maum hills, where gradients reach a lung-busting twenty-five degrees in parts. Fortunately, the bike section leads back to Westport, where those who are still able and willing run the last four-kilometre stretch back along the greenway and into Westport town.

Just reading the course description leaves me exhausted.

I click on pictures from last year's Croagh Patrick Mountain ascent. I see skinny men dressed in tight triathlon suits looking way too fit for their own good. They also look totally shattered, however, as they crawl their way up Croagh Patrick's boulder-strewn, precipitous slopes. Thick mist swirls around them as they attempt to find the summit, and all around them thick snow impedes their progress and freezes their naked, shaven legs.

I feel cold and tired just looking at these images. But if I am to keep my post-natal racing promise, I have no choice but to enter this Sea to Summit race.

I soon discover the reason why the photos are full of fit and thin sportsmen and women. Sea to Summit is the last race on Ireland's National Adventure Race Series calendar. Athletes are signing up in their droves to earn much-needed points for their final rankings before the season ends. This also means that thousands of competitors will attend the event. There is no risk of last-minute race cancellation this time around.

I tell Eamonn about my reluctant decision. 'Go for it,' he says as he shuffles my training schedule around to suit this change in plan.

With my first race scheduled, training starts to tick along quite nicely. It has taken a while, however, to get into the swing of things. Babysitting obligations have caused a bit of back and forth with Eamonn about how to fit sessions in. We've finally worked out ways to ensure I'm not out of the house for more than ninety minutes. Where there are two sessions to do, they are both done in the morning rather than staggered over the day. Rest days are moved around to fit into random baby activities.

There is something about this formal, structured training that is really working for me. Maybe it's the fact that each session has a defined purpose, whether it is to build strength, aerobic capacity, or a chance for me to rest. With Eamonn involved, I don't have to think about what session I should do, or why.

My own mother also comes to my aid to help facilitate my training. Twice a week, I hand Aran over to her, and she looks after him.

'Are you sure you're okay with this, Mum?' I ask, as I am about to head out for my bike spin on one of her designated days. Even though Mum is totally up for babysitting Aran, I still feel like I am abandoning her as much as I am deserting my own child. Will I ever get over this irrational guilt complex I have of leaving Aran with someone else?

'You know I love looking after Aran,' Mum says, flashing her grandson a mighty grin. 'Now off you go, my dear,' ushering me out the front door.

She may be in her seventies, but Mum finds a new lease of life when she's around her new grandchild. I have no idea what they get up to while I'm away, but I have my deep suspicions. I arrive in after my bike ride, with the kitchen in total chaos. There are cuddly toys and baby books strewn all across the floor. Aran's seat is deserted.

'Mum, Mum, where are you guys?' I call.

'Shhhhhh,' she says, before whispering loudly, 'We're in the living room.'

I make my way to the other room, stepping over some

rattles and blocks on my way. I had left the place spotless. I come back to find it booby-trapped.

I see Mum plonked down on the sofa, with half an eye open. Aran is fast asleep on her belly, with a cosy blue blanket draped across both of them.

'How did it go?' I ask, thinking I might already know the answer.

'We had great craic altogether,' Mum says. 'Though I might have tired Aran out a little bit.'

Aran looks peaceful as he snuggles himself up close to his granny, who looks like she could do with a little nap right now as well.

'Thanks for looking after him, Mum. I think I can take it from here.'

'Not at all,' Mum says. 'Sure leave him here with me, and go have a shower or something.'

I hate leaving Aran with others longer than I need to, but I get the impression that Mum is trying to get rid of me. Aran and Mum are becoming best buddies. It seems to me that Mum is trying to spend as much time as she can with him.

Between Granny, the crèche and Pete, Aran now has someone to look after him most days of the week. It allows me to train consistently. However, I still have much to learn about how to train properly. I go for a ninety-minute bike ride one day and upload my data once I'm home. I think I've done a nice fast session and wait for positive feedback to come. Instead, Eamonn takes one look at my heart rate graph and scolds me. 'Your heart rate was too high for the session,' he writes on my plan. 'It needs to be more stable.'

I look at the data Eamonn has just slated. When I bike uphill, my heart rate soars. And when I freewheel downhill, the heart rate drops dramatically.

'It needs to be close to a flat line,' Eamonn tells when I speak to him next. 'I shouldn't be able to tell what type of terrain you're going over.'

'So I need to hold back when going uphill, and push harder going down?' It is the total opposite of what normally happens when I go out biking with a group.

'For this type of session, yes, that's exactly what you need to do,' Eamonn explains.

Though I severely doubt what Eamonn is telling me, I figure he's the coach in this relationship. There must be some sort of method to his madness if he comes so highly recommended.

Not many people want to ride their bikes in the way Eamonn is instructing me. I struggle to find anyone who wants to pedal at a pace that is dictated solely by how fast my heart beats. The time of day I go training now is also governed by childcare availability. Not many amateur athletes are available, however, to train at 10 am on weekdays. These two mitigating factors mean that, if I want to adhere strictly to my training plan, I have to train on my own.

Though I initially doubt I am training hard enough or long enough, my fitness levels start to improve. Eamonn has me checking my resting heart rate in the morning, as soon as I wake up. The beats slowly decrease week on week, dipping below forty as the Sea to Summit race approaches. Having a lower resting heart rate is a sure sign that I am doing something right.

The day before the race, Aran, Pete and I pack up our gear and make our way to Westport. We arrive in the town at 5 pm, just as it is getting dark. The early sunset time is a sign that winter is truly setting in.

There is so much to do before I can race tomorrow.

First I have to collect my race number. However, I forget to bring my mandatory kit to registration, and have to run back to the car to get it. I need to show the officials a first aid kit, a foil blanket, a whistle, a jacket, and my bike helmet before they will hand over my number. All these things I also need to carry on the course tomorrow in case of any accidents.

I open the car boot and start to rummage around in my bags to find the required items. Unfortunately, with it being night-time already, I can barely see a thing. I wasn't prepared to present them at registration, a failure on my part to read the final event instructions. I had packed them away safely before travelling, thinking I would put them together just before the start. Pete, Aran and I are all tired and grumpy from the long day's journey. Looking for a whistle in a stack of bags is the last thing I need right now.

I manage to get the required bits and pieces together and present them at registration. In addition to my number, I get a timing dibber and a sticker for my bike.

'You need to drop your bike down to Westport Quay now,' the official tells me, as I'm about to leave the building. Westport Quay is a five-minute drive from the centre of town. Bike needs to be there all ready and waiting for me tomorrow morning, after the first four-kilometre run.

It is pitch black when we park our car at the quays. There are no streetlights installed in this deserted part of town. Normally empty at this time of night, the place is now buzzing with cars, loaded with racers and their bikes. This time I'm organised, and I have Bike already kitted out with his sticker, a full bottle of water, and my cycle helmet. However, some are not so fortunate, and are trying to pump up tyres and fix brakes under the gaze of weak head-torch beams. I cycle the short distance to the racks and drop Bike in his allocated spot. I leave him there, wishing him a safe and sound night.

Pete, Aran and I drive back into town and find our accommodation, a local bed and breakfast.

'Welcome, welcome,' the lady of the house says as she opens the front door. B&B hosts are notoriously friendly in this part of the country. 'My name is Helen. And you must be Pete and Moire. And who's this little man?'

'This is Aran,' I say. 'He'll be four months old next week.'

'Ah, will you look at the cute baba. Doesn't look any trouble at all.'

If only she knew the full story.

Helen shows us up to our room, which comes complete with a travel cot installed. It's the first time we've seen such a contraption up close. 'So you've come to do tomorrow's race?' our host says, directing her innocent question at my husband.

'Ah, yes ... Well, no,' Pete says. 'My wife is doing the race, not me.'

I plunge my hands deep into my pockets. I don't know who's more embarrassed, Pete, me or Helen.

I know it sounds completely crazy to compete in an adventure race less than four months after giving birth. But I want to explain to Helen that, in fact, more and more women are proving that it can be done. Having a baby doesn't automatically mean I have to stay at home and forsake forever my identity. In fact, the training I've done after Aran's birth, and the goal of racing again, has kept me happy and healthy during these post-natal days.

But I don't tell Helen any of this. I just shrug my shoulders and thank her for the room.

I regret entering the race as soon as I arrive at the start

106

line. Fifteen hundred participants have gathered in the early morning darkness outside Westport's Castlecourt Hotel for the start of the Sea to Summit race. The skinny triathletes have arrived en masse. I feel intimidated. These girls and guys have been busy competing and winning all round them for an entire season. In addition to the superb looking triathletes, I also see Fiona Meade and Marie Boyle, the current top two females in Ireland's National Adventure Race Series. I recognise them from my trawl of last year's race photos.

What worries me most is not the race, but leaving my baby for the next four hours. The longest I have left him thus far is two and a half, by which time he was starving and bawling for milk. So, on the pavement outside the hotel I give him a top-up feed, before leaving him with Pete and a promise to be back before one o'clock.

On the stroke of 9 am, the adventure racers are let loose and take off at a gallop. I see Fiona and Marie sprint off at great speed. Much as I want to join them, I know I will never keep up. I opt instead to run at my own pace and see how I get along. After the four-kilometre run, we arrive at the quays and our bikes. I am currently the fifth lady, a position I am happy with. Bike and I team up, without Bump this time, and we draft as much as possible on the short cycle to the base of Croagh Patrick.

For many, ascending Croagh Patrick is Ireland's ultimate penance, the country's Holy Grail of pilgrimages. Legend has it that Ireland's very own patron saint fasted here for forty days and nights in AD 441, preparing Patrick for his mission to convert the Irish to Christianity. At seven hundred and sixty-four metres in height, Croagh Patrick is certainly not Ireland's highest peak. But its steep, rocky paths have put the fear of God into many who have attempted to scale its slopes. And it is to this very top that the race route now beckons me.

I can quickly tell I haven't mountain run for a while. The ascent is sharp and painful, forcing me soon to walk. I stutter and stammer over the boulders that litter the entire track. And as the path steepens towards the summit, my lungs beg for this torment to come to a merciful end. I touch the top and turn to run downhill, but notice I have lost descending courage. I skid to a stop on the rocky descent, then lurch down the rest with short, uncertain strides. Still, my time earns me the second fastest woman on the mountain, and by the bottom, I have worked my way up to third place.

Much to my surprise, my family are at the base of Croagh Patrick to give me some welcome support. Pete is there, smiling and clapping softly as Aran slumbers in his wrap. I give both of them a quick peck on the cheek and assure them that all is good before continuing on with my race.

I grab Bike and head out towards the Maum Hills. By now racers are spaced out along the road, the Croagh Patrick ascent having separated the field. The road steepens to ridiculous slants, forcing me to dismount Bike. Eventually, as we get to the top of the final hill, I remount Bike, and together we push hard all the way down to Westport. I cycle as fast as I can, knowing that brilliant triathletes and bikers are just behind me. But despite their foreboding presence, I get back to the bike transition without another girl passing me.

The last four-kilometre run nearly kills me. I failed to bring enough water and am now dying of thirst. I grab an abandoned bottle I find on the roadside and slug its entire contents. I am so tired I don't give a damn whose mouth it was previously around. It gives me just enough sustenance to shuffle back to town, all the time waiting for a woman to pass me and take my podium place.

I reach the finish in three hours forty-seven minutes, well under the four-hour time limit I had set myself. And less than a minute later, another female competitor crosses the line behind me.

'Third place!' Pete shouts. 'Well done!' he says, giving me an enormous bear hug. Aran is in the wrap on Pete's chest, and gets squashed in the celebrations. I am too exhausted to reciprocate his embrace, though I silently share his excitement.

'I'm so proud of you, my amazing wife!' he tells me as we walk back together to the B&B.

And I'm so proud to be married to such a wonderfully supportive partner. Though, of course, I'm too tired to tell him this myself, to vocalise those grateful words out loud. Hopefully I'll remember to reciprocate his thoughts and feelings once I've had a little lie-down.

Later than night we return to the Castlecourt Hotel for prize-giving. The hall is full of adventure racers, all clean and dolled up for the after-party. Pete and I look distinctly out of place in our obviously sleep-deprived state. Aran, on the other hand, snoozes through the event, snuggling up to my bosom in his wrap. Afraid to wake him when my name is called, I carry him up with me to share in my third placed result. There's a minor gasp when the partygoers realise the bundle I'm carrying holds a tiny baby.

Pete, Aran and I can't stay awake long enough to take part in the celebrations. Gone are the days of racing hard and partying to all hours afterwards. Instead we slink back to our beds and slip back home the next morning.

10

Stress

I am on a high after the Sea to Summit race. Not only did I manage to come third overall, but I've proven my post-pregnancy body can still race after all. I am also so proud that Pete and I managed to travel across half the country with a young baby, and that we successfully looked after Aran while so far away from the safety of home.

But the elation doesn't last long. A few days after the race, I develop a painfully sore throat and a rattling cough. When I tell Eamonn of this unforeseen sickness, he is not surprised. He could tell my body was unwell from my training data and elevated heart rates. It seems like I can hide nothing from this man.

Eamonn gives me a few days' rest to let my body heal. With loads of free time now on my hands, I decide to go along to the water babies' classes I had signed up to at Sure Start.

The changing room is crammed full of babies the same age as Aran. I didn't realise so many women were busy reproducing at the same time as me. I do, however, seem to be one of the oldest mothers at the swimming pool. Maybe bearing children on the cusp of forty isn't really what's done around here. Fortunately, we are all in the same boat when it comes to our post-natal bodies; all of us are struggling to hide sagging bums and tums under our swimming costumes.

As soon as we're submerged though, our bodies can't be seen. Most of the babies start to bob around in the pool without the slightest flinch. Aran appears too busy sucking his fist to be bothered by the water lapping around him. It's only when I see one mum arriving with her baby girl that I realise not all babies are partial to the pool. The child has no more than her toe in the water than she starts to squeal violently. The poor mother is startled by the child's reaction, confined then for the rest of the session to the water's shallow edge.

'Well, hello everyone,' the female instructor says as the session begins. She tells us to make a circle, each parent holding their respective child. 'So, let's start with singing our water songs,' she says, clapping her hands with glee.

Water songs? Oh no, you're not serious. I don't like singing. I despise nursery rhymes. And I definitely don't bob around in a pool with other mums and their offspring reciting silly songs. Are we not meant to be teaching our kids how to do breaststroke and butterfly? When do we teach them how to dive underwater, like on Nirvana's *Nevermind* album cover?

Only memories of Pete's warning stop me from fleeing the swimming baths. I could still be a target for the child welfare watch list if I refuse to participate in mother and baby stuff.

Before I know it, the instructor breaks into verse. 'Hello Aran, Hello Aran, Hello Aran, we're glad to see you here.' All the mothers are holding their babies' hands, and waving them directly at my son. I avoid all eye contact with these women by staring down at baby Aran. He is too taken with trying to catch a plastic duck floating past him to register any sort of shame. Well, if this set-up isn't embarrassing Aran, I guess I can suck it up for his sake.

Fortunately, the song's next victim switches to the kid right beside me. 'Hello Thomas, Hello Thomas ...' There are ten babies in this circle. This song could take a while.

I am next inflicted with renditions of *Incy Wincy Spider*, *Five Little Ducks went Swimming*, and the ultimate classic, *Do the Hokey Kokey*. Aran seems happy enough to endure it all, as he floats around in the water. I am surprised how proud I start to feel about Aran, who is obviously coping so well. I can't help but compare him to the other children, especially those who are not taking to swimming like proverbial ducks. But my pride in Aran is soon, unfortunately, annihilated.

The instructor decides it's time to sing *it's raining, it's pouring*. As we hum along, the instructor comes around and sprinkles the entire contents of a plastic watering can on top of Aran's head. As the water makes contact with his eyes, Aran starts to wail. 'Oh, poor, poor Aran,' I say, hugging him, then chuckling a little, trying to humour him. Little does Aran know that he has just gone way down in my estimation.

The humiliation continues as we leave the pool and return to the changing rooms. I overhear the other mothers swapping stories about their sons and daughters.

'Our John is nearly crawling,' one mum says. 'Really early for his age.'

'Our Linda never cries,' I hear another mum telling her friend. 'Such a happy baby.'

'Oh, Brian is a great sleeper. Has slept through the night ever since he was three months old.'

I wish I could draw solace from such storytelling.

It seems like these mums really appreciate the friend-ships they make through these swimming sessions. But hearing how well their kids are doing doesn't make me feel supported. Instead it makes me feel like a terribly bad parent. Aran still pees and poos in his nappy. He is nowhere near walking or talking. And I am lucky if he sleeps more than three hours in a go. These comparisons with other children do nothing for my confidence. I quickly slip away before the mums notice I don't even have a stroller or plush travel system to carry Aran back to the car park.

Aran's short sleeping blocks are proving particularly problematic to our household. He is nearly five months old, but still wakes up at least two or three times a night for a quick breastfeed. The midwife told us that Aran should sleep in the same room as Pete and me for the first six months of his life. That means Aran wakes both of us up when he's feeling a little peckish. Pete wants to get up and help, but there's absolutely no point. Well, not unless Pete wants to start lactating as well.

More importantly, Pete is now our sole breadwinner. It is important that he gets a good night's rest so that he can go to work the next day. Pete doesn't function well when his slumber gets disrupted. In fact, neither of us is coping well with all the interrupted nights.

Eamonn too is on my case about having insufficient kip. My training timetable has a column solely dedicated to the subject matter. Every day I have to note down how much rest I've had and Eamonn comments on it. Though he fully understands my situation, and knows it won't last forever, I get totally wound up every time he reminds me to get a bit more rest.

After a particularly bad night, I lose my rag with Eamonn.

'Aran just keeps waking up!' I say. 'And there's nothing I can do about it. I can't let him cry too long, or it will wake up Pete, then Pete will be a nightmare to deal with the next day.'

Sometimes I think I treat my poor coach like my personal agony aunt. All I seem to do these days is complain about being sick and tired.

'Listen, try to sleep when Aran does,' Eamonn replies very calmly. 'If Aran has a nap during the day, just lie down with him.'

'But I can't sleep during the day!' I say. There's part of me that just wants masses of sympathy from Eamonn instead of a practical, proactive solution.

'You don't have to sleep,' Eamonn says. 'Just close your eyes for fifteen minutes, and get to that point where you're just about to drool.'

It's not a pretty vision, but I suppose anything's worth a shot.

Meanwhile Pete is trying his best to chip in with Aran whenever he can. He holds Aran after a breastfeed, wiping his spew from his shoulder when Aran vomits it all back up. He bounces Aran up and down on his lap when I'm busy, even if Aran is kicking and screaming, wanting just his mammy. Pete changes Aran's dirty nappies, even though he still can't stand the sight and putrid smell of baby poo after all these months.

Pete is trying to be a good husband and a modern man. Something my own father is particularly perplexed by when he sees us interacting with our son.

'Never changed a nappy in my life,' my father says to Pete and me repeatedly, without a hint of shame. Pete shrugs his shoulders and looks in my direction.

'Is that daughter of mine forcing you to do all this baby

stuff?' Dad says, reading into Pete's glance. Dad is puffing on his pipe, in strongman Popeye style.

'No, Dad, it's got nothing to do with me,' I say. 'But these days, if men want to have children, then they are expected to also lend a hand.'

'Children should be seen and not heard,' Dad continues, divulging his antiquated parenting philosophy.

Pete and I stay quiet. Having Aran has really shown us how everyone has an opinion when it comes to child-rearing. I know there were people who frowned at me for exercising while pregnant and so soon after giving birth. There are some who covertly criticise me for disrupting my entire family's rhythm just so I can train and race. There are others who raise their eyebrows at the fact that I'm staying at home to look after Aran while wilfully letting my career slide.

We find it especially hard when these alternative views come from our own nearest and dearest. At times, their voices make us sincerely wonder if we are doing the right thing. Though we fully understand and appreciate their opinions, there are other times when we know we have to stand our ground, and do what we believe in.

It takes me several days to recover from the cold I contracted after the Sea to Summit adventure race. Finally, after what seems like forever, Eamonn allows me to go back training. But as soon as he starts giving me sessions, I regret that I am well again.

The racing season is over for the year. Now that it's winter, and officially off-season, athletes have to do long gruelling mileage on the road and trails, and they are forced to hit the gym.

I hate going to the gym. It's far too much hard work. What makes it worse is that Eamonn has me on the rowing machine, the ultimate instrument of torture. It provides a total body beating, working every one of my major muscle groups. My legs, hips, and glutes heave with every stroke. My back, shoulders, and arms strain with every pull, while my trunk and core strain to keep the peace between my upper and lower bodies. What makes it even worse is that I'm not allowed to just sit down and simply row-row-row my boat. I have to push hard for a couple of minutes, and really grunt and sweat. I'm then allowed a little break for a minute or two, before rowing hard again. It is a truly evil exercise.

The only advantage I can see to gym sessions is that it allows me to train inside. Wet and windy weather has arrived in Ireland with all its wintery might. It makes biking outside miserable to say the least. However, when I complain to Eamonn about the weather, he tells me it's character-building.

I'm not in a particularly good mood when I drop Aran to the crèche one day before going for a bike ride. I really don't want to do the session Eamonn has assigned me. It's far too long and hard. I reluctantly wheel Bike in through the crèche's front door, past the admin office, then place him as usual with the other baby buggies in the crèche's corridor. After taking a few minutes to hand Aran over to the kind crèche staff, I take Bike by the handlebars and, using all my powers of self-control, I will myself outside. But before I can reach the front door, a member of the crèche administration calls me into her office. I'm sure she has something to tell me about Aran; I'm worried it may be bad news.

'You can't leave that there,' she says, pointing out to the corridor.

It takes me a while to realise she is referring to Bike.

'No, of course I'm not leaving it there,' I say, laughing at the slight misunderstanding. 'I'm going for a bike ride.'

'No, you can't leave it there when you're dropping off Aran,' she says, trying to clarify her point. She is sitting behind her desk, looking far too important. But I don't want to get into a fight.

'But I can't leave my bike outside on the street,' I plead. 'Someone might run off with it.'

I try to explain how expensive Bike is; how irreplaceable he has become to my life. I explain there is no car parking close to the building, so I have to bring Bike along when I drop Aran off.

'One of the staff can mind your bike outside while you drop off your son,' she says, before returning to her paperwork.

'But that's ridiculous,' I say. 'I can't be forcing your staff to stand outside in the cold while I settle Aran inside.'

'Sorry,' she says. 'Buggies can be left in the corridor. But bikes are definitely not allowed inside. It's one of our key health and safety policies.'

I am so incensed by this ridiculous rule that I don't care if I'm making a scene now.

'I don't even have a buggy to carry Aran,' I say. 'Bike is my baby carrier.'

Even as I say it, I can see her health and safety radar sound the red alert. I have lately been riding my bike with Aran strapped to my back, a slightly risky mode of transportation.

I try to reason with the manager, but I get nowhere. I go for my bike ride with a pounding headache. And when I return and collect Aran from the crèche, with Bike briefly relegated to the road outside, I resolve to never bring Aran and Bike back there again.

By the time I return home to Pete, I have worked myself up into a total rage.

'I just can't believe it,' I say, holding Aran a bit too tightly. 'Why do all the other mothers get to leave their four-wheeled buggies in the corridor while my two-wheeled bike is banned?'

Pete pulls Aran out of my arms; he must be afraid I might squeeze the life out of our only child. 'Well, she might have a point,' he says, playing devil's advocate. 'Like what if your bike fell on someone?'

'I only leave it there for two minutes!' I protest. There is no way that anyone but me is going to win this argument today. 'Aren't crèches meant to be there to support parents, to look after their children so they can do other things? And just because my "other thing" is biking, and not study or work or a mummy support group, then it's strictly not allowed?'

'Look, I'm not trying to fight with you, Moire,' Pete says. 'But she was probably just doing her job.'

I'm just sick of being told what to do and how to parent, of being tortured by Eamonn with ridiculously hard sessions and being forced to sing ridiculous songs in the swimming pool. I can't take it any more.

I start to sob uncontrollably.

'Look, I know it's been a hard couple of months,' Pete says. He is snuggling up to Aran, trying to make him laugh. I can't help but be distracted by this playful paternal bonding.

'Why don't we go away for Christmas?' Pete says, totally out of the blue. 'Maybe get out of here for a while?'

I feel tired by the mere idea of travelling over the festive period. But then again, maybe a change of scenery would do me a bit of good.

'I've been offered a six-week contract in Cambodia,' Pete says, giving this piece of news to Aran rather than directly to me. 'I was going to turn it down as it would mean being away from home for too long. Why don't I accept it, and you guys come with me?'

My mothering instinct knee-jerks in.

'But what will people think? Aran isn't even five months old.' I realise he is due his sixteen-week vaccinations soon. He can't go without them.

'You really care what other people think at this point?' Pete says, now the adamant one. 'I certainly don't. Let's just go, and escape the lot of them.'

I think about it for a while, and eventually agree on the condition that Aran's doctor gives the final go-ahead. Both Pete and I have lived and worked in Cambodia previously, so we know where to go and what to do there. Cambodia is also lovely and warm in December, unlike Ireland's increasingly dark and dank weather.

But most importantly of all, childcare possibilities in Cambodia are plentiful, ridiculously cheap, and don't have any heavy-handed health and safety rules.

11

Abroad

Before escaping to Cambodia for Christmas, Pete and I make a major purchase. Our spending decision is based on the fact that Aran is now almost able to sit up straight on his own. It means that, finally, he is allowed into a running buggy.

I have been dreaming about running buggies for ages. I already know the exact specs I need. It has to have pneumatic tyres that can negotiate tough, off-road terrain. I want a state-of-the-art, adjustable suspension system to provide Aran with an exceptionally smooth ride. A wrist strap is non-negotiable, so the stroller doesn't roll away from me while heading down hills. And it needs a fixed front wheel for directional control while running, but one that can also swivel when out and about in the shops.

The Bob Revolution Stroller meets all my stringent conditions. Only the four hundred pound price tag makes me balk and reconsider its acquisition. Placing this stroller inside our Citroen Xsara doubles the car's value instantaneously. I ultimately rationalise this expenditure by calculating that the buggy is the equivalent cost of eighty hours of childcare. If I use the buggy for more than eighty hours, I will actually start saving money.

The Bob buggy proves to be the purchase of the year. It means I can go out for a run with Aran at anytime of the day, regardless of childcare availability. Bringing Aran with me also means I don't worry that he is causing havoc back at home, something I normally do. And, more often than not, Aran really enjoys coming for the ride. He rarely cries when he is whizzing along in his new seat, and is often fast asleep by the time I pull into our drive.

Pete and I decide to bring the buggy with us to Cambodia. It turns out to be the only additional piece of child-related baggage that we eventually take with us. We are exceedingly lucky in that we have child-friendly accommodation to stay in for the whole six weeks.

Two of our friends, Aine and Richie, live in the capital, Phnom Penh. They are going home to Ireland for Christmas, right around the time we arrive. They have a two-bedroom apartment that they have generously allowed us to housesit. They also have a two-year-old son, which means their place is packed with all the necessary equipment for taking care of young Aran.

It takes about thirty hours' travel time to get to Cambodia from Ireland. I am dreading the journey before we even leave the house. Normally I struggle with flying, as well as airport transits and jet lag. God only knows how baby Aran is going to cope with his first-ever global voyage.

We arrive really early at Dublin airport to make sure we get checked in without incident. Aran is already fast asleep in his buggy when we present our tickets and passports at the flight desk.

'Did you book seats with a bassinette?' the airline lady asks.

We had heard that babies could reserve their own special flatbed cots for long-distance flights.

'Yes, we did,' Pete says, before quickly adding, 'Does the bassinette come with bulkhead seats?'

'Yes it does, sir,' the lady says, as she prints out our three boarding cards. Pete can barely contain his excitement. Thanks to Aran's presence, Pete just got extra legroom.

Pete wheels Aran off to the boarding gates, while I struggle behind them with our trolley. Though we have already checked in our main bags, I still have to go to the oversized luggage counter to hand in my bike bag. Pete thinks bringing Bike along is hassle due to its bulky rectangular size. But we are going away for nearly two months. There is absolutely no way I am abandoning Bike and leaving him at home all alone.

We settle down at our boarding gate and wait for our flight to be called. Aran is still pretty content, gazing around at all the airport's various sights and curiosities.

'Can passengers with children please present themselves first for boarding?'

'Yeesssss!' shouts Pete, jumping for joy straight out of his plastic chair. Finally, after all these years of budget travel, Aran has handed us a priority boarding pass for free.

Another couple soon joins us in the bulkhead bassinette seats. They also have a young baby boy, who is a few months older than Aran. Pete tries in vain to get Aran to become best friends with the other child. I sit there, hiding my face in shame. Pete's attempts at socialising Aran are a little premature for his age, I feel.

'You've such a good baby,' the other mother says to me halfway through our twelve-hour flight. Aran has indeed been good, much better than I had expected. He has cried only a little, and sat quietly most of the time. He has even used his bassinette and taken a nap in it.

She, on the other hand, is battling with her infant. He wants to crawl. He wants to explore. He wants to get the hell out of the airplane. Though my initial reaction is to gloat over how good Aran is in comparison, I know that Aran is a ticking time bomb. It will not be long before he too will refuse to sit still for a second.

We arrive at Phnom Penh airport early the next day. The sky is bright blue. The air is warm and sticky. The heat from the sun is intense. It is the total opposite of what we have left behind us back in Ireland.

Pete and I are jaded from our long, sleepless flights. Aran however is wide awake, thanks to the consistent sleeping strategy he adopted throughout the journey. I am so jealous of how well Aran is adapting to this holiday already.

Our own tired eyes are soon revived, however, when we climb into a taxi and zoom straight into town. I had forgotten how crazy Phnom Penh is. Motorbikes whiz past on both sides of our vehicle, manically driven by beautiful little ladies with long, black, flowing hair. We pass brightly coloured markets laden with exotic, pungent fruit. We drive past vast Buddhist temples, with saffron-cloaked monks spilling out from their wide ornate gates. And beside the temples, we see crass neon-flashing signs advertising the latest mobile phones. The teeming humanity and its accompanying contradictions shake awake our senses and our minds.

Aine and Richie's apartment is perfect for all our needs. There is a kitchen, a large bedroom with en-suite bathroom, and a sitting room with sofas to sprawl on. There are soft play tiles, as well as plenty of books and toys to amuse Aran. Not that Aran's needs are much these days. All he requires are nappies, a bed, and breast milk.

One thing I need though is someone to look after Aran. Even though we are on holiday, my training regime continues. I have bike, run, gym, and swim sessions to complete while we are away from home. And with Pete working long hours on his consulting contract, I need some additional childcare help.

Fortunately Aine and Richie employ a full-time nanny named Sophea, who is happy to work for us while our friends are away. Sophea comes to visit us the day after we arrive. I initially think she must be a mere teenager when I see her petite figure and flawless facial skin. However Aine and Richie have already informed us that Sophea is in her mid-thirties and has a young child of her own. When she enters the apartment, Sophea spots Aran and picks him up without thinking.

'Oh, look at the lovely baby!' she says, before formal introductions are even made. 'What is your name? What is your name?'

I feel I must intervene. 'His name is Aran. And I'm Moire. And this is Pete.'

'Hello, Aran, hello, Aran,' she says, crinkling her nose up as she tickles his belly with her long, slender fingers. Aine told me that Sophea is great with children. I see now exactly what she means.

'So Sophea, can you look after Aran for a couple of hours, maybe three days a week?'

'Yes, no problem, no problem,' she says, still entranced by Aran.

'And can you come early, maybe around 7 am?'

'No problem at all,' she says. 'And if you want, I can do laundry. And some cooking and cleaning as well.'

No way. One-on-one childcare with housekeeping services thrown in? All for less than three US dollars an hour? Is this for real? We agree with Sophea that she can start later in the week, once we've properly settled in.

Once Sophea has gone, Pete suggests we visit his former workplace, a local microfinance bank called AMK. We hitch a ride in a tuk-tuk, a quasi open-air chariot pulled by a motorbike. Aran seems to love this novel taxi ride. He is tucked in close to me, peering out of his wrap at the exotic Asian sights and sounds flying by. Meanwhile, Pete and I hang on for dear life as the tuk-tuk driver speeds down the road, overtaking other vehicles using a range of well-rehearsed illegal moves.

Pete worked as AMK's CEO for two years. We got married just before he left the job. Now he is making a grand return to the bank, sporting a brand-new child. The Cambodian staff are thrilled to see that Pete is now a dad.

'Can I hold him? Can I hold him?' is all I hear around me as soon as we enter the building. Four Cambodian ladies have surrounded me. They want a closer look at Pete's baby.

'Oh, look at his eyes,' one says, as she grabs Aran out of my arms. 'They are so blue.'

'And his blond hair,' another says, giggling from the novelty. Pete and I are standing there, amazed by their fascination.

Another Cambodian lady takes Aran and gives him a massive cuddle. 'My goodness,' she says. 'He is so white!'

Cambodians are blessed with the most beautiful brown skin, dark eyes, and black hair that I have ever seen. But when confronted with a Caucasian blond-haired, blue-eyed baby boy, it seems Cambodians are totally smitten.

Aran is oblivious to these women swooning all over him.

His thoughts are solely focused on the source of his next feed. Suddenly I see him turn his head towards the breasts of one of Pete's former female colleagues, searching for a suck. The lady shrieks with shock, dropping Aran in the process.

'Oh God, I'm sorry,' I say, catching Aran before he hits the ground. The four Cambodian ladies giggle uncontrollably.

'So what is his name?' one lady asks, once she's managed to stifle her laughs.

'Aran,' Pete says.

'A-ran,' she repeats back, but this time with emphasis on the second syllable. 'You gave him a Cambodian name?'

'Really?' Pete says. 'No way!'

Pete and I had struggled to find a suitable name for our baby. We first of all wanted a name that showed he has Irish roots. But we also wanted one that could be easily pronounced and spelled in case we moved abroad again. It meant we had to rule out popular boys names such as Darragh, Eoghan, Gearoid, and Ruairi. In short, we couldn't use ninety-nine per cent of traditional Irish names. Eventually we selected Aran for its short and simple spelling, and its link to Ireland's Aran Islands. Pete is now delighted to claim that it's also a Cambodian name.

Pete continues to proudly parade Aran around his former office. I hear coos of admiration emanating from every office and glass cubicle. Aran soon tires of all this adulation, and cries to be rescued by his mummy. But if Aran thinks all this attention will stop once he leaves AMK, he will be sadly disappointed.

The next morning, my training timetable instructs me to go for a run. It is still cool enough to exercise outside first thing in the morning, so I leave just before sunrise at

6 am. Pete is still asleep, so I slip out of the apartment, taking Aran with me in his Bob buggy. We jog together down the wide boulevards of the old colonial part of town. The pavements are cracked and uneven around here, so we opt to run on the road that is still car-less at the crack of dawn.

I run past Independence Monument, towards the Mekong River with its sweeping, wide waters dotted with boats and barges. Then I turn towards Diamond Island, where I intend to do some laps.

Diamond Island is an enigma within Phnom Penh. It is piece of reclaimed land where Asian capitalism has been let loose. A network of speed-bumped concrete streets covers the island, and these are lined with casinos, fast-food joints, and gigantic wedding halls. At 6 am, these fine establishments are yet to open, meaning the streets are empty and quiet enough for a baby-laden buggy and mother to run around. The traffic lights flash green, then red, with only Aran and I present to heed their commands. Only the occasional construction worker appears from around random corners. I see them congregating in an area crammed with fake Parisian architecture, where they are currently building high-end apartments for the emerging Cambodian elite.

By 7 am, I leave deserted Diamond Island and make my way back to the mainland. It takes great skill to manoeuvre Aran and his buggy back to our apartment, dodging the swelling rush-hour traffic along the way. We arrive back, both a bit sweaty from the rising heat, but happy to have made it home without incident.

The following morning, Sophea arrives at the apartment good and early so I can go for a bike ride. Eamonn has given me a ten-kilometre time trial to do today. I am a little apprehensive, as I know how much time trials hurt. I am also not sure how my body will cope with the heat under such pressure. But these issues should be the least of my concerns. Something much more deadly awaits me.

Phnom Penh is already swarming with motorbikes and cars when I wheel Bike out on to the street. I opt to cycle the least busy road out of Phnom Penh, towards the Vietnamese border. But even this tranquil road is hectic first thing in the morning. I put my foot down regardless and start the clock. But as soon as I accelerate, I come close to hitting a tuk-tuk. I then slam on my brakes as a lorry turns right in front of my wheel. Young school children run into my path, waving and shouting at me. I slow down to make sure I don't run over any of them.

It goes from bad to worse. Chickens run the gauntlet, while lazy dogs won't budge from my lane. The odd buffalo and donkey also wander over and try to impede my way. In the end, I have to abandon my time trail. I tell Eamonn the reasons for my slow time, despite how far-fetched they all seem.

I'm so depressed by my morning session that I decide to unwind with a massage. I bring Aran along with me rather than go alone. Even though Sophea is great with Aran, and I'm sure she'd appreciate the cash, I still feel guilty about leaving Aran for so long, and for taking Sophea away from her own child just so she can look after mine.

I choose a ninety-minute hand and foot massage at the ridiculously cheap price of ten dollars. I ease into the reclining comfy chair while Aran lounges on my lap. The Cambodian masseur can barely speak English, and I know no Khmer. Normally I feel uneasy in this situation, the westerner lying there receiving such indulgent attention. But somehow, with Aran with me, this unease thaws a little. The lady seems so happy to see this little baby, and vice versa, that the massage seems a little more convivial this time.

Aran's appeal just keeps on giving throughout our entire stay. One evening, Pete, Aran and I go for dinner at a high-end restaurant called Metro on the Mekong riverfront. It is well known for its attractive, slim waitresses who wear short, figure-hugging, Robert Palmer style black dresses. They are very cool, calm, and collected when they take your order or serve you. But again, Aran's presence immediately pierces their tone of professionalism and causes a frenzy in the serving bay.

'Oh, look at the baby!' one shouts as they all congregate around our table. We know by now just to hand Aran over, and let them ogle him from up close. It keeps the staff happy, Aran likes it, and we get a free babysitting service thrown in.

'Isn't it great how popular Aran is?' Pete says.

'Totally,' I say. 'It's amazing how much Cambodians love kids.'

'Does it not make you wonder what it would be like if Aran grew up here in Cambodia?'

I had a feeling this question would eventually surface during this trip. Pete loves Cambodia, and would move back here in a heartbeat. He just needs to convince me to come along with him.

'I actually like looking after Aran,' I say, surprised I'm even saying such a thing. 'If we lived here, we'd be expected to have a nanny, even if I didn't have a job.'

'I am sure you could choose how many hours the nanny works,' Pete says.

I'm not sure that would be the case. Having a full-time nanny is very tempting when you can give them your kid to mind at any time of the day. But it can feel quite intrusive if a nanny is round all of the time, especially when they can watch every detail of your life.

'You know how household staff tidy up all the time,' I say. 'They'd end up hiding your stuff.' We had a part-time maid when we lived in Phnom Penh before, to help us with the cleaning. The maid used to pick Pete's socks off the floor and put them in the wash unsolicited. It drove Pete demented. He ended up hiding his socks from her so that he could wear them more than once.

'And look at the traffic, Pete. It's total gridlock some days,' I say. I know Pete hates traffic jams with a passion. 'It's too dangerous to ride my bike, and it's not going to get any better, what with the rate of construction that's happening in the city right now.'

Pete does his customary shrug, dismissing my latest argument. I'll have to come up with a more persuasive case if I want to avoid moving back to Cambodia.

'And I like living in Ireland,' I say. 'I like the mountains there and I like the climate.' But this isn't just about me. And I want Pete to realise that. 'I think Ireland is good for Aran too.'

'There's no way he'll be as popular with the ladies at home!' Pete seems to have fast-forwarded to Aran's teenage years.

'Seriously, Pete, both our families are in Ireland. Isn't it important for Aran to know his relatives? Sure look how much my mum adores hanging out with Aran. It'd break her heart if Aran moved away.'

Pete twists his wine glass. I wonder if he is planning his counterargument.

'Aran,' he says suddenly. 'Aran! Where's Aran?'

I look around. The waitresses have gone.

'Shit! Where's Aran?' I shout, leaping out of my seat. 'ARAN!'

I rush into the serving bay, only to find some waitresses inspecting their nails.

'Where's my baby?' I say, sweating now from distress. A waitress looks up from her cuticles, and shrugs her shoulders dismissively.

Oh shit, someone has kidnapped him while Pete and I were busy talking.

I run out of the restaurant, on to the street, unsure of which direction he could have gone. The road is swarming with tourists, tuk-tuks, and taxis. I can't see my blond-haired, blue-eyed baby anywhere.

'Aran!' I scream. 'ARAN!' I turn and burst back into the restaurant to see Pete searching behind the bar.

'Pete, I've no idea where he's gone,' I say. 'Oh God, what are we going to do?'

My shouts must have alerted the chefs, as Aran appears within seconds from behind the kitchen doors. He is smiling brightly at the beautiful waitress who's carrying him, totally oblivious to the drama that has just unfurled.

'We were showing Aran around the place,' the waitress says.

I take Aran back into my arms and hug him very tightly. 'Pete, seriously,' I say, when I return to the table with our son. 'I really don't think I can live here.'

Regardless of the pros and cons, soon fate dictates where we will live next. Before we even leave Cambodia, Pete is offered an interim CEO job based in Dublin. Though it is only a short-term contract, it is an ideal career move. It seems like I have won the argument, at least for now.

12

Change

With Pete starting work in Dublin, we have to find somewhere nearby to stay. His contract is only for a couple of months, however, way short of the minimum one-year commitment Dublin landlords look for. My close-knit mountain running network fortunately comes to our aid. I ask around, and find a fellow mountain runner who is also looking to rent out her place for a short period of time. Her house is in Greystones, a small coastal town and seaside resort just south of Dublin City.

Greystones is extremely popular with sports enthusiasts. It is a great base for heading west and straight into the Wicklow Mountains for road biking, hiking, and running. It also has a web of mountain bike trails in the nearby Glen of the Downs and Kindlestown Woods. And for those partial to water sports, the sea is right there, with Greystones having its very own harbour as well as several stunning beaches. Triathletes are often seen practising their strokes at the crack of dawn in this part of the Irish Sea.

Greystones is not, however, just for outdoor adventurers. It has also a reputation for being yummy mummy central. The village is packed with young, immaculately manicured mothers, with their trendy kids in tow. Greystones caters for them perfectly, with high-end coffee shops, cool vegetarian restaurants, and local designer stores.

I am an athlete and a mother. I hope I will fit in to this new place.

We move into my friend's house in mid-January, in the depths of Irish winter. It is dark, cold, and raining when we drive down from Derry to Greystones. It is a long and stressful four-hour journey. Our hatchback car is weighed down with everything we need for our stay. Aran is squashed in the back, his bulky car seat taking up much-needed space. Tom is curled up under my feet in the front passenger seat. There is barely enough room for him to breathe. Bike drew the short straw and is strapped on to the outside of the car. In doing so, Bike blocks Pete's view through the rear-view window. I know from Pete's prolonged silence that this obstruction stresses him out. It is not an ideal start to our stay.

Pete's alarm goes off the next morning at 5.30 am.

'Oh God, why so early?' I say, rolling over in bed and pulling the duvet around me.

'I got to get up and go to work, you know,' Pete says.

I hate it when he says things like that, as if I've never worked a day in my life, like I don't know what it's like to have to get out of bed at a godforsaken hour.

'Turn that thing off before it wakes the baby.' Aran is six months old now, but still wakes up two or three times a night. At 3 am this morning, Aran decided to stay up for a whole hour. His sleep routine is slowly torturing me to death.

'I need to get the 6.30 am train,' Pete says, as he slams hard on the mobile screen and silences the annoying, repetitive beep. Greystones is the last stop on the DART train service that heads north into Dublin city centre. This is the main way commuters from this area get in and out from work.

'But why so early?' I say.

'Well, I have to walk to the train station first, then get the train, then walk to the office, then start work.'

'But that means you'll be in the office around 8 am.' Still sounds very early to me.

'Look, it's my first day. I need to get my head around things if I'm to hit the ground running. And I can't do that if I show up late on the first day.'

'Fair enough,' I say, conceding. 'What time will you be home?'

'I don't know,' Pete says, searching for his glasses. He sounds really exacerbated.

'It's just, what time will you be home for dinner?'

'I . . . don't . . . know,' Pete says. He looks quickly at the clock on his mobile screen. 'Look, I gotta go.'

Pete gets up and performs his morning ablutions. While Pete is gone, Aran wakes with an abrupt, shrill cry. I pick him out of his cot, pull him out of his grobag, and carry him gently downstairs.

Pete is in the kitchen making a cup of tea. He doesn't look too pleased to see us.

'Can I make you some toast or something?'

'No, I don't have time,' Pete says, taking great slurps from his mug. 'I'll grab something in town.'

'Well, dinner will be ready around 7 pm,' I say. 'I presume you'll be back by then?'

All I want is an answer; a definite time when he'll be home. Then I'll know when I can look forward to having adult company once more.

'Look, I have no idea what time I'll be home,' he says. He grabs his bag and coat, and places a hand on the door handle. 'Sorry. I'll text you once I know the train times.'

And with that, he opens the front door and makes a hasty escape.

Pete only left a moment ago, but already I feel so horribly alone.

I stare out the window at the pelting rain. This is what I feared from the very start, even before I got pregnant: that I would be left at home all day on my own, stuck minding the baby Pete literally begged for in the first place.

After wallowing in self-pity for several hours, I tell myself to get a grip. I'm going to go and find some decent childcare in this place. At least then Aran will be surrounded by happy, smiling people who are qualified in childcare; a much better prospect than Aran being stuck at home with me, his depressed, ignorant mother.

What with Greystones being a family hub, there is a good selection of crèches to choose from. After shopping around, I opt for a place called Puroga on the outskirts of town. It is a brightly coloured, well-lit place with friendly, welcoming staff. I sign Aran up for three mornings a week, for a total of ten hours.

Within seconds of registering Aran, my foul mood starts to lift. But what makes me happiest is the fact that Bike is welcomed by the crèche. I can park my car outside the building and leave Bike there while I settle Aran in. I can then take Bike straight out of my car and begin my cycle directly from the crèche's front door. It seems like such a small thing, but it makes a huge difference to me.

I am ridiculously excited to tell Pete about this progress when he eventually comes home from work. He has already texted me to say he'll be home for dinner at 7 pm, as I

135

originally proposed. But as soon as he enters the house, I can tell by his demeanour that he is not too happy to be home.

'How was work?' I say. He drops his laptop bag on the kitchen floor. It lands with a wet, heavy thud. Outside it is dark and raining relentlessly.

'I had to walk home from the train station in this friggin' storm,' he says.

'I'm sorry,' I say, even though I am not responsible for the current state of the weather. 'Do you want something to eat?' I add, playing it safe with my subsequent line of questioning.

'What's for dinner?'

'Pasta.'

'Oh,' Pete says. 'Okay if I get a take-out?'

I am this close to tipping the saucepan of hot pasta right over his flippin' head. I've been stuck all day at home minding Aran. I spent an hour making the pasta sauce. And I get total crap from my husband when he comes home from work.

'Fine,' I say. 'Do what you want.' I turn back to the stove, and stir the sauce, hoping my hot angry tears will fall silently into the pot.

'You forced me to come home early,' Pete says. 'And now you're giving me this attitude.'

'Early?' I say, pointing the wooden spoon directly at his face. 'Pete, it's 7 pm. You've been gone for nearly thirteen hours.'

'I have work to do. And if it doesn't get done, I'll get behind, and have to spend more time away from home.'

I stare at him, wondering if I should make some idle threats as well.

'Look, I'm sorry,' Pete says after a moment's thought. 'It's just I'm not sure I can do this.'

136

'Do what?' What's his issue now? Is it work? Or Greystones? Our marriage? Having babies? Or can he just not stand life in general?

I hate it when Pete has problems. We are a team and I need him, depend on him, to be strong. The suggestion that he is now floundering worries me deeply. I simply don't have the energy or expertise to take charge and guide both our lives through whatever storm is brewing.

'This job,' he says, clarifying my query. 'It's really a lot of work. And I'm going to have to put in some serious hours.'

'That's fine,' I say, though it isn't fine at all with me. Maybe he should have considered all this when he accepted the position and when he persuaded me to have a child in the first place.

'And the commute is killing me. It's a three-hour round trip and there's standing room only in the train on the way back.' He has done the commute only once, for the first time today, and already he has written it off completely. His daily commute in Cambodia has obviously spoiled him. In Phnom Penh, his own personal driver would pull up in a tuk-tuk outside our front gate. Pete would then be chauffeured to the office, in less than ten minutes, with a stop at his favourite coffee shop along the way.

'Do you want to move back home then?' I say. 'Or do you just want to quit?'

I really don't care what we do at this point. I just want a quiet life.

Pete is silent. He looks over at Aran, who is sleeping soundly in his chair.

'No,' he says, easing himself into a seat at the dinner table. 'It's fine. It's only for a couple of months, I suppose.'

I put a plate of pasta in front of him and he sets about

137

devouring it, having forgotten all about his sinister take-away threat.

Regardless of Pete's hatred of the commute and his new job, he still gets up at 5.30 am the next morning to do it all over again. I hear him leaving the bedroom as Aran mutters his early morning cry. I pick Aran up out of his cot and bring him into bed with me. A quick breastfeed quietens him instantaneously.

I lie in bed with baby Aran snuggled up against me, his head resting lightly on my arm. I dare not go downstairs to the kitchen in case Pete bawls us both out of there. I soon hear Pete rummaging in the hallway, and then the front door slamming behind him.

How exactly did my life come to this? I know I agreed to look after Aran while I'm breastfeeding, and I know Pete has to work so that we have an income. I was also the one who pushed to live back in Ireland rather than Cambodia. But now I'm seething that Pete has all this freedom that has been rudely snatched from me. Or is it my own fault? Did I just give away my freedom all too easily?

There is one way I can, however, get back a little of my independence. At six months old, it is time for Aran to start eating solid food, and to slowly be weaned off breast milk. My community health worker, Bridgeen, has given me all the information I need for this new, daunting development stage. She has informed me about purées and the foods that should be in them. She has told me about the importance of graduating soon to foods with lumpy bits. But she has also let slip about a new alternative method; something called baby-led-weaning.

Baby-led-weaning is a fancy term for letting a baby feed itself. Food is cut up into finger-sized portions, then placed in front of the kid. Six-month-old babies are just about able to grasp hold of these assorted pieces. And they are at an age where everything, edible or not, goes straight into their mouths. What it means is that I don't have to spend hours smashing up foods into mush. I can ditch feeding spoons from the get-go. And I will not have to pretend to be an airplane or chu-chu train to entice Aran to open his mouth.

I like the idea of baby-led-weaning and decide to give it a go. In doing so, Aran is not only reducing his reliance on breast milk, he is also becoming a little more independent himself, feeding himself what he likes, whenever he likes. I go straight to IKEA and buy Aran a high chair with a large serving tray. I then get busy, chopping up bananas and cooked carrots into long, fist-sized chunks. I place all the yellow and orange blocks on to Aran's new table, then wait to see what happens.

Aran immediately goes for the banana and tries to pick it up. His hold is too hard however, and the fruit dissolves into mush. Regardless, he sticks his fist into his mouth and sucks on the foreign food. Aran consumes approximately one per cent of the banana. The other ninety-nine per cent falls back on to the table or lands with a splat on the floor. Having worked out what the yellow thing tastes like, Aran now makes a beeline for the carrot. The carrot survives Aran's handhold a little better, but still gets pretty beat up. Aran still has no teeth, but he manages to tear chunks off it. He chews the carrot pieces in his gummy mouth, and then ceremoniously spits them out.

Tom soon comes into the kitchen to check out the latest goings-on. He spots the pieces of carrot and banana smattered on the floor beneath Aran's chair. He takes a quick sniff at the fruit and veg, and licks up all the carrot pieces he can find. If Tom is willing and able to clean up Aran's mess, he could prove very useful in this whole baby-led-weaning process.

With Aran getting to grips with proper solid food, I figure it might be time also to change his source of milk. I decide to give Aran some powdered formula. If I can wean him off breast milk, Aran will become less dependent on me. It also means my boobs can shrink back to some sort of normality.

Getting formula feed into my child is the first obstacle I must tackle. With Aran still belligerent when it comes to bottles, I try giving him a cup. Much to my surprise, this change in tactic works. Aran takes little sips of formula feed from the two-handled mug. I feel like I am making real progress when it comes to feeding my kid.

The next morning, Aran's digestive system delivers bad news. I undo his nappy to find the most disgusting poo ever seen by mankind. It is liquid diarrhoea laced with carrot bits and black banana seeds. But the worst thing is that the formula milk has gone right through his system, burning the very skin off his baby bum. I try to put on nappy rash cream, but there is no skin left for it to stick to. Instead the cream slides straight off the burn marks that cover his entire bottom. Once I clean Aran up and put him in a new nappy, his tears dry up and he forgets the whole incident immediately.

However, I am so traumatised by the sight of Aran's wounded arse that I abandon my formula milk plan completely. Aran is going to be breastfed for the next six months, until he reaches the age of one and can handle normal cow's milk.

One of the bonuses of using a baby-led-weaning strategy is that Aran can basically eat the same food as

140

me. It also means we can share all our meals by dining at the same time. My coach Eamonn has also asked me to keep a food diary to see how my nutrition is going. The diary shows that I eat six times a day. This is in perfect harmony with Aran and his tiny stomach that needs frequent, small snacks. The diary also shows the wide range of foods that I consume. There's porridge, toast, scrambled eggs, cucumber, cheese, sweet potatoes, broccoli, roast chicken, Greek yoghurt and berries on a given day. I share a little of all these things with Aran, and let him pick and choose what he wants. The extensive menu, much of which ends up on the ground, also fascinates Tom. He gobbles up everything with a protein base, and slowly starts to expand his carbohydrate taste range.

The one thing that Aran doesn't partake in is my frequent coffee consumption. I know caffeine should only be taken in mild doses in case it affects athletic performance, but I need regular intake to keep me going these days. I haven't had a full night's sleep for nearly half a year, and coffee is the only thing that sustains me. I also have a duty to catch up on all the coffee I didn't consume during the nine months I was pregnant. I am not surprised therefore when Eamonn advises me to cut my number of coffee breaks. I do as I am told, halving the number of coffee cups I take, while doubling the size of the mug I use. Coffee is too critical to my current survival strategy for me to sacrifice a single drop.

The last few months have been difficult to say the least. I still can't get over the amount of turmoil Aran's arrival has caused. So when it comes to my birthday, I decide not to celebrate. I instead send a huge bouquet to my own mother, with a note saying, 'Happy Giving Birth-Day.'

As soon as Mum receives it, she gives me a ring. 'Thank

you so much for the flowers,' she says. 'They are so beautiful!'

'Least I can do, Mum,' I say. 'I suppose birthdays will never be the same again for me, seeing that I have given birth myself.'

'Sure it was a pleasure looking after all of you,' Mum says. She has an amazing ability to always put a positive spin on past events.

'But how did you manage to look after us kids?' I say. She cared for three of us, while I am struggling to mind just the one.

'I suppose you just get on with it,' she says. 'But really, I'm so proud of you all. And I think about you all the time.'

I hope I'll be as gushing about motherhood as my own mum when I look back at all the nappies and vomit and sleepless nights I've endured. But going through this has definitely given me a new-found respect for my own long-suffering parents.

With Pete practically gone for most of the week, I start to settle in to Greystones and get on with raising Aran. We soon discover lovely cafes, playgrounds, and beaches where we can hang out together. We find a local community centre with a baby swimming pool where we regularly go for a splash. In Derry, I paid one pound for a thirty-minute baby swimming session. Here in Greystones, in the rip-off Republic, the same session costs ten Euros, eight times the price. Seeing that I already know the baby songs and actions, Aran and I choose to conduct our own private session in the swimming pool at no additional charge.

While things get slightly easier with Aran, Eamonn has other ideas. It is during our weekly call that he reveals his latest cunning plan.

'Can you get yourself a power metre?' he asks.

'Power what?' I say.

'Power metre. It's for your bike. It will help us see how efficiently you are riding,' he says. 'It will tell me how fast or slow you're pedalling, and how hard you're working with each stroke.'

Already Eamonn knows exactly how hard my heart is working when I run or bike. He knows how fast I go, precisely where I go, and how many calories I burn. He knows also what I've eaten to refuel, and how must rest I've had. At this stage, Eamonn knows more about me than I do about myself.

I get a power metre that is fitted into the front chain-ring. I pair it with my Garmin GPS, and go for a bike spin. When I upload the data, I am overwhelmed by the onslaught of new-fangled graphs. All of a sudden, I can see my cadence, power output, and balance. Eamonn has a quick look and straightaway gives me feedback.

'You are using your right leg more than your left one,' he tells me on a call.

Who would have thought that was even possible?

'Your left leg is providing forty-seven per cent of the power, and your right leg fifty-three per cent. You need to be trying to get more of a consistent fifty-fifty balance.'

As if this wasn't complicated enough, Eamonn wants to make my bike sessions even harder.

'I want you to start power sets on your bike,' he says. 'You are to do a two-and-a-half-hour session. In the middle, you need to do twelve sets of two-minute efforts.'

'Wooh, stop right there,' I say. 'What's an effort?'

'An effort is just a way of saying you work harder for a set period of time,' Eamonn says.

I still don't get what he means.

'Listen, you'll be wearing a heart rate monitor during your session,' Eamonn says. 'So, for two minutes, I want you to have a heart rate between one hundred and forty, and one hundred and sixty-one. Then, I want to see your heart rate drop to between one hundred and nineteen, and one hundred and twenty-eight for three minutes. That will be your recovery time.'

My eyes begin to glaze over. My head is starting to hurt.

'But Eamonn, I'm not sure I can do a session like that,' I whimper. 'Like, it sounds really ... hard.'

'I know you can do it,' Eamonn replies, in a surprisingly adamant tone. 'Believe me, I wouldn't give it to you if I thought you weren't able for it.'

I think about it for a second. Even though I doubt my own ability, Eamonn's professed confidence flicks a switch in me. It's at times like this, when I lack self-confidence, another's trusted opinion can make me do a U-turn. I suppose that's why I need someone like a coach to help me train harder, to help me become faster, to help me believe in myself.

I tell myself I've nothing to lose by giving the session a try. And anyhow, biking is my weakest discipline. I need to work on it if I'm to stand any chance of making the podium.

I take a spin out towards the N11, the main dual carriageway between Dublin and Greystones. Cars and trucks whizz past me, breathing out toxic fumes, as I pedal precariously along the hard shoulder. It is the only road I know where I could possibly do such a session without encountering roundabouts, traffic lights, or major inclines. It is also unlikely I will encounter random chickens and donkeys straying across my path like they did in Cambodia.

I warm up for twenty minutes, then start the first effort. Within a matter of seconds, my legs start to hurt. I watch my heart rate go up and up, until it hits the magic number of one forty. I know I am working hard as my breath becomes more laboured and fast. Thirty seconds done. Ninety more to go. Oh god, I don't think I can make it.

Only the thought of Eamonn's comments makes me continue on. If I didn't have to upload my data and let him dissect it, I'd turn around right now and start to freewheel slowly back home.

My clock says twenty-two minutes have passed. With the initial warm-up taking twenty minutes, that means I have done my first two-minute effort. I immediately stop pedalling, and try to catch my breath.

Okay, so that's the first effort done. So now I have a three-minute recovery. That means I have to start my second effort when the clock says twenty-five minutes.

The number twenty-five appears quicker than I expect. I push hard again on my pedals, increasing my cadence and power digits. But just as I am in the middle of the effort, my brain starts to malfunction.

Is this my second effort, or third? Am I meant to stop at twenty-seven minutes or twenty-eight? Is my heart rate meant to be above one hundred and forty, or below it? Tiredness causes me to forget. And these efforts are tiring me out so quickly I am unable to do simple arithmetic.

The tiredness and stress of motherhood is also aiding the decline of my short-term memory. Now when I think of it, I don't even remember what it was like being young, single, and childless any more.

13

Fight

With Pete working long hours and long days, I spend more and more time with Aran on my own. And at seven months old, Aran is actually becoming slightly fun. We play peek-a-boo for hours, Aran never tiring of my hiding and reappearance. His ceaseless giggles make me want the game to never end. I read picture books to him and do impressions of sheep and lions that send him into fits of laughter. We look at ourselves in mirrors and pull all manner of faces. I never thought I would ever enjoy doing this sort of thing with a real live baby, let alone a baby of my own.

Aran also comes along with me sometimes when I have running training to do. We drive together to a nice flat place and, once there, I strap him into his buggy. Often we run up and down the promenade in the neighbouring town of Bray. We sprint past the holidaymakers as they lick their ice cream cones and stare contemplatively out to sea. We weave in and out of the prom walkers, dodging dogs with their owners, and little old ladies taking their morning stroll. Sometimes we drive into Dublin itself and visit one of its many lush parklands. We do circuits around Marley Park, through the woodlands, past the expansive pitches, and around the stately home that is Marley House. If we have time, we stop at the teahouse after our ninety-minute run. Together we share a slice of freshly baked banana bread, while I indulge in a nice warm cup of tea.

Back home, Aran also assists me with my indoor exercises. I have become much stronger with the regular strength and conditioning sessions Eamonn has given me. I use Aran as a weight to increase the resistance, holding him close to me while I perform squats and lunges. He lies down beside me as I do my planks. I tickle his tummy to keep him focused on the workout.

However, Aran is starting to behave in a way that is incompatible with using my bike rollers. Aran is learning to crawl. At first, I wasn't too sure what was happening. I just kept on finding him wedged beneath the sofa and kitchen table. In his attempts to crawl forward, he pushes himself backwards and reverses under the furniture. But as soon as he works out how to use his forward gears, he crawls everywhere and anywhere he can go.

I initially put him in a playpen to contain his movements while I ride my bike indoors. But he cries so much that I have to lift him out and abandon such stationary bike sessions entirely. I don't want the neighbours to hear his screams, and think I am neglecting my child.

Eventually I find out about a marvellous contraception called a jumperoo and immediately purchase one. It looks like a pair of large elasticated knickers attached to three big springs. I place Aran in the pants, and he immediately starts to jump up and down with great abandon. If he bores of bouncing, he is also surrounded by a massive circular tray, on which there is a riot of colourful toys that rattle, shake, and spin. It is the perfect device for keeping Aran amused while I ride my bike inside.

I place Aran in the jumperoo one day when I have a particularly difficult bike session scheduled. I know it will take me at least ninety minutes to complete the warm-up, efforts, recovery times, and warm-down. I balance myself on Bike as I watch Aran starting to bounce around. I'm not sure how long Aran will last in his jumperoo before he will demand to get out. I start my first effort, a one-minute sprint at a heart rate over one forty. It is cold outside, weather that requires cycling mitts and waterproof over-shoes. But inside, it is twenty degrees, and the sweat starts to drip off my body straightaway, landing in great drops on the kitchen floor. Aran watches me closely as I finish the effort, and I pedal slowly to recover. He then hits the music button on his play tray, and starts to blast out Old Macdonald on endless repeat. I suppose I'll have to put up with this incessant nursery rhyme if I want a quiet baby who'll let me do my training in peace.

I do the next effort, already fighting to keep the pace. Aran is equally struggling with his present confinement. Aran watches me. I watch him, wondering which one of us is going to crack first. But all credit to the lad, Aran manages to jump up and down for a full ninety minutes, while I strain to complete my own session.

Even when I leave Aran in crèche to do workouts on my own, Aran proves to be a perfect child. I hand him over to the childcare staff who welcome him warmly. Aran goes to them without the slightest whimper or complaint. I am so glad he doesn't cling to me, or cry whenever I leave. It makes my departure so much easier, especially when I still suffer from guilt attacks about selfishly leaving him so I can do my own thing.

As soon as I am out the door, however, I know I have made the right choice. Without Aran, I can now go trail running. I take the coastal path that leads out of Greystones, and heads north towards Bray. I follow it as it curls up around the rocky hill of Bray Head with its sweeping views over Dublin Bay. I climb the steep cliffs up to the hill's summit, and touch the imposing stone cross. I breathe in the salty, sea breeze, and enjoy the brief solitude.

Eventually I turn around and jog back to Greystones. Even though I've had a long run and my legs are tired, there is a lightness in my step. Aran spots me as soon as I return to the crèche. A smile spreads quickly across his face. He gets himself on to all fours, and crawls towards me at great speed from right across the room. I drop to my knees and open wide my arms as he crawls right into my lap, where he receives a massive hug.

But while Aran and I are becoming best buddies, relationships are strained at home. Pete's absence from day-to-day affairs means Aran barely acknowledges him these days. Pete has made a habit of coming back to the house after dark. When he tries to say hello to his son, Aran recoils and clings to me fervently. I don't want to rile Aran further by going near my husband, so I just give Pete a welcoming nod. Pete has no other option but to turn his unfulfilled affections towards Tom.

'Who's a good dog then?' Pete says, cuddling Tom in his arms if he is a baby, albeit a very hairy one.

'You are not to start putting that dog in Aran's wrap,' I say, half-joking.

'But why not?'

'Well, he's dirty,' I say. 'Don't you see where he sticks his nose?'

I have also become estranged from Tom due to his lack of hygiene. I spend so much time washing my hands these days, after nappy changes and when feeding Aran, I don't want to have another reason to have to scrub them clean again. If I pet Tom, I will have to wash my hands before going near the baby. So these days, I also prefer to acknowledge the dog with a mere perfunctory nod.

Tom is also perturbed by his radical change in status. Before, he occupied a position of rank, as the beloved pet in a household full of doting adults. Now, he has a rival for my affections, in the form of baby Aran. Aran is, however, unaware of the dog's recent and drastic demotion. He is instead fascinated by this white hairy beast that walks around at his eye level.

While Tom is the happy recipient of Pete's abundant affection, he is terrified of Aran. Tom hides from him in his covered crate that transported him back from Asia. But this refuge is insufficient to protect Tom from Aran's persistent intrigue. I soon find Aran crawling into the crate in hot pursuit of our dog. Tom has his back up against the end of the box, growling at Aran, warning him to get the feck out of his home. Aran is totally oblivious to what this growling sound means. It is only when I hoist Aran out by the scruff of the neck that he realises the crate is now off limits.

Even Bike has to take sides in this ongoing family feud. With Aran annoying the hell out of Tom, Pete puts Tom's crate near the back door, where Aran will have difficulty finding him. This is, however, where Bike is normally placed. Pete is not too happy having to squeeze past Bike to get to his beloved dog.

'Why don't you put this thing in the shed?' Pete says. He comes very close to kicking Bike's wheel to indicate which 'thing' he is referring to. If he dares touch Bike with his foot, I swear I'll castrate his dog.

'Bike is way too valuable, Pete. There's no way I'm leaving him outside.'

'But can't you just move it somewhere else?'

'No, Pete. I can't,' I say, staring him down. 'Bike stays right there.'

Pete stomps upstairs in a mood. The household pecking order is now officially complete. Aran, Bike, and I are in charge. Pete and Tom are second-class citizens in their own home. The gulf between these two groups, however, has something sinister lurking within.

With all the training I am doing, I have lost considerable weight. The bathroom scales say that I am even lighter than I was before getting pregnant in the first place. My fingers are getting noticeably thinner, and with that, my wedding ring is now a little loose. I need to be careful in case the ring falls off altogether, and my marriage with it.

I wonder if I should talk to someone about all that's going on. Mothers with babies often hang out together and share their respective woes. But when I think about calling up a friend for coffee, I feel too stressed by the idea. Most of my friends are either childless, or had their kids a long time ago.

I tell myself to wise up, that my friends will understand my predicament. But I have this terrible worry that I'm just not that interesting to talk to any more. I used to be able to converse about world politics and exciting countries I've visited. Now all I can talk about is babies and training, in ridiculously minute detail.

Some friends do reach out and tell me to call round to theirs any time. A few of these pals have chosen not to have kids of their own. I wonder if they want to see me in the flesh just to confirm that they've indeed made the right decision. And though I truly appreciate their invites, I use Aran as the perfect excuse not to go. 'Sure he'll wreck your place now that he's crawling,' I would say. 'He might be asleep in the afternoon. Best we give it a miss.' My own chronic sleep deprivation is also making me avoid interacting with others. Even when out shopping, I find myself starting a sentence, then halfway through, forgetting what I originally wanted to say. If I can't even communicate while buying groceries, how will I ever be able to hold a proper conversation about anything substantive?

My problems with communication fail to end there. Even Pete can't seem to get simple messages across to me now.

It is 8 pm on a weekday evening when he gives me a call. I'm sitting in front of the TV, watching nothing in particular.

'You won't believe it,' he says. 'I've missed the Greystones train.'

'Can't you get the next one?' I ask, idly clicking the remote.

'It's not for another half an hour.'

So?

'I'll just get the train to Bray, and see if there's anything from there,' he adds.

There's a brief silence on the line.

'Well, okay,' I say. 'Aran is fast asleep here. So we'll see you when you get home.'

I've already hung up before I start wondering, am I meant to collect him from Bray? I don't even know where the train station is in the town. And I don't want to wake up Aran by throwing him into our cold car.

It is past 9 pm when Pete finally collapses through our front door.

'So you got the last train back in the end?' I say when he comes into the sitting room where Aran and I are snoozing.

'No thanks to you,' he says.

Tom is prancing around Pete's feet, furiously trying to greet his master, but Pete doesn't even notice this warm canine welcome. This is very strange behaviour.

'What? Did you want me to go collect you?'

'Of course I did,' Pete screams, his face turning bright red. 'Do you not listen any more?'

'Listen? You didn't ask me,' I say. 'You did not say the words, "Please come and collect me from Bray Station".'

'I feckin' fell asleep on the platform, I'm so wrecked. Some guy had to come and wake me up to catch the next train.'

I look straight at him. I don't know what to say.

'Look, we're living in Greystones because of you,' Pete spits out from nowhere.

'But, I thought you liked . . . ' I say, stopping short. I'm not actually sure I know what Pete likes or even thinks any more.

'All you seem to do these days is train,' Pete says, suddenly on a roll.

I'm gobsmacked. I thought we'd already agreed to these terms and conditions. And he knows full well I used to suffer from selfish runner syndrome, racing at least once if not twice a week. I was convinced I was a lot better now, and was a bit more considerate about my training habits.

'And another thing: you seem totally incapable of compromise,' Pete continues, his voice rising to fever pitch. 'I work hard all week, and then when I'm finally home at the weekends, you're off biking or running for hours.'

'Well, you're not the one stuck doing all the cooking and cleaning and shopping and laundry,' I shout back in retaliation. I've had enough of his crap. 'You come home and you don't even have to lift a finger.'

'What? Do you expect me to do all the housework as well as be the sole breadwinner?' Pete says. 'Do you have any idea how stressful it is when I'm the only one bringing home money?'

'I am sick of this shit!' I scream, my hands gesticulating wildly. 'I was totally fine going out to work and earning before you even came along.'

We are so busy roaring and fighting with each other that we forget all about Aran. Our raised voices wake him abruptly from his sleep. Pete hurries to pick Aran up from his seat just as he begins to bawl.

'Give him to me,' I say.

'No. I'll calm him down.'

'Stop it. Don't be ridiculous.'

Aran's cries start to crescendo, until neither Pete nor I can hear each other speak. Pete turns and walks out of the room with Aran, and opens the front door.

'Where are you going?' I shout, fearing they're about to disappear forever into the dead of night.

'Standing outside,' Pete says, rocking Aran in his arms. 'It seems to calm him down.'

I severely doubt his strategy, but I am quickly proven wrong. Aran breathes in the fresh night air, and snuggles into Pete's chest.

How is this little baby going to survive his parents if they're fighting all the time?

154

'Look, we can't go on like this,' says Pete with a sigh. 'We need to make this work.'

I lean heavily on the front door post. 'Come inside. And let's talk.'

We sit down together in the sitting room, and agree not to raise our voices. Pete wraps Aran in his blanket and settles him on his knee.

'So, is Greystones the problem?' I ask.

'No. It's not that,' Pete says. 'It's just ... the work. It's so much pressure.'

'Well, do you want me to find a job then?' I ask. 'Will that help at all?'

Pete thinks for a moment. 'Probably not,' he says, stroking Aran's head absentmindedly. 'Money's not the problem. And if you go back, it means that we'd have to put Aran into full-time childcare. I'm not sure I want that right now.'

I'm not sure I want that either. I sort of like being Aran around, but lately I've been feeling guilty that I've not gone back to work yet. Even though I know that, if I do start back, I'll then feel guilty about leaving Aran with full-time childminders.

'Let's get another car,' Pete says out of nowhere.

'Well, if you want to,' I say. 'But how will that help?'

'Then I can drive up and down to the train station,' he says. 'And I won't get caught in the rain again.'

'Fair enough,' I say. 'I'll ask around to see if anyone's selling anything cheap,' trying to help him out with his plan. 'And I'm sorry if you think I'm training all the time. But honestly, Pete, it's the only thing that keeps me sane and gives me a break from Aran.'

'No, I'm sorry too,' Pete says. 'It's just, I didn't realise it was making me feel so frustrated.'

I assumed that, when Pete's home, he'd want to just spend time with Aran, and that I could disappear for a while. I didn't realise Pete wanted me to hang out with them as well, and be like a 'normal' family.

'Listen,' I say. 'I promise never to train on Saturdays. And I won't do big sessions on Sundays.' There goes the hope I'd had of joining a local cycling group and going for three- to four-hour spins at the weekend. Now there's some *real* compromise on my part. 'And maybe we could get some sort of backpack for Aran,' I say, trying to solve as many of our issues in one fell swoop.

Pete looks a little confused.

'I've seen how you still struggle to tie the wrap on to yourself,' I say. 'But Aran really does like being carried. I could get one of those holders with clips that are easy to put on and take off.'

Pete goes quiet for a minute. He must be thinking of how a cheap used car and a simplified baby carrier could potentially affect his quality of life. But if an automobile, a backpack, and less weekend training on my part can save our relationship, then I'm all for giving them a try.

'I just don't get it though,' I say, sensing a chance to speak to Pete about something that's been bothering me for a while. 'It seems to me that we've been really lucky. Like Aran is a great baby, healthy and everything. And we have no major worries to deal with.' I look up to see if Pete is still listening. 'So how come having a new baby is so incredibly hard? Like, how do others even begin to cope if their baby is sick, or everything isn't okay at home? How do single parents survive? How do people manage when the kid isn't biologically theirs?'

'I have absolutely no idea, really I don't,' Pete says. 'But it's definitely given me a whole new level of respect for people who manage to bring up children in difficult circumstances like those.'

I nod silently in agreement.

'Listen, I knew it was going to be difficult having Aran,' Pete says. 'And, trust me, I definitely have no regrets. But at times I think both of us are really pushed to our limits.'

I suggest we sit for a while and drink a bit of wine. I rarely drink these days, seeing that I'm still breastfeeding, but I feel like it might be a good way for us to reconcile.

I hand Pete his glass as he makes himself comfortable on the couch.

'We should have a date night,' Pete says, as I clink my glass against his. 'Like, get a babysitter or something.'

We've not been out together without Aran since he was born last year. We used to go out every night for dinner when we lived abroad. It's amazing how a new arrival can change your lifestyle so radically.

My initial reaction is to say no. Where would we get a babysitter? Where would Pete and I even go? Then I realise that a night out now and then might make our relationship a little healthier than it is right now. Dinner out might actually spur me on to wear something a little classier than the spew-drenched rags I seem to throw on every day. Thanks to nursing Aran, I have an actual cleavage, for the first time ever. I might as well make the most of this development, which I know won't last.

'Okay,' I say. 'I'll ask at the crèche if there is someone who can look after Aran for an evening. And maybe we can go for dinner at one of the restaurants in town.'

It sounds so ridiculously simple when I say it all out loud. But it's amazing how long it has taken us to formulate this straightforward plan.

Pete relaxes back into the sofa and beams the widest smile I've seen in years.

'So, if I get a date with my lovely wife, what do you need to make you happy?'

I don't even need to think about it for a second. 'Can you look after Aran on the odd Sunday morning, so I can go mountain running?'

14

Adventure

Although the Wicklow Mountains are a stone's throw from Greystones, I rarely manage to reach them. It is a minimum twenty-minute drive to get to any decent hill, meaning travelling alone takes a whole forty-minute chunk out of my allotted crèche time. This, in my mind, is an inefficient use of childcare.

With Pete agreeing to mind Aran at home on Sunday morning, I decide to indulge in a couple of guilt-free hours of mountain running. The Irish Mountain Running Association have scheduled a race out of Glendalough in mid-April, coinciding nicely with our new babysitting pact. The race promises twenty-eight kilometres of running over three peaks, with nearly one thousand four hundred metres of climb. It sounds like a perfect way to get reacquainted with the hills.

Long mountain races don't attract many women. So I'm not surprised when I am the only lady at race registration. Even the men are far and few between, put off by the long distances, steep climbs, and tricky navigation.

With five minutes to spare, a car speeds up to the start. A somewhat flustered Niamh throws herself out of the passenger seat. 'I'm so disorganised!' she giggles, throwing a map into her back pocket and sprinting past me towards the registration desk. The last time I saw her was two years ago, when she lugged her newborn baby into the crowded pub. She is a transformed woman from the one I saw that day. I had heard on the grapevine that she has returned to her old winning ways. Just a few weeks ago, she triumphed at a major half-marathon trail race through the Wicklow Mountains. And by the looks of her new streamline, svelte self, she could easily float up and down a mountain or two today.

At the stroke of noon, the race director waves us off. The pace is fast from the start as we climb the forest road and head towards St. Kevin's Way. I try to keep in step with the leading men. But my haste for speed means I fail to think about the direction in which I am heading. Niamh takes a clever shortcut through the forest, and hits the trail right in front of me. I push to catch up with her, cursing my error, and together we run shoulder to shoulder towards Scarr Mountain.

All of sudden, out of the corner of my eye, I see Niamh flinch.

'Oh no!' she exclaims. But even with something obviously wrong with her, Niamh refuses to slow.

'What's up?' I say, between my laboured breaths.

'My pelvic floor's just gone.'

Before having Aran, I would have stayed silent, too embarrassed to enquire about her sudden incontinence. But, having gone through childbirth myself, I totally understand what she means.

'Oh God, I thought that was just me,' I say, forgetting all about the race. 'I have to be careful not to wet myself, especially when I sneeze.'

'You should talk to Maeve,' Niamh says, barely

breaking from her stride. 'She can't run downhill any more without her bladder giving out.'

With that last piece of highly personal information, Niamh edges past me.

We battle each other up and over Scarr, then down into Glenmacnass. But as we start the long boggy climb to Tonlagee's top, Niamh leaves me defiantly in her tracks. I put my head down and keep trudging on, wondering if her descending skills will be up to speed, or if her pelvic floor might crack once more.

Unfortunately for me, neither of these possibilities comes to pass. I commence the final ascent of Camaderry Mountain with one last-ditch effort to catch Niamh before the line. Every now and then I catch glimpses of her on the horizon, just enough to give me hope. I am so busy trying to chase her down that I barely notice overtaking several male competitors. They can't work out what is up with the ladies today. Niamh and I seem hell-bent on destroying each other and any men who dare to come in our way.

In the end, I fail to catch up with Niamh. She edges me into second place by nearly two minutes. I am convinced she is speedier now than ever before, even after having a few kids.

I come home and tell Pete about my battle with Niamh on the hill. He is in the bathroom, perched on the toilet, supervising Aran's bedtime bath.

'That's amazing,' he says. 'She's never beaten you by this much before.'

'I know!' I say. 'It's really quite a comeback.'

My attention diverts to Aran, who is manically splashing the bubbles. It's amazing how much enjoyment he gets from a little bit of froth.

'How many children did you say she has?'

'Two,' I say.

'Maybe we need to bang out a few more so,' Pete says. 'Might make you faster as well.'

I have dreaded the day when Pete brings up the possible extension of our family. Before Aran, ignorance was bliss. But now I know *exactly* what pregnancy and childbirth entails, and it ain't to my liking at all.

'Aran isn't even one year old,' I say. 'Will you just give me a break?'

'Sure my mother was already pregnant with my brother when I was Aran's age.'

'Back in the 1970s?' I say. 'I think family planning in Ireland was a little different back then.'

'You know I want four kids,' Pete says, looking up at me wistfully from the toilet seat.

We've had this conversation already. Pete wants to emulate his younger brother who already has four children. But I feel way too old to reproduce three more times.

'You can have two. That's it,' I say. I can see the value of Aran having a sibling to play with, and occasionally to beat up. But given how we've struggled caring for just Aran, I can't imagine how we'd cope with one more, let alone two or three new additions.

'Okay, three,' Pete says.

'This is not a negotiation.'

'All right,' Pete finally concedes. 'Let's just try for a second, and then we'll see.'

I lean heavily against the bathroom door. It's hard work changing my husband's mind.

'So when do we begin?' Pete says.

I pat him on his head as he flashes me an expectant,

cheeky grin. 'We'll see,' I say, before turning and making a hasty retreat from the bathroom.

The answer is, I don't know when we can begin. There's part of me that wants to compete in this year's racing season and use all the training I've done. The last race is usually in October, so maybe we can hold off until then?

However, there is a bigger issue for us to deal with; my periods have yet to return. Breastfeeding can often make periods completely disappear. I thought, however, that once Aran started on solid foods three months ago, his reduced number of feeds would allow them to come back. I'm still waiting, and waiting, and there's no sign of any yet. Not that I'm complaining, but without any periods, there's little chance of me getting pregnant again.

Apart from that, I don't have much time to think about another baby. I am too busy running after Aran who is getting into everything. He has discovered the stairs and the excitement that comes from climbing up them precariously. He has found out that drawers can bang and clatter when they are opened and closed ad nauseam. Aran has worked out that he can climb into kitchen cabinets as well. I find him one day perched on a cupboard shelf, hiding behind a mixer and several Pyrex bowls.

Not even Bike is safe from Aran's reach. Tom and Bike now live together at the back of our hallway, and Tom has managed to teach Aran, through some strategic growls, the importance of keeping away. Bike, however, cannot give such verbal warnings. Aran gets great joy out of spinning Bike's pedals incessantly round and round. He pulls hard on the chain and gets black greasy oil on both of his hands. It is when he starts venturing near the sharp, spiky rear cogs that I ban Aran from Bike. Those metal things could do real damage to small, soft limbs.

163

I also set about trying to solve our issues of another car and an alternative wrap. I finally manage to find a strap-on baby carrier that allows both Pete and I to easily transport Aran around. The Ergobaby Performance model fits the bill to a T. With two simple clips, we can strap Aran on to our fronts and keep a close eye on him. Or we can place him behind and carry him around like a backpack. Pete immediately realises the benefits of this design. He can throw Aran on to his back and mow the lawn with his son. Aran is ecstatic with this new elevated, scenic view. And I'm glad that Pete has finally learned how to multitask, skilfully combining lawn cutting with babysitting.

We also succeed in resolving Pete's car dilemma. We buy a second-hand Renault Kangoo people-carrier van for four hundred Euros from a friend of a friend. It is cheap and cheerful, and breaks down with amazing regularity, but it allows Pete to drive down to the train station and back home again when it rains. The extra couple of minutes he can spend in bed in the morning, and the certainty of dry work clothes, make an amazing difference to Pete's mood.

The added bonus of Kangoo is that Bike can now come and join us inside our new car. Gone are the days when he has to hang on for dear life off the hatchback door. With Bike stretched out in our spacious boot, Pete now has an unrestricted view outside the rear window while driving. The sliding van doors and higher roof make Aran's car seat entry and exit much less of a contortion act. Tom has more room to roam around on the floor and underneath the seat. Such small things, but Kangoo makes a world of a difference, and an element of harmony is restored to our family.

With the feuding factions now reconciled, I can turn my attention to the racing calendar. My training thus far has been geared towards one-day adventure races. The Sea to Summit race I did when Aran was four months old was tough but totally thrilling. I enjoyed the epic challenge of climbing Croagh Patrick Mountain, pushing myself to the limit to reach its lofty top. I loved biking around the narrow rural roads, pedalling hard up and over the Maum Hills. And the thrill of racing against top class competitors in these disciplines really spurred me on.

Sea to Summit was the last race of 2013 on Ireland's National Adventure Race Series. I look up the Series website to see what races are lined up for this coming year. I see events as far south as Dingle and Killarney, and as far North as Donegal. I see races in the west of Ireland, along the wild Atlantic Way, and others in the Wicklow Mountains, in Ireland's ancient east. With such a range of territories and terrains, I am sorely tempted to enter. There are nine races in total, with your four best races counting towards your final score. Within seconds, I have decided. The National Adventure Race Series is what I will aim for.

However, my series-racing plan gets off to a disastrous start. Days before I am scheduled to compete in the first event, the Beir Bua Waterford Adventure Race, Aran gets really sick. All the breast milk he has consumed since his birth has made his immune system rock solid. But finally, at the tender age of ten months, he succumbs to an ear infection and bad cough.

I bring him to the local doctor to get him checked out. She gives me some strong antibiotics and sends me on my way. What with it being the Republic of Ireland, this consultation is not free. I fork out thirty Euros for the doctor's visit, and an extra tenner for the medicine.

The next morning, Aran's ear infection has got no better. He still has a hacking cough. But to make matters worse, he has developed a horrific rash all over his back. In a blind panic, I call the doctor, fearing he may have contracted deadly meningitis. She tells me to return straightaway, fortunately this time at no extra charge.

It turns out that Aran has contracted pneumonia. He is also allergic to the type of antibiotics he was originally given, hence the sudden rash. This means I have to get a different type of medicine, which I also have to pay for. This experience starkly reminds me to be grateful for the National Health Service available in Northern Ireland, where such appointments and treatments are provided free of charge.

I am so busy caring for my sick child that I barely notice when I start to feel unwell myself. I first experience a sore throat, but then the same cough as Aran's arrives. I start to spit up putrid, yellow-coloured phlegm. I call my coach to inform him of my illness, and ask him what I should do.

'Don't train,' Eamonn says, with an authority I've not heard from him before.

'Are you sure?' I say. Normally I would have just battered on with my training schedule, and hoped I'd get better soon.

'Your body needs rest. Get some meds and take today off,' he confirms. 'We'll talk again tomorrow and see how you feel then.'

I hang up the phone, upset that the day's session is cancelled. I feel like a failure that I couldn't suck it up, and just go out and train. But soon this sense of regret is replaced with total relief. Someone else has told me to rest. It wasn't me who chickened out. If I had opted out by myself, I would have second-guessed the decision a million times. But now that Eamonn has instructed me to stop, I have no problem obeying his strict command.

I head to the chemist to buy some medicine to flush away the phlegm clogging up my throat. The chemist gives me some Exputex and instructs me to take it three times a day. I take one dose as soon as I get home, then wait for it to work. The belligerent phlegm refuses to budge, even after several hours' wait. I decide to take another spoonful to accelerate the process. I idly glance at the bottle label as I pour the liquid out.

'Do not take if you are pregnant or breastfeeding' is written right across the glass.

Oh shit.

I forgot that breastfeeding precludes a wide range of medication. I return the bottle to the pharmacy and get a full refund. Now I have no choice but to let my body heal itself without outside assistance.

I take a day off, then another. I wake up every morning, hoping I'll feel better, but instead spend my waking hours coughing and spitting up phlegm. The race gets closer and closer. I am running out of time to get well.

Eamonn calls me two days before the race.

'How are you feeling?' he says, cutting to the chase.

'Better,' I say, sounding relatively optimistic. 'Got a fair amount of phlegm still coming up though, to be honest.'

'Right, you don't race,' he says.

'What?' I splutter, realising I should never have told him the whole truth. 'But ... but I've already paid the race entry fee.'

'Doesn't matter,' he says. 'Let's aim for the next race after this one.'

There's no arguing with Eamonn. He is adamant on this

167

issue. And though I am bitterly disappointed, ultimately I know he is right.

When the Beir Bua Waterford Adventure Race results appear online, I can't help but look them up. And there I see it. Fiona Meade, the spectacular winner of Sea to Summit, has claimed the first Series victory of 2014.

I take the next few days easy as I try to return to fitness. Already I have lost a whole week to this illness. But while Aran and I slowly battle with our infections, Aran is fighting on an additional front. His teeth are erupting out of his gums, making them painfully sore and red. He wakes at night, tossing and turning from the pain that is exploding inside his head.

His fitful nights disturb my own sleep patterns, and we both wake up grumpy and tired. But what makes my life even more unbearable is breastfeeding this little Dracula. I keep forgetting that he has teeth in his mouth when I place him on my nipple. Aran sucks away as normal, then bites down hard on my poor defenceless breast. The pain emanates quickly and spreads throughout my body. I screech, he screams, and we both end up crying from self-pity. I've really got to get this little monster off breast milk as soon as possible.

By the time Dingle Adventure Race comes around three weeks later, my phlegm has well and truly gone. Pete and I pack up our bags, and head with Aran and Tom to the race start. The Dingle Adventure Race is a forty-eight-kilometre course around Kerry's scenic Dingle Peninsula. Starting on road bikes, the route takes you high up and over Conor Pass, before descending via steep, winding country roads for twenty-five kilometres to remote Cloghane village. There the bikes are dumped for a ten-kilometre hike up Mount Brandon. From sea level, you climb a steep, rocky thousand metres to the top, before descending via a gentle grassy slope back to civilisation on the other side of the peninsula. Then it's a ten-kilometre road run back to Dingle, where boats await for a kayak section near the marina. And if your legs haven't cramped or you've not sunk your boat by then, the race ends with a one-kilometre sprint back into Dingle town, where lies the ultimate finish line.

I arrive at the start line early on Saturday morning to try to calm my nerves. Straight away, I see Fiona Meade, the current Series leader and today's firm favourite. I also see previous Dingle winner, Emma Donlon, eyeing up the competition. All I can hope is to make my own mark on this, my first adventure race of 2014.

I see Fiona lining up on the start, alongside the main male contenders. My only hope is that I can hang on to these cyclists and not lose too much ground on the initial climb. My hopes are quickly dashed, as Fiona sprints off through the streets of Dingle, and blasts up the mountain pass. I push hard, but before I know it, I am in no man's land. Soon I hear the gentle breaths of a girl on my shoulder.

'I'm Emma,' she says as she glides past me into second place.

'I'm Moire,' I gasp in return, taking her third position. I wonder if I should continue chatting with Emma, but before I can think of a conversation topic, she is well and truly gone.

Reaching the pass, I let go of the brakes and descend as best I can, praying not to fall off the cliffs on my left or slip on the wet patches on the road. I soon catch up with a guy pedalling furiously along. I suggest to my new friend that we work together, and we draft each other all the way to Cloghane.

'You're second lady,' a marshall calls as I drop my bike at the village.

'No, you're wrong,' I want to say. 'I'm third. Fiona and Emma are ahead.'

But then I turn and see Fiona on the roadside, leaning against her bike calmly. She is chatting and laughing with some random bystanders. She is not racing at all.

I don't have time to ask what the hell Fiona is up to, whether this is a clever race ploy. If I'm second, Emma is first. I set off up the mountain in hot pursuit.

I look up and catch a glimpse of Emma's T-shirt. She is only a few metres ahead of me. But my closeness to Emma is short-lived. Emma has run for Ireland. There's no way I'm going to catch a capped athlete on the mountain. I follow the narrow and rocky path up Brandon, sliding on the patches of wet bog that intersperse the track underfoot. To my left, I catch the sight of beautiful shimmering lakes, with only a sharp precipitous drop separating me from their cold waters. I pick my way carefully up the mountain, praying that I won't slip down a surrounding cliff.

After nearly an hour of climbing, I encounter a massive wall of stone. There is no obvious way up and over this section, until I see another athlete snake his way up through the strewn boulders. It looks like we're entering Valhalla, and there is no other way out of here than up.

I manage to find the summit just as an old adventure-racing pal passes me.

'Good to see ye back racing,' he says.

Despite the pain, it is definitely good to be back again.

I relax as I run down the mountain, following the white pilgrim markers at first, then enjoying the fast grassy descent. Emma is nowhere to be seen as I reach the road at Bally Braic. Pete, Aran, and Tom are waiting for me at the transition with news I do not expect.

'Emma is four minutes ahead of you,' Pete shouts. 'But she is looking pretty tired.'

I flash him a quick smile as I set off down the road. I push hard to see if I can make up some of this precious gap. Pete takes off after me in the car. He loves a good photo finish.

Soon I can just make out Emma's blue T-shirt in the distance, but she still seems so far away. The road section is relentless after the freedom of Mount Brandon's terrain. I hammer the tarmac for what seems like an eternity, trying hard to catch the leader.

After fifty minutes of running, I reach the kayak section. Pete is already there with Aran and Tom, waving his arms excitedly.

'She's only ninety seconds ahead of you,' Pete shouts. 'You can do it!'

I stop to allow the marshals to throw a lifejacket on my body. But the sudden stop and pounding road have battered my full bladder. My weak pelvic floor can't cope. All of a sudden, urine gushes down the inside of my leg.

'Oh no!' I shout, without thinking.

'What's wrong? What's wrong?' Pete says, worried I might have pulled a muscle or something.

I don't have time to explain to Pete that I have accidentally wet myself. I jump into the kayak and hope I don't leave a puddle behind in the seat when I exit.

The sea is choppy from the wind. Immediately I feel the boat wobble beneath me. My heart beats fast, fearing I might overturn and take an unexpected swim. All of a sudden, out of nowhere, I start to sing out loud. 'Hello Aran, hello Aran, hello Aran, we're glad to see you here.'

Oh my God, why is the baby swimming song belting out of my mouth? This is not the time or place to be shouting silly songs. But surprisingly, it seems to calm my nerves. The thought of Aran splashing around is a perfect distraction from the waves.

I paddle hard, reaching the shore with Emma now forty seconds in front. She must have heard me coming, as she bolts out of her boat and sprints down the road. Despite my best efforts, I fail to close the gap and take second place, thirty-four seconds off the pace.

'Was that you singing in the kayak?' is the first thing Emma says to me as I cross the finish line.

'No, not me,' I reply. 'Must have been the wind you heard.'

I soon find out that Fiona Meade never intended to finish the race. She used the road bike section as a training session, and was happy to leave it there.

Pete, Aran, Tom, and I drive back to Greystones the following day. I am looking forward to more adventure races, now that I have some points on the Series board.

We are still not sure though if Greystones is the right place for us to live. Fortunately, the decision is soon made for us: my friend tells us she wants to sell her house. It's a perfect excuse for Pete to finish his job and for us to move back north and home to Derry.

15

Pain

The next race up in the Adventure Race Series is Gaelforce North, three weeks after Dingle. It takes place in the far north-west reaches of Ireland, in the remote wilderness of County Donegal. Being so far away from major urban areas, it means that the vast majority of athletes refrain from travelling and participating. It means that Fiona and Emma will not be there. I, on the other hand, live in Derry, a mere sixty-minute drive from the start. It is a perfect event for me to go to, to capture some series points.

The sixty-four-kilometre race takes in some of Donegal's finest features. An initial run through Glenveagh National Park and along its unspoilt lake leads you to a short kayak section on Gartan Lake. Then it's a road bike through vast barren bog lands to the foot of Donegal's highest mountain, Mount Errigal. A quick hike up and down its rocky slopes is followed by an off-road bike leg westward to the Atlantic coast, with the finish in the coastal fishing town of Bunbeg.

I complete the race in first position, and take a maximum score of one hundred series points home. It is good preparation for my next challenge, Gaelforce West, one that I am secretly dreading. Gaelforce West is the fourth race this season, with five more to come later in the year. With the overall Series still up for grabs, and my post-natal body still somewhat fickle, I need to turn up to earn some much-needed points.

Gaelforce West is one of Ireland's toughest adventure races. The course probes the depths of one of the wettest, wildest, but most beautiful places in Ireland, the area of Connemara. The race itself traverses sixty-seven kilometres of Connemara's remotest beaches, mountains, and waterways. Starting at Glassilaun beach, on the very western edge of Europe, the race embarks on a thirteen-kilometre run inland along the old Famine trail, where in the 1840s starving Irish trekked to the coast to escape the Great Potato Famine.

Competitors flee this track by kayaking across the cold choppy waters of Killary Harbour fjord. Back on dry land, a short run across rutted bog leads athletes to their bikes, where they embark on a thirty-four-kilometre cycle along relentless, narrow, rural roads. As they pedal, the shadows of Croagh Patrick Mountain loom ominously large, beckoning them to its top. Croagh Patrick is also the pinnacle of the Sea to Summit adventure race that I competed in last November. But this time, instead of the popular northern route that pilgrims trod, Gaelforce West brings you up via the mountain's southern slopes that are seldom visited.

No sooner have you summited the mountain than you are thrown back down again, your feet balancing on boulders as big as your head, your body falling in bog holes concealed under ankle-tripping heather, your eyes watering from your runaway descending speed and the icy gusts that whip up from the Atlantic Ocean far below.

And then you are back on your bike. It's a mere

eleven-kilometre cycle to the finish line in Westport, yet two of these kilometres span rough, puncture-inducing off-road tracks, over which the wiser competitors carry their bikes on their backs. A short sprint on foot through the grandiose grounds of Westport House transports you to the finish line.

The most fleet-footed females will make it home in around four hours. Those less able may have to endure this course for well over ten.

Before I can even think about tackling the course, reaching Westport with Aran in tow poses my first logistical challenge. Westport was the starting place for the Sea to Summit race. And just like Sea to Summit, Aran must accompany me on the journey as I am still breastfeeding him. I live in Derry, in the far north-west corner of the Emerald Isle. This race is as far west as I could possibly travel.

Registration is at Killary Adventure Centre, a five-hour drive from my home. If I were still young, free and single, this long trip would be a piece of cake. Now it is a journey I dread.

A key task is to find a babysitter for Aran while I race. Pete is out working in Cambodia for several weeks before Gaelforce West. We have agreed that he'd be back in time to look after Aran while I compete. His flight, however, does not get into Dublin until Friday morning, just as I need to leave Derry to make my own way to Westport. It seems like our ongoing parental juggling act gets more complex with time.

After a flurry of internet searches, Pete works out that he can catch a train from Dublin that will deposit him in Westport at 4 pm the day before the race. We agree that I will finish registration just in time to pick him up from the station.

Aran and I set off in our spacious Kangoo bulging beneath all our needs. I intend to set off good and early, but it takes a little longer than expected to get Aran fed and clothed and changed. Despite this delay, we make good progress along Donegal and Sligo's network of minor roads. Aran thankfully dozes off to sleep within half an hour of leaving.

Aran eventually stirs from his sleep halfway through our journey. There is no gradual yawn or loving sleepy smile at Mummy. He starts screaming wildly, flailing his arms around, and tearing out his blond toddler hair. 'It's okay, it's okay,' I say, throwing random glances in the rear-view mirror while trying to keep one eye on the road. His squeals grow louder and louder, while my stress levels escalate.

Suddenly I spot a pub ahead with a large parking lot to one side. 'Are you hungry, little one?' It is an educated guess. The easiest thing is to pull in, grab him out of his car seat, and stick him on a boob.

It works. The sobs subside as he sucks long and deeply until he is finally satisfied. I stick Aran back in his seat, and pray that this will be our first and last unforeseen pit stop.

Killary Adventure Centre is found on the remote southern banks of Killary Harbour. Ideally situated as a staging post for wild and remote exploration, the centre is less suited for the onslaught of over a thousand participants who need to park and collect their race numbers on the eve of race day.

Fortunately, we make it to registration in the early afternoon without any further delays. Aran is wide awake as I pull in to park. I cannot leave him in the car alone. I pick him up and carry him inside, hoping he will be on good behaviour. Aran soon spots the stairs that lead up to number collection. He wriggles and writhes out of my arms. He wants to climb up the steps, one by one, all of them without Mummy's help.

Slowly, he puts one foot on the step and grasps on to the handrail with all his might. With one long pull he heaves himself up, his other leg dragging behind him. This is going to be a very long stair ascent. I dare not lift him less he freaks out and causes a terrible toddler scene. But I have to get moving. I have my number to collect, my bike to drop, and a very jet-lagged husband to collect from the local train station.

I seem to be the only one carrying a baby into registration. I feel embarrassed. I can't work out if everyone else has wisely left their kids at home, or if there is some kind of mother apartheid system. Or maybe the others were astute enough to realise in advance that having offspring might complicate, or even severely curtail, their adventure-racing plans.

Having a child in tow does, however, prove somewhat advantageous. The crowds part out of pity and I pass smoothly through the process.

A quick nappy change in the centre's loos and we are off to nearby Delphi Centre for the bike drop. But though we are in deepest, darkest rural Ireland, traffic is at a standstill. Cars laden with racing bikes squeeze along the slender roads designed for farmers and their sheep. The race organisers have imposed a one-way system, but this does nothing to relieve the gridlock. I am delayed even further, painfully aware that Pete's train is relentlessly chugging its way to its final destination.

I eventually arrive at Westport train station very late. Pete is sitting on the platform, idly scanning through a book.

'I am so sorry,' I say, as I jump out of the car to greet him. Aran is crying, hungry again, but I have not had time to stop and feed him.

Pete is silent. We hug without warmth.

'I am so sorry,' I say again, but I know this will not cut it. He has flown halfway around the globe, then travelled the width of Ireland just so I can race. He is sleep-deprived, his face is unshaven, and his clothes smell of stale sweat.

Being late is understandable. But it is also unforgivable.

Before Aran arrived, there is no way I would have apologised so repeatedly for my lateness, or so obviously tried to make amends. I would have resolutely stated that it wasn't my fault that I got delayed, and that therefore an apology was unnecessary. Now, with a child on the scene, Pete and I know that arguments must be quickly resolved and relationships healed for the greater good of our family. Marriages can easily break up over the wrong word said too many times. The greatest casualty, in our case, would be Aran.

'Is the Bed and Breakfast far?' Pete asks as he slumps into the passenger seat.

'No, not at all,' I reply. 'Really close in fact.' I am eager to smooth things over and to start the weekend again. I hope the proximity of the B&B will do something to lighten his mood.

I had struggled to find a place for us to stay. Having a baby that moves by himself means our choice of accommodation is somewhat curtailed these days. It needs to be family-friendly, with big enough rooms for a double bed and travel cot and all our bags. It also needs understanding owners who do not mind if we pace the corridors with a baby squealing blue murder at midnight.

No one has thrown us out of a B&B yet, but I know

that several proprietors have been happy to see the back of us.

All is soon well again. The B&B is fine and functional. Pete is able to shower in the en suite and settles down for a snooze. Aran is happily deconstructing the room, opening and banging closed every drawer and door that is within his infant reach. And I am all ready to go race-wise.

Training has been good. I am as fit as I could possibly be at this stage of the year. The form guide suggests that I am one of the pre-race favourites based on my Gaelforce North win. Now all I need to do is rest, relax, and wait for tomorrow.

Or at least, that's what I think – but all is not well in Westport town.

It does not start as anything major, just an overwhelming need to lie down. 'Shift over in the bed there, Pete,' I say, pushing his jaded jet-lagged body over to one side.

He grunts and turns as I curl up in a ball beside his back. 'Pre-race nerves?' he slurs out of his hazy slumber.

'I don't know,' I reply. 'Probably.' Hopefully no more than that, but something is just not right.

I pull myself closer to his body, and scream. 'Feck! That hurts!'

Pete jumps up. 'What? What? What's going on?' His eyes dart around the room, trying to work out where he is and who I am. He comes through, looks down, and sees me screwed up, tight as a foetus, clutching myself in agony.

'My boobs!' I scream. 'They feckin' hurt.'

'Calm down. You'll upset Aran,' Pete whispers, though it is clear that Pete is the one most upset by this confusing scene.

'I think I've got mastitis,' I groan through a contorted

179

grimace. I have had mastitis before, but never as bad as this. My right breast is as hard as a rock. It is noticeably larger than the other one. The slightest touch makes me scream in agony. A glance with a feather would be sufficient, but instead, curling up beside Pete's back has started this painful onslaught.

'The milk,' I try to explain. 'It must be stuck.'

I have been rushing around all day. First to get packed up and go, then to drive halfway down the country to the race. I had to do all the administration and bike drop before finally picking up Pete from the station. Aran had fed just once that day and from only one single breast. There had not been enough time that day to stop and feed him from the other side. The milk has now built up in the neglected boob. It looks like an over-inflated balloon that is on the verge of bursting.

If only it would burst, that might alleviate at least some of this agony. By now the localised pain is being augmented by sweeping waves of nausea.

This is ridiculous. How could a blocked milk duct inflict so much bodily grief?

'You can't race in this state,' Pete says. 'We better just go home.'

'Home?' I shriek. 'You're kidding me. I need race points for the series.' Even as I say it, I know it sounds ridiculous. But I have prepared so much and travelled so far. I have even made my husband literally travel from the other side of the world so that he can babysit for a few hours. I cannot give up so easily.

'Well then, do you want to go to hospital?'

'No. No. Please no,' I say. 'All I have to do is get the milk out.'

Pete stands over me as I cower on the bed. The pain

180

and feelings of sickness have now been joined by flu-like symptoms. I feel hot, then cold, then shiver constantly. My body aches all over. I am a total mess.

I slowly sit up and try my best to squeeze some milk out of the offending breast. But the mere touch of my hand starts me squealing again, this time out of inconsolable frustration.

'How can I help?' Pete asks.

'Aran,' I whimper. 'I need Aran to get the milk out.'

Pete finds Aran in the bathroom, investigating the water in the toilet bowl. He picks him up and hands him to me. I gingerly tilt his head towards my body.

Aran is having none of it. He was having a great time splashing in the latrine. He arches his back, kicks his legs, and contorts violently away from me. Not that I blame him. Getting milk out of my mammary glands now is akin to sucking blood out from a stone. He is not interested in such hard work, especially when he still has a whole bathroom right there that he intends to explore.

I placate Aran for a while as he unravels the toilet tissue and drapes it over the towel rail. Finally, hunger gets the better of him, and he agrees to finally suck. Aran manages to latch on and soon the milk begins to flow.

'Ahhhhh,' I purr. 'Oh God, the relief,' as I feel the liquid leaving.

Once Aran starts the milk flow, the milk struggles to stop, so I pump and dump as much as possible. But even with the milk levels low, the damage has already been done. The breast is still sore, the flu-like symptoms persist, and the mere thought of food makes me want to vomit.

I have booked us into a lovely restaurant, An Port Mor, for a bit of fine dining before the race. Despite the current circumstances, I figure we might as well use the

181

reservation. Pete is starving after a day of airplane and airport food, and Aran needs some solids after his liquid lunch and dinner.

'I'll have the Connemara smoked salmon to start with, and the maple glazed pork belly for the main,' Pete instructs the waiter. An Port Mor is renowned for its excellent local fare, hence why we made the booking.

The very idea of consuming such flavoured food renders me instantly queasy. But I still cling to the idea of competing in the race tomorrow. 'I better eat something, just to keep up my strength,' I say. So I keep it simple and order the chicken.

Aran is not interested in the dishes on offer. He is much more intrigued by the street outside, and decides to go for a wander. The waiter sees our predicament and kindly seats us outside.

'You have your starter,' I say to Pete. 'And I will keep an eye on Aran.' So I follow Aran as he waddles up and down the pavement. When he stumbles, I am there to catch him. He is still learning to walk without falling.

Pete is left alone at the table while I keep tabs on our son. He downs his salmon mechanically, without savouring the slightest mouthful. Rare are our days of intimate dinners, enjoying a glass of wine together and appreciating each other's company. Eating food is now a perfunctory task, done hastily before Aran cracks up or toddles off.

As Pete finishes his starter, our mains soon arrive. 'My turn,' Pete says, as we tag-team the parenting role. He gets up and jogs after Aran, who is threatening to round the corner and disappear out of sight. I look at my food, delicious and delectable, and feel like I want to puke.

When both of us have eaten as much as we can, Pete,

Aran and I start our short walk home. The food I force-fed myself at the restaurant makes me feel a little better, but I am still a little wobbly on my feet. Pete loops his arm around mine and I am thankful for the support. I am so woozy, however, that I nearly miss the duo walking towards us on the street. I glance up and at the last minute realise that Emma Donlon is one half of the couple.

The last time I saw Emma was at the Dingle Adventure Race two months ago. After a gruelling three-hour battle, she won the race, beating me into second place. But Gaelforce West is a race that plays exactly to her strengths. She won it in 2011 and 2012. She is now back to reclaim the title. Emma is also a personal trainer, with qualifications in pre- and post-natal exercise.

'Hi, Emma, how's things?' I ask. We don't know each other that well, but Irish adventure-racing circles are exceptionally small.

'Grand, thanks,' replies Emma. 'All ready for tomorrow?'

I hesitate. I always play it cool before a race. I never admit to any weakness. If it had been any other female competitor, I would have told her I was all good to go. But, knowing that Emma trains women who have just had children, I am desperate for some advice.

'Not sure I will make it the starting line tomorrow, Emma,' I reply. I glance up at Pete and make the under-statement of the year. 'I've got a bit of mastitis.'

'Oh no,' Emma says. 'That's horrible! It's really painful, I hear.'

'Yeah, I'm not feeling the best. Any tips about how to get over it?'

'I'm afraid I'm not too sure,' replies Emma. I lean a little heavier on Pete. 'My sister had it once while breastfeeding.

Screamed in agony, she did. It got infected and she ended up on antibiotics.'

Oh God, I think. If it is that serious, there is no way I will be able to get antibiotics in time. It is late on Friday evening and I have no idea how to even find a doctor in Westport.

'That's a shame,' Emma adds. 'I was really looking forward to going head to head after the race we had in Dingle.'

She wishes me a speedy recovery, then Emma and I go our separate ways.

'So are you going to race tomorrow?' Pete asks when we get back to the B&B.

I think for a moment. 'I still don't know,' I reply. 'We have to stay the night anyhow, as it's too late to head back home. I suppose I'll just see how I feel in the morning.'

The alarm goes off at 4 am. If I want to catch the 5 am bus to the start, I have to get up now. The night was restless. Sleep had come in fits and starts. Pre-race nerves had stolen some slumber, but at least the nausea is gone. Before lying down for the night, I had put my sports bra on under my clothes to keep my breasts strapped firmly in place. And though the offending breast still feels sore, it is not as bad as yesterday.

I decide to get up and go. Maybe it is the fact that I have already paid my race entry, that I spent money on new puncture-proof tyres, and that I have dedicated hours and hours of training towards competing in Gaelforce West. So much has already been invested that it seems silly not to at least toe the line.

Dawn breaks as I arrive at a blustery Glassilaun beach. Two hundred other competitors are milling around the dunes waiting for the elite start at 6.30 am. I spot Paul

Mahon, my former adventure-racing teammate, warming up on the shore. We were racing together on the twenty-four-hour Cooley Raid Adventure Race when I figured out I was probably pregnant, unbeknownst to my team.

'Howaya, Moire?' Paul asks as he limbers up. 'All ready for the race?' This time, I refrain from disclosing my current feminine issues. I sincerely doubt anyhow that Paul can give me any reasonable, practical advice.

'Sure, we'll give it a lash,' I reply.

'Ye better,' he says. 'Emma is looking well fit these days. She'll be definitely hard to beat.'

We line up under the inflatable starting arch that has been shipped to this remote beach for the day. Before I have time to concur with Paul about Emma's current form, the horn blasts, and everyone sprints off on the run. I see Emma's heels kicking up sand just ahead of me. Within seconds, she is gone. I have no choice but to let her go as there's no way I can match her pace.

I take it handy as we race along the rutted, rocky famine track that traces the southern bank of Killary Harbour. After sixty-six minutes of running, I reach the second stage, the kayak north across the harbour. Emma is nowhere in sight, but I am at least in second place.

The waves beat against my single kayak as I struggle to steer it towards the opposing shore. The Atlantic wind too plays its part, buffeting my little boat's bow. And as I fight to keep the vessel afloat and going in the right direction, my stomach decides to add to my maritime woes. It feels at first like seasickness, but I know its true source. I slowly start to drown in the same waves of nausea that the mastitis drenched me with yesterday. Any race plans I might have had sink slowly into the waters below.

I struggle to reach my bike that I had so fastidiously

placed in Delphi Centre just the day before. With not finishing a real prospect, survival is now the new plan. I drink heavily from my water bottles on Bike, drawing a little strength from the sugar suspended within. I then work out the pace that I can just about manage without feeling I have to get off my bike and vomit on the roadside. The slightest change in heart rate, and I know my stomach will rebel.

It takes me ninety minutes to cycle to the base of Croagh Patrick Mountain. Much to my surprise, Pete is there at the bike drop. He is holding Aran high up on his shoulders. Pete's wide, friendly smile melts my race woes for an instant. Normally he tells me I'm looking great, but today we all know such a statement would be totally untrue.

'She is ten minutes ahead of you,' Pete shouts, finding something else positive to say. 'You can do it.'

Ten minutes! That's forever in adventure racing. The mountain section is only five kilometres long, and then there is a mere eleven-kilometre cycle to the finish. I flash a quick smile to thank him for the info, and start to ascend the mountain.

It takes me a quarter of an hour to climb the heathered terrain that leads towards the rocky cone summit. Just as I hit the steep, stony section at the mountain's shoulder, I see my mate Paul flying down the slope.

'She's just ahead of ye,' Paul shouts as he negotiates some steep scree. I look up at him incredulously. But before I can tell him where to go with his lies, he rapidly disappears.

I look up the mountain to see how far it is to the top. And just before the summit, I can just make out Emma's shape. I can barely believe it. I push hard, hoping that my body will hold out. Another couple of minutes, and I dare to look up again. She is closer, much closer.

I overtake her just as we arrive at the peak. Not wanting to pass by without saying something, I place my hand on her back and say hello. She is quiet. She looks tired and confused. Her usual strong stride has gone.

I don't understand what has happened her, but I don't have time to ask or wonder why. We have a race to run and I need to get back to my bike at the base of the mountain. I slip, stumble, and slide my way down its slopes in under fifteen minutes. Pete and Aran are at the bottom, waiting.

'Where's Emma?' Pete shouts.

'Up there,' I yell, thumbing back up the mountain. 'Gotta go!' are my last words to my stunned husband and son as they watch their wife and mother pedal frantically away.

The last bike and final run are a bit of a blur. I dare not look back lest I see Emma hunting me down. I finally reach the finish line in just under four and a half hours. And amazingly, I am the first lady home.

Emma arrives in Westport five minutes later.

I approach her as she crosses the line and congratulate her on the race. We have had the head to head that Emma hoped for, but neither of us had anticipated the final result.

'What happened out there?' I ask out of curiosity.

'I just bonked on the mountain,' Emma admits. She had tried to race on a minimum of food, and just ran out of energy before the end.

I went into the race feeling pretty miserable. But I suppose you never know how others are feeling, what injuries or illnesses they might be dealing with on the day. I doubt though that there were many other competitors lining up at Gaelforce West that morning dealing with a major bout of mastitis.

16

Killarney

After my debilitating attack of mastitis, I resolve to wean Aran off breast milk forever. He has just turned one, and so is well capable of digesting normal cow's milk by now. However, my commitment to stop this habit is met with violent resistance. When he wakes in the morning, Aran looks for his usual breastfeed, and instead is handed a hard, inanimate plastic cup. He duly flings the container across the kitchen floor, telling me in no uncertain terms that he despises this change in plan.

I pick up the cup of cow's milk and give it back to him, then sit him on my knee for a nice grown-up chat. I tell him that this is his new breakfast drink and that it is very yummy indeed. My logical explanation is drowned out, however, by blood-curdling screams. Suddenly, he throws his whole body backwards in protest and nearly topples off my lap. He doesn't seem to understand or care how dangerous such sudden movements can be.

He bawls and bawls, until I finally can't stand it anymore. I slip him under my shirt for a quick feed. His screams stop as soon he gets the liquid fix he craves, while I sit there cursing him for disrupting my weaning plan. I can't help worrying though he'll be addicted to breast milk forever. For the time being I'm just glad to have quelled Aran's manic tantrum; that is, until the next time he feels a little thirsty.

Now that we are back home in Derry, Mum can hang out with Aran again. She loved looking after him as a baby because of all the afternoon naps they could share. But now that Aran is a fully-fledged mobile toddler, the fun Mum and Aran can have together has increased immeasurably.

I leave Aran with Mum one day so that I can go for an hour's run. It is a warm, mild afternoon, so they head straight out into the garden to see what trouble they can get up to. I see them making a beeline for the pond, something that would spark fear in most parents of a wobbly toddler. But I need not worry, as Mum holds Aran firmly by the hand, stopping him from toppling in and accidentally drowning. They peer into the pool's murky depths, and start searching around for frogs. Aran lobs a few stones into the water to frighten them out into the open. When they fail to find amphibians, Mum produces some Peppa Pig bath toys. They spend the next hour throwing George Pig, Suzy Sheep, and Zoe Zebra into the pond, and then fishing them out again.

I come back from my run, glad to see that Mum and Aran are still dry and alive, and are keeping each other well entertained in the back yard. I pick Aran up and give him a big hug.

'Thanks for looking after him, Mum,' I say. 'Sure I can take it from here.'

'No problem,' Mum says. 'We had great fun altogether! Didn't we, Aran?'

I carry him towards the house to get both of us something to eat.

'I think I'll just stay out here,' Mum calls after us. 'There is a flower bed I want to weed.'

Back at the house, I put Aran down on the kitchen floor while I open up the fridge. Aran totters off out of the kitchen, to his hoard of toys that litter the nearby sitting-room floor. One of these days, I really must clear them up.

I don't hear a bang or any sort of violent thud. All I hear is the wailing sound of Aran's voice. I drop what I am doing at the kitchen counter to see what's up now. And when I finally find Aran in the next room, all I can see is blood spouting from his mouth.

'Oh my God! Oh my God!' I shout, not knowing what the hell to do next. Aran is crying so loud, I can barely hear myself think. I pick him up and hold him close to my body, cupping my hand around his head. I then rush out to the garden, where I find Mum knee-deep in her flower bed.

'Aran's bleeding badly,' I shout, my voice breaking from the stress. Mum gets off her knees and comes running to my aid.

'Oh God, how did that happen?' she says, looking straight at Aran's mouth. The sleeve of my running T-shirt, which I've not changed out of yet, is now totally soaked in Aran's blood.

'I have no idea,' I say frantically. 'We were in separate rooms, and next thing I heard was Aran screaming.'

Pete hears the noise from our office where he has been working up until now. He comes out to see what all the fuss is about.

'Oh good Jesus,' he says, covering his own mouth. 'We need to get him looked at. We have to go straight to A & E.'

'Are you sure?' I say. 'Take a look first and see where the blood is coming from.'

My worst fear is that he's somehow hit his chin and dislodged one of his new teeth.

'Oh my God,' Pete says, as he peers inside Aran's mouth. 'I think he's cut his tongue in half.'

A jolt of pain rips through my body. It is a sharp, cutting sense, a type that I've never, ever felt before. It is like I'm enduring Aran's actual pain in my very own flesh. This injury might as well have been inflicted on me, the feeling is so strong.

Pete and I rush Aran to the local hospital. As soon as Pete drops us off at the front entrance, I run up to the reception desk clutching Aran as if it is my own life that's at stake.

'It's my son,' I say. 'I think he's cut his tongue.'

She asks me Aran's details, but in my total fluster, I can barely recall any of them. Remembering his full name, date of birth, and doctor's surgery are way beyond what my brain can cope with right now.

'Take a seat and you'll be called by the doctor soon,' the lady behind the desk commands.

I find a spare chair, and place Aran on my lap. He has gone very quiet, and is sitting there motionless. I see other patients looking at Aran and wondering what is wrong. The bloodstains on my own top only raise their curiosity.

I feel so guilty having let this injury happen to my son. I decide to give Aran a quick breastfeed to calm him down, as well to soothe my own nerves. But the sucking motion he makes with his tongue only opens up the wound again. Blood starts to stream out of his mouth and straight on to my bare skin. I jump up screaming. Aran is still in such shock that he fails to make a sound. Pete soon arrives to distract me from this horror story that is unfurling.

Because Aran is so young, we don't have to wait long

before a doctor is free to see us. We are brought into a cubicle, and wait for him to come.

'And how did the injury happen?' the doctor asks me straight off when he arrives.

'I guess he must have fallen,' I say. 'But I'm not really sure. I wasn't there.'

It sounds so negligent. I had taken Aran off Mum's hands only minutes beforehand. He was my responsibility, and I failed horribly in my duty of care.

Though his mouth is obviously the issue, the doctor sets about examining Aran's entire body. I fully understand there might be other injuries sustained that we know nothing of. But the fact that he is looking for other marks and bruises makes me wonder if we are coming under scrutiny. Does the doctor think we did this on purpose? Is he wondering if there were other incidents that we intentionally failed to report? I hug Aran a little closer to show the doctor we really do love our child.

Eventually, he gives up his extensive search of Aran's body when he finds nothing to report. He looks inside Aran's mouth and investigates the blood's source.

'Looks like he cut his tongue,' he says, confirming Pete's suspicion. Pete takes a look too and provides more graphic detail.

'His tongue has been sliced in half on one side,' Pete reports back.

'He probably fell and hit his chin, and then bit through his tongue in the process,' the doctor tells us, taking an educated guess. 'There's no point in stitching it. Just leave it alone and it will heal itself.' And with this succinct advice, he bids us good day and farewell.

'But...But ...' Pete says, trying to stop the doctor from

192

abandoning us in this sterile space. 'Are you sure there's nothing you can do?'

'Mouth injuries can bleed a lot,' the doctor says, turning to reassure us. 'But they also heal very quickly as well. If we try stitching the wound, Aran will probably struggle so much that it wouldn't be worth it. Best we leave it alone. Believe me, it will mend itself.'

I breathe a hesitant sigh of relief. Poor Aran will be okay in the end. And though I'm reluctant to believe that the tongue will pull itself together under its own steam, it does exactly that over the coming days.

Aran's accident and subsequent tongue wound unfortunately does nothing to deter him from continuing to tear around the house. I would normally be fine to let Aran be as noisy and destructive as he pleases. The problem is that Pete is now attempting to work from home, having managed to negotiate a contract whereby he can do some of his job from our place, with trips to Dublin when required. Working from home, however, requires a certain level of peace and quiet. Aran's manic energy, heightened curiosity, and increased mobility unfortunately causes maximum disturbance instead.

I thought it would be nice to have Pete work from home, so that we could see him a bit more often. I was also glad that we could move back to Derry and be in familiar surroundings again. But the current daytime arrangement, of Pete and one-year-old Aran residing in the same location, causes unprecedented levels of stress. I am just desperately hoping that this is a phase with Aran, something that he'll grow out of ASAP.

Pete's presence at home provides me, however, with an unexpected opportunity: I have a two-hour bike ride to do one day and my regular childcare options have fallen

193

through. I knock at his office door and poke my head around.

'Are you busy?' I say.

Pete is sitting down and thumbing his mobile phone, scrolling through a long list of unanswered emails.

'Sorta,' he says without looking up. 'Why? What's up?'

'I was just wondering if you could look after Aran for an hour or two today?' I say, hope in my voice. 'It's just that Mum isn't free to mind him.'

'Are you serious?' he says, giving me his full attention. 'Can't you just skip the session?'

'I could, I suppose,' I say, disappointment in my tone. 'But I'd prefer not to.'

'Well, I'm not free,' Pete says adamantly. 'Can't you see I've got work to do?'

He returns to his mobile phone, and goes to put in his headset.

'But surely you'll have some time this evening?' I say, refusing to take his hint and go.

'Can't you just be at least a little flexible?' Pete says.

I thought I *was* being flexible by suggesting I train this evening rather than this morning as usual.

'Please, Pete,' I beg, getting a little desperate. There's nothing I hate more than failing to do something I've committed to.

Pete pushes his chair back from the table, and turns to face me head-on. 'My God, Moire, why are you so feckin' *disciplined*?'

'I thought you liked that about me!' When we first met, he said it was one of my most attractive qualities.

'It is a positive thing from afar,' Pete says. 'But God, is it painful to live with!'

I turn to leave. It upsets me when my spouse hates

194

something that is so part of my personality. I don't want him to see me cry.

'Stop,' Pete shouts, getting up to prevent my exit. 'You just have to understand, Moire, you're just not like most people. Most people would just skip the session and not think twice about it.'

I think he's probably right: most mums would prioritise family harmony over their own personal commitments. 'But you know full well that this is my way of coping with the daily grind of motherhood,' I say, throwing my back against the wall.

Pete stares at me for a second. I hold my breath, unable to guess what he'll say next.

'Look, it's okay. I'll mind Aran this evening if you want,' Pete says, his expression more relaxed now. 'But please, just try and be a bit more flexible in the future.'

I leave Pete's office chastened. Though I know that my training can't take precedence over everything, and sometimes I will have to indeed forgo sessions, I resolve to plan my training and childcare so it clashes less with family members.

There is one last race I want to do this year as part of the National Adventure Race Series. The Killarney Adventure Race is one of the oldest and most prestigious on the racing scene. The town of Killarney itself is Ireland's outdoor capital. It plays host to the two-hundred-kilometre Kerry Way walking trail, the Ring of Kerry cycling and driving route, as well as providing access to Ireland's tallest mountains, the McGillyCuddy's Reeks. If you're seeking adventure within Ireland, this is the place to head.

Aran is fourteen months old by the time the race comes around. The good news though is, after two months of painful persistence, I have finally forced Aran to kick his breastfeeding habit. With Aran now off the boobs, he doesn't have to accompany me to the race. But Pete has started to enjoy these family weekends away, with a chance to see some adventure-racing action as well. He enjoyed watching Emma and I fight it out in Dingle and at Gaelforce West. Now he wants to come along to Killarney to see what battles lie in wait for me.

The event takes place in October, when Ireland's warm summer months are well and truly gone. October in Killarney can be cold and wet, with winter fast approaching. The race itself starts bright and early on Saturday morning at 7.30 am. Pete, Aran and I travel down to Killarney the day before so that I can register and drop my bike.

I head late afternoon to the bike drop at Kate Kearney's Cottage, at the mouth of the Gap of Dunloe. The race starts from Kate's house with a nine-kilometre run up and down Strickeen Mountain. The route then returns us right back to the cottage, where we collect our bikes from Kate's back yard for a thirty-five-kilometre cycle to Muckross Lake.

I take Bike carefully out of my car boot, and wheel him over to the stands. Bike's wheels begin to turn for the first time after being stuck in the car for seven hours. But instead of them spinning in silence, all I hear is a horrible, grating noise. This isn't good. Bikes can easily get knocked about in the back of cars, especially when they have to share their space with luggage. Pete and I often fight if one of his suitcases accidentally touches Bike during long-distance car journeys.

I bend down and turn the pedals manually to see what the problem is. I soon realise that it's my back wheel that is making a rather unhealthy crunching sound. I poke

196

and prod at various metal bits before concluding there is nothing much I can do. It could be just a bit of mud stuck somewhere unobtrusive. Or it could be something far more serious. With no bike mechanics around, I reluctantly leave Bike at the start and hope he'll be better by the morning.

My rear wheel dilemma is made all the more stressful knowing whom I am about to compete against. Fiona Meade, who did only the bike section in Dingle, has since been crowned Irish National Road Racing Champion. Though Killarney's course is well known to favour mountain runners due to its ascents of both Strikeen and Mangerton, I can't lose too much time on the route's two intervening bike legs. A banjaxed bike wheel would be enough to hand Fiona the win.

Buses ferry us from Killarney to the starting line early on Saturday morning. As luck would have it, I see Peter Cromie, who sold me Bike, also on the bus.

'Oi, Cromie,' I shout out to him as we disembark. 'Any chance you can take a quick look at my bike? I think it has an issue.' I sound a little desperate, but it's definitely worth a shot.

'No problem,' he says. 'Which one is it?' I know I am distracting him from his own race warm-up, but Cromie is the sort who's always happy to lend a hand regardless.

I jog up to Bike and present my rear wheel to Cromie. He takes one look at it and pronounces it race worthy. 'The tyre was just put on a little off-centre, so it's rubbing a bit. But it should be fine to get you round the course.'

I don't tell Cromie that I'm the one who put the tyre on the rim. If there are any issues during the race, there's no one to blame but me.

With that worry sorted, I move on to my next concern:

today's female competition. I look around the starting line but can't see Emma anywhere. Though she beat me in Dingle, it seems like she has opted out of Killarney. It means that Fiona is the one I must focus on.

Fiona means business from the start. As soon as the gun goes, she sprints off up the pot-holed road towards Strickeen Mountain. I push hard to overtake her, as I want to get to the narrow mountain path section first, where passing options become severely limited. Up the rocky zigzags, I keep a handy pace, bouncing up and over the bog and stones to get into a nice rhythm. I reach the summit first, but as soon as I turn, I see Fiona coming right towards me. I hightail it out of there and throw myself back down the mountain, hoping the rough rock-strewn path will slow Fiona down slightly.

I grab Bike as soon as I reach Kate's Cottage, and whisper a silent prayer that his rear wheel will behave. Little do I know that this mechanical issue will be the least of my concerns. It rained heavily last night, making the tarmac slippery smooth. This, combined with the course's steep descents, hairpin bends, and a low glaring autumnal morning sun, makes cycling totally treacherous. The marshals at the safety briefing warned us to be careful. I get a stark reminder as I crest the steep Gap of Dunloe and see an ambulance all ready and waiting.

I keep my fingers on my brakes as I descend into Black Valley. All the time, I am listening hard to hear any rear-wheel grating sounds. Bike, however, puts my worries to bed, and glides effortlessly along the rural roads in total silence. I pedal hard towards Moll's Gap, before hitting the main road to Killarney. All the time I am waiting for Fiona to come flying past me. At Ladies View, I round the corner to see a lad sprawled across the tarmac floor, his bike in bits beside him. I hear later he missed the bend, then fell off and broke his collarbone. The marshals were right to warn us about slowing down.

I reach the bike transition at Muckross Lake with still no sign of Fiona. I know she is a strong paddler, so I still can't hang around. I run the short distance to the lake and jump into a boat. I see Pete and Aran on the shore, madly clapping me on.

As soon as I start to paddle, my legs decide to cramp. I must have pushed really hard on the bike for them to rebel this early on in the race. I adjust the way I'm sitting, and use my legs a little less on each paddle stroke. Luckily the water section takes most of us only fifteen minutes to complete.

I crawl out of the kayak and back on to dry land. I glance back out over the waters and see two women paddling straight towards me. 'Fiona was three and a half minutes behind you on to the water,' Pete shouts. 'You can do it!' he adds. I flash him an already tired smile.

The race started two hours ago. I know, however, that the real race begins only now. The eighteen-kilometre run up and down Mangerton Mountain is where winners and losers are made. With this in mind, I run towards the mountain, happy to be done with the bike and boat sections for now.

The initial section through a forest is farther than I expect, and I end up running alone for long stretches. Occasionally, I forget I'm racing as I jog through these pretty woods, daydreaming as if I'm on a training jaunt. I am rudely awakened, however, when I emerge from the trees and see Mangerton Mountain rising impressively from the ground before me.

The ascent is boggy and rocky, and too rough to run

in parts. But I know this is where I have to make up time if I am to break clear of the opposition. After an hour on my feet, I realise I am near the top when I see the leading men sprinting down the hill towards me. I dodge out of their way just in time, leaving them free to continue their masculine battle.

At the turnaround, I check my watch to see if I've gained any precious minutes. By the time I cross paths with Fiona coming up the mountain, I guess I am around ten minutes ahead. However, anything can happen descending the mountain given the jagged terrain, so I carefully pick my way back down.

I reach Bike just as my watch tells me I've been going for four hours. I jump on my trusty steed and carefully negotiate the six-kilometre ride to the finish. Despite all my doubts, Bike has performed superbly. He brings me home safely without the slightest mechanical hitch. I cross the line, the first lady finisher. But more than this, with this victory and my three other race scores, I have clinched the 2014 National Adventure Race Series title.

Peter Cromie is at the finish line to congratulate me.

'I should never have doubted that Bike could make it round the course,' I say, a little embarrassed about how stressed I was before.

'No worries,' Cromie says. He has had a good day too, and is the first over-forty male home.

'So how's your little man?' Cromie asks, enquiring after Aran.

'Good,' I say. 'He was out spectating on the course with Pete today. And how's your wee one doing?'

'Ah, sure grand as always,' Cromie says, before thinking for a split second. 'Remember how I told ye that one child was plenty?'

I remember indeed how, at the Inishowen adventure race while I was pregnant with Aran, Cromie told me how a single child is enough. He seemed pretty adamant about that at the time.

'Yes,' I say, 'it has made me think whether we'll stop with just Aran.' Considering how hard I've found it raising just one child, the thought has definitely crossed my mind.

'Well, my wife convinced me to try for another one,' Cromie says. 'And now we're expecting twins.'

I cover my mouth just in time to stop myself guffawing. But my laughs aren't at Cromie's predicament, but from my own sudden onset of nerves. I am totally petrified I could also end up in his same shoes.

My husband Pete appears from out of nowhere, holding Aran aloft. 'Did you win? Did you win?' he says, knowing full well I probably have.

I smile a shy grin, and nod my head sheepishly. 'And how was your morning with Aran?' I ask, curious how Pete managed to entertain our son for a full four hours' duration.

'Good,' Pete says. 'Only that, when I tried to change Aran's nappy in the front seat of the car, he peed right in my face.'

Just like that, I am brought crashing down from the highs of racing and winning, landing with a loud thud right back into the murky realities of motherhood.

17

Again

It is November 2014 and the adventure-racing season is over for the year. This means I have a few luxurious weeks without scheduled training when I can do whatever I please. However, I quickly tire of all this free time I now have on my hands. My attention turns instead towards our garden, which has been severely neglected since Aran's arrival. While Pete is away for work, I order ten tonnes of gravel, and with the help of my elderly mother, we spread it all over the driveway. I then procure a hundred sacks of washed-up seaweed and spread it on the flower beds as fertiliser. It's heavy, dirty work that leaves me totally wrecked. I think I might be the type of person who needs constant exercise.

With Aran finally weaned off breast milk, after fifteen months of no monthly cycles, my periods return. This unfortunately wipes out my primary excuse for not trying for a second child.

Even though I dread getting pregnant again, I know now would be perfect timing. I conceived Aran two years ago around this time of year. He was born towards the end of the summer, allowing me to skip a full year of races, then slot seamlessly back into a winter training regime. Getting pregnant now would mean missing the entire 2015 season, but I would be raring to go by spring 2016.

Eamonn and I have already signed off on our training agreement for the year. We had originally planned that he would get me fit again after childbirth, and coach me for the 2014 National Adventure Race Series. Having successfully completed our arrangement, Eamonn has told me to get back in contact if I want him to coach me again next season. Thankfully there's no pressure from his side, which is good, as I've not made up my mind myself. I am stuck in this painful conundrum of not knowing the future, namely if I'll be pregnant or not next year.

Even though I've managed to get pregnant before, there's no certainty I will be able to a second time. I am approaching the decrepit age of forty, with my fertility decreasing all the time. It's now or never, so Pete and I decide to try again.

One month on, and December arrives. I soon realise I need to continue on with life as if I won't conceive. If not, I'll be hanging around every month on tenterhooks, doing nothing except waiting for a positive pregnancy test. That's not how I want to spend my time. So I get back in touch with Eamonn, and I suggest training again together with an eye to competing next year. Eamonn is happy to oblige, and immediately suggests I compete in a winter five-kilometre road race.

I hate short distances, and I despise races involving tarmac. Basically, my interest level plummets to zero when faced with anything less than three hours in duration and that doesn't involve mountain terrain. But my protests to Eamonn are met with deaf ears.

'It will be a good to find out what kind of time you can do over that sort of distance,' he tells me.

I remain unconvinced. But there is often method to Eamonn's madness, and he has proven me wrong before. So I put my trust in his suggestion, and go to the local Parkrun on a cold Saturday morning. Parkruns are free five-kilometre timed events held every Saturday throughout the country the whole year round. Derry's Parkrun is a scenic out and back course along the sweeping banks of the River Foyle. The route climbs up and over the Peace Bridge, put in place after the Good Friday agreement. The bridge joins the two once-divided sides of the city, the largely unionist Waterside with the predominantly nationalist Cityside. The route then delves in and out of the thickly wooded Saint Columb's Park, named after Derry's very own patron saint.

The course is not fast, thanks to its many twists and turns. But it is all that's available to me now that the road-racing season has gone largely dormant with the festive season approaching.

I turn up good and early on Saturday morning. The weather was bitterly cold last night, so I want to do a good warm-up. However, even if I warm myself up really well, it will not be enough to melt the thick sheets of ice that have since frozen to the ground.

I find a Parkrun official to see what the story is.

'The Parkrun is off,' he tells me. 'Far too slippery out there.'

I feel slightly disappointed but, at the same time, hugely relieved. I need a really good excuse to give Eamonn if I'm going to bail from this race.

'If you want to run it and time yourself, you're more than welcome,' the official says.

I jog up to the starting line to consider his offer, and in the process, nearly fall flat on my face when I hit a patch of black ice. There is no point risking a broken ankle for the sake of a local time trial.

I go back home, glad to have dodged a bullet. However, even after this lucky turn of events, I've a terrible feeling something else is up.

I've only had one period since Aran was born. If my calculations are right, my next one should be due very soon. But if that's correct, I should be experiencing full-blown premenstrual syndrome right now, and my stomach should be really sore. But I feel fine, far too fine in fact.

I rush to the local chemist to buy an early detection pregnancy test. I'm just not in the mood to sit around and wait for my next period to not arrive. As luck would have it, Pete is currently in Cambodia working. He was also in Cambodia when I found out I was pregnant with Aran. So yet again, I have to take the test alone, with no one nearby to calm my unsettled nerves.

My hand shakes when I open the kit and read the test result. The positive line is faint, much fainter than before, but it is most definitely there. With Aran, it took us several months of trying before I finally got pregnant. Now, at our first window of opportunity, we've hit the mark bang on. I suppose practice does make perfect, but this is totally ridiculous.

The bottle of red wine is all ready and waiting for me on the kitchen counter. As tradition dictates, I pour myself a large glass and make a call to Cambodia. Pete whoops and hollers down the line as I tell him I'm pregnant once again. My only hope is that this is the last time I have to drunk-dial him with such news when he's halfway around the globe.

My next issue is how to deal with Eamonn. I've recently committed to training with him for next year's racing season. Fortunately, our weekly call first focuses on the Parkrun cancellation.

'It was really icy and slippery out there, so wasn't wise to run,' I tell Eamonn.

'Look, you did the right thing,' he says, confirming my suspicion. 'But how are you feeling otherwise?'

I hesitate for a split second. To be honest, I'm feeling totally grand, all things considered.

'It's just I see that your resting heart rate jumped five beats over the weekend,' Eamonn says. This would be perfectly normal if I had actually done the race. My body would have been tired from all that extra exertion. But I've not done anything difficult training-wise in the last couple of days. 'Are you getting sick?' he asks.

There's no hiding anything from this man. I can't help but blurt out, 'No, I'm pregnant.'

'Congratulations, young lady!' Eamonn says straightaway.

I'm a little taken back. I thought he would be disappointed that I've just written off next season.

'Please don't tell anyone,' I say immediately. 'Pete knows, but I've not told my parents yet.'

'Your secret is safe with me.'

I don't even know why I'm begging for his silence. Eamonn is the most discreet person I have ever met. To this day, I still don't know who else he trains or even how many athletes he works with. He never mentions a single name or even tells me random anecdotes that might permit me to deduce their identities. I suppose when he knows so many personal details about so many sporting individuals, it is best he keeps all that information closely to his chest.

But even though Eamonn knows my situation, there's a more pertinent issue that needs resolved.

'Would you be able to guide me through this pregnancy?' I ask Eamonn, fearing that his answer will be no. I have really appreciated Eamonn's support since Aran's birth and throughout my return to racing form. However, my experience with fitness professionals while pregnant first time around was that they didn't want to touch me with a barge pole.

Eamonn doesn't even hesitate with his answer. 'Of course, I will. No problem.'

I breathe a huge sigh of relief. At least this time round I will be told exactly what to do and specifically what to avoid. In addition, I don't want to lose all the fitness I've just recently gained. I also hope to hit the ground running once this baby is born.

With competitive racing off for the next nine months, Eamonn gets me to do other exercises that are typically sidelined when preparing for events. He instructs me to get someone to take a video of me running on a treadmill, from the front, side, and rear. I do as I'm told, and send him the results. I doubt that he will find much wrong though with my current running form.

'You're heel striking,' Eamonn says as soon as he watches the film. 'You should be landing more on your mid-foot.'

I am taken aback. I thought I had corrected that issue years ago when I was trying to improve my running efficiency and decrease the amount of injuries I sustained.

'You need to lift your knee more when you are running,' Eamonn explains. 'Think about where your heel is during your knee lift, and try to shorten the gap between your heel and your glutes.'

Changing your running style is easier said than done. Thankfully, Eamonn is well aware of this challenge. He tells me that, when I do skipping as part of strength and conditioning exercises, I should try to have high knee lifts to mimic this new action.

The next time I take up the skipping rope, I attempt to do as Eamonn suggests. I throw the rope in front of my body, and jump with my knee in the air. The rope gets caught in my raised foot, and my skipping motion abruptly stops. I try again, but my exaggerated bum kick means the rope gets stuck elsewhere. How is this change in skipping style meant to help me run more efficiently, when I can't even complete one jump?

Eventually I get the hang of this exaggerated leg motion while skipping on the spot. The question is whether I can do this while trying to run forward simultaneously. I take to the tarmac and start to jog along. I lift my knee, pull my heel towards my glutes, and concentrate on landing mid-foot. I feel like I am prancing around like a palomino pony. Is Eamonn trying to make me into a dressage horse while I'm pregnant?

When I look down at my watch, I realise I am going ludicrously slow. Though I complain about this reduction in pace, Eamonn tells me to persevere. It's a good job that I'm pregnant right now and not preparing for any events. If I had to compete with this new running style, I would definitely come last. I will just have to wait and see whether, once I've delivered, this new prance will make me any faster.

Meanwhile, Pete is on his continued crusade to never spend Christmas at home. Last year, he carted us halfway across the world to Cambodia. This time I put my foot down and insist on a European destination. I just don't have the energy to bring eighteen-month-old Aran all the way to South East Asia. And, what with being pregnant,

I'd prefer to avoid the scenario of having to take anti-malarials again like I did in Ethiopia. I'm not interested in constantly worrying about damaging this new baby.

We search around for destinations that are relatively warm in December. We happen upon a small town in southern Spain called Salobreña, where the temperatures are in the teens. Pete finds a cute little traditional villa high up on the hillside overlooking the Mediterranean Sea. He books us in for three weeks over Christmas and New Year's.

We fly into Malaga two days before Christmas. And after a short ninety-minute drive, we reach our final destination. In my child-free days, I would have loved the villa. But with a toddler now in tow, it is a total nightmare to stay in.

Within seconds of entering the house, I find Aran dismantling the kitchen cupboards. They are simple shelves without doors and are filled with breakable earthenware jugs and bowls.

I start the arduous task of childproofing the place. Everything has to be removed and placed on shelves that are least one metre above the ground. Aran is not happy with this new arrangement and immediately starts to bawl.

Next, I discover a set of steep stairs without any stair gate in place. Aran loves going up and down stairs at the moment, but I only allow such exploration when I am there to supervise. I move a large armchair in front of the steps to slow Aran's approach. I can't block them off totally, or Pete and I won't be able to go downstairs to the bathroom or bedrooms on the ground level.

Unfortunately, there's nothing I can do about the rock-hard quarry tiles that cover the villa's entire floor. I resign myself to the fact that Aran will leave the villa with multiple bruises and scrapes from silly falls.

The CDs and books that our host has provided for our entertainment are relocated to lockable cupboards. And I instruct Pete that there's no lighting the fire at night, as Aran will undoubtedly burn himself on the hot cast-iron frame.

Pete is not happy at all with this new décor. He finds the place cluttered and constricted by my assorted barricades. But I know what Aran is like, seeing that I am with him every day. With Pete spending so much time away from home, he hasn't yet witnessed Aran's latest phase of compulsive demolition.

It is not long, however, before Aran puts on a show for Pete. He has seen the stairs, and wants to go down them, but the armchair is blocking his path. Aran tries to push it to one side, but I pull him quickly away.

Aran is not pleased with my intervention. He arches his back and throws himself backwards, screeching at the top of his voice. Aran's skull speeds towards the tiles with incredible velocity.

'Oh God, mind his head,' Pete shouts, hoping I'll intercept this touchdown.

Fortunately, I know this signature move of Aran's well, and catch him just before he makes full contact. I lie him down on the ground, and watch over him closely as he wriggles and writhes in frustration.

'What's wrong with him?' Pete says.

'Oh, don't worry,' I say. 'He's having a tantrum. He'll be fine in a few minutes.'

I had tried to tell Pete that Aran is becoming a 'terrible two', but Pete didn't believe me, as Aran is only a year and a half old. Even when I described his violent actions and vocal outbursts, Pete remained the ultimate doubting Thomas. However, Aran seems determined to put on an up-close exhibition for his daddy right now.

Pete is so perturbed by Aran's behaviour that he tries to pick him up and physically restrain his son.

'Leave him, Pete,' I say. 'Seriously. He'll calm down in a bit.'

I am so busy explaining to Pete the importance of not reacting that I fail to see Aran getting back on to his two feet. Aran launches himself toward the nearest wall and headbutts it at speed.

Even I am shocked by the dull-thud sound Aran's head makes when coming into contact with concrete. Aran seems also a little surprised at the painful outcome of his latest attention-seeking outburst.

Both Pete and Aran start wailing.

'Oh good God, is he all right?' Pete says, lifting up Aran's fringe and checking his forehead. 'Do we need to get him to hospital?'

We're not even in the country twenty-four hours, and already Aran might need medical attention. But when I look closer, there's barely a mark. Aran has harmed himself just enough to get our full, undivided attention.

'Headbutting is a new one for me, I must admit,' I say, taking Aran into my arms while walking away from the stairs' edge. I've learned that distraction is the best technique to deal with his tantrums. I need to find something else for Aran to destroy, instead of allowing him to total himself on the villa's stone stairs.

Pete soon finds the ideal diversion for his temper-tantrum-prone son. He discovers a playground in the centre of town, and takes Aran there every day. Aran runs around the swings, slides, and roundabouts for several hours, expending energy safely outside, instead of wrecking the interior of our rented villa.

While Pete and Aran get to spend quality time together, I get to ride Bike. Bike, as an integral part of our family, has also come along on our winter holiday. Eamonn has also customized my training regime to take into account my pregnant state. Seven weeks in, and he has scheduled a two-hour bike without efforts. This would normally be considered an easy ride.

I find a wide road that leads out of Salobreña and follows the Mediterranean coast west. I cycle through the sunny tourist towns of Almuñécar and La Herradura, and then turn around after one hour. Though I don't feel the effects of my pregnancy, my speed data shows otherwise. I ride painfully slow and my heart rate is proving hard to control. The next day I go for a gentle one-hour run. And though I should be well able for such a session, I feel like death warmed up as I shuffle along the road. I barely make it home, having to walk up the final hill. I collapse in a heap on our villa's doorstep and burst into tears. I am only seven weeks into this pregnancy and already I feel totally shit. How am I going to cope with the thirty-three weeks of baby-making that are still ahead of me?

I soon realise that the pregnancy is not solely responsible for my sorry state. The day after my disastrous run, I start to feel unwell. I go to the bathroom and hack up tonnes of phlegm, green crusty stuff that clogs up the plughole.

No one else in the household is sick. Only I have succumbed to this illness. I had read that pregnancy can make your immune system shift down to a lower gear. The advantage of this suppression is that my body doesn't fight off the baby, who is technically a foreign invader. But the downside is that my body struggles to fight off

212

common colds that it would normally shift in seconds.

Already feeling sorry for myself with a stuffy nose and sore throat while on holiday, all of a sudden, morning sickness arrives with a vengeance. It is New Year's Day and I should be celebrating with plentiful paella at a beachside restaurant on Salobreña's spectacular coastline. Instead I am staring at the bowl of coloured rice and crustaceans that Pete has ordered, feeling like I want to puke all over it.

When I was pregnant with Aran, I thought Ethiopian food was responsible for making me feel so sick. Now I realise the *injera* and spicy meat on offer had nothing to do with it. It was the foetus growing inside of me that had made my stomach lurch. And if I thought that the second time round I'd be more prepared for this feeling, the sickness is actually twice as bad as it was first time around with Aran.

I spend the next two weeks unable to train due to my unshakable cold. Bike sits there in his bike box, trying to comprehend why he has come all this way to Spain for just one single solitary ride. And while Pete enjoys chorizo, soft cheese, Rioja wine, stiff espressos, and everything wonderful that Spanish cuisine has to offer, I can barely stomach a few oranges and the occasional sip of Coca-Cola.

God, I so hate being pregnant.

18

Exhaustion

I arrive back home in mid-January, into the depths of a dark and cold Irish winter. I hated every moment of our break in Spain, what with my body letting me so badly down. But at least there were blue skies and warm weather in Salobreña, something I bitterly miss now.

Ten days after our return, I go to see the local surgery for my twelve-week antenatal check-up.

'So you're back for a second one?' the midwife says with a smile.

'Yeah,' I say, before immediately adding, 'but this is so definitely my last.' I am just coming out of a hellacious first trimester. I really hate feeling so unwell. I still can't believe some women go through this voluntarily.

'I see last time you had a water birth,' she says, reading my hospital notes.

'Yes,' I say. 'It was great. Apart from the childbirth part.'

'Well, seeing that it's your second child, and you're a low-risk mother, do you want to give birth at home?'

I think about it for a moment. A good friend of mine once opted for a home birth. She told me the midwife bagged up her placenta after she delivered, but

214

subsequently forgot to dispose of it. My friend's father then accidentally stepped on it when he came to visit her and his new grandchild.

Though my friend and I laughed about it afterwards, I'd prefer not to go through anything remotely similar. 'No, thanks,' I say. 'I'll just go for the water birth again.'

I've come to the conclusion that, if something worked first time round, there's no point in deviating from the original plan.

'Well, if you're twelve weeks along now, that gives you a due date of the twentieth of August.'

Oh God, that sounds so far away. Fingers crossed the baby will arrive on or before then.

The midwife takes my blood to do the usual checks. She then gives me my antenatal file that I must carry to all appointments between now and the birth.

Carrying that bright green file is a dead giveaway that I'm expecting a baby. Even though I've no bump or anything, it identifies me as a marked woman. So when I meet Bridgeen, my community health worker, on my departure from the surgery, she immediately knows that congratulations are in order.

'That's great that Aran's going to have a wee brother or sister,' Bridgeen says.

'That's the only reason I'm doing this,' I reply.

Bridgeen nods. She understands. She's heard this rationale before.

I wonder then and there if I can share with her a different issue that's also been bothering me lately.

'I'm just worried though that they'll be totally different temperaments,' I say, knowing how silly my concern already sounds. 'It's just that, we've been so lucky with Aran, like he's so healthy and quite easy to deal with, in retrospect. I'm just wondering if our luck is going to run out with this second one.'

Bridgeen laughs and tells me not to worry.

'No, seriously, Bridgeen,' I say, trying to justify my fear. 'I've friends who have had a lovely first child, and then produced a devil child the second time round.'

I am sure she has heard concerns like these, and probably worse, from an assortment of mothers-to-be. It seems like every mother has worries; they just differ from one child to the next.

'Everything will be fine,' she says, patting me on the back. 'And I'll see you once this second one arrives.'

Now that I've entered the second trimester, I start to feel semi-normal again. And though the nausea has gone and I've found some of my old energy, Eamonn still gives me pretty conservative sessions to do. He gets me back in the pool and starts me swimming again, for an hour each time I go. He makes me do bike sessions with mini thirty-second efforts, and most of these are indoors on rollers. I struggle, however, to raise my heart rate over one hundred and forty beats per minute even when I'm going flat out. My pulse seems to have gone on strike.

Eamonn also gives me plenty of strength and conditioning exercises to do as I prepare to carry the baby's extra weight. I find, however, that everything seems much more of an effort this time around. By mid-March I have to reduce the number of squats and lunges I can attempt in one go. When I do planks, I collapse in a heap gasping for breath after less than a few seconds. Luckily, as soon as I struggle, Eamonn adjusts my training and reduces the next session's load.

Though Eamonn is trying to keep me moving, I am the cautious one now. Gone are my gung-ho days of training and racing regardless of how I look or feel. I do eventually manage to take Bike outside, but am incredibly careful about how I ride. At one stage, a group of six lads catch up with me on a road spin. With a slight push, I could easily have stayed with them and drafted along. But my new prudent self stops pedalling on purpose to let them go past. I want to go at my own pace, not one dictated by somebody else. Not long after, a large plump man on his bike appears on my shoulder. He has just seen me dropped by the group that is now ahead.

'Couldn't stay with the big boys, eh?' he says as he draws alongside me, sweating from the considerable effort he's making to catch up with me.

'Not at all,' I say without thinking or losing breath. 'I'm pregnant, so don't want to risk crashing in that group.'

He stops pedalling for an instant, digesting what he has just heard. 'Oh,' is all he can muster up in the end. And, with no more smart-arse comments at his disposal, he pedals hard to pass me out. The idea of a pregnant lady biking faster than him is obviously too much for him to handle.

Even though I am keeping well within safe limits, I often still find myself totally worn out. I just can't understand it. I am only in my second trimester, when I should be full of energy. Around this time in my first pregnancy, I was hiking up and down mountains in the Lake District and competing in adventure races. Now, if I go for a thirty-minute easy run, I need to go to bed for the remainder of the afternoon. However, having such rest is easier said than done.

Ever since Aran was weaned off breast milk, I have struggled to get him to sleep during the day. Before, all he needed was a quick breastfeed, and he was off to la-la land in broad daylight. But now, the only way I can make him doze off is by putting him in the car and driving him round and round for at least half an hour. It costs us a fortune in petrol. The strategy also comes close to causing several accidents, as I frequently check in the rear-view mirror to see if he has conked out. But I am so desperate to make him sleep, so that I can lie down too, that I will drive anywhere and everywhere to make sure it happens.

Pete has no sympathy though for how tired I am.

'You should be fine,' he says. 'Sure isn't Aran sleeping through the night these days?'

It has taken a full eighteen months for Aran to finally stop waking up in the middle of the night. I get a solid nine hours rest nowadays, but even this seems insufficient. I get up most mornings, and within an hour, desperately want to go back to bed.

The problem is, not only am I dealing with the exertions of pregnancy, but I'm also running after a hyperactive toddler. And Aran is getting up to all sorts of mischief these days. He has learnt how to open doors, which is an unfortunate development. Even if Pete shuts his office door to try to do some work, Aran has learnt how to slip through this line of defence, disturbing Pete right in the middle of important business calls. Pete doesn't take this interruption kindly, and reads me the riot act. He knows if he gives off to Aran, it will have zero effect. It may even encourage Aran to disturb him more often so he can see Daddy's hilariously funny reaction when he loses the plot.

As soon as we find keys to lock our interior household doors, Aran discovers the wonderful world of cars. He somehow works out how to open Granny's car door and, once inside, experiments with all the control buttons. He switches on the blinking hazard lights, turns on the windscreen wipers, and puts the headlights on full blast. It is only the next morning, when my mum tries to start her car, that she realises Aran has run down its battery.

Aran doesn't realise yet that doing such things can make him very unpopular. It is only when Mum buys Aran his own toy car dashboard that flashes and bleeps and distracts Aran endlessly that Granny can finally forgive her grandson.

Aran never fails to amaze me with the mischief he can get up to. I only find out he has stolen my mobile when I'm browsing the phone's photos section and find hundreds of random selfies. Most of them are of the ground or of Aran's knee. He then works out how to reverse the camera and take photos of the kitchen ceiling. It's only when he takes a burst of fifty or more photos, and uses up all the memory, that I ban him from touching my cell phone.

Stopping Aran from doing what he wants to do, however, has its consequences. He hurts my ears with his screams; he bruises my body with his tantrum kicks and punches. And even though these outbursts are troubling, I find Aran's silence even worse. If I can't see Aran or hear what he's up to, I have to search him out. If Aran is quiet, it means he is getting into some sort of trouble, like unravelling toilet rolls or scribbling on walls or sticking his fingers into plug sockets. If Aran is banging something or crying uncontrollably, at least I know he is still alive and can easily track him down by following his sound waves.

While I am busy running after Aran, Pete decides he wants to get in shape again. Before we met, Pete would keep fit by doing the occasional marathon. However, since we got together nearly eight years ago, Pete hasn't completed such an event. I've teased him mercilessly that he only ran those long-distance races to keep him slim and attractive to single ladies, and now that he's married and settled, he has let it all slide.

'So, what kind of session do you think I should do today?' Pete asks, as he prepares himself for his first training jaunt. He announced only yesterday that he is entering the Belfast City Marathon in three months' time.

I look up at him from the kitchen table, where I'm seated with Aran on my knee.

'I've no idea,' I reply. 'I thought you've trained for marathons before.'

'Yes, but you've had a coach for the last two years,' Pete says. 'Surely you've learned a thing or two from Eamonn.'

Pete is adding insult to injury. Not only is it unfair that he gets to go out and train while I bumble around the house pregnant, but now he expects me to be his personal in-house trainer.

'Eamonn trains me for adventure races,' I say. 'Not marathons.'

'But you must have some sort of idea of what I should do today,' Pete says, lacing up his Brooks.

In fact, I have no idea what Pete should do. That's because I don't fully understand the ins and outs of the training I do myself. Eamonn does the thinking for me, and I do as he says. Even when Eamonn does explain the purpose of each session, I find my brain is unable to comprehend this physiological gobbledygook.

But Pete is looking for an answer. I need to suggest something or risk an impromptu argument.

'Well, I suppose you could do some strength and conditioning exercises,' I say. 'That could help improve that calf issue you always complain about.'

Pete looks at me, and then his watch. This wasn't the answer he was looking for.

'Or you could do a seventy-minute run with some efforts, say one minute on, three minutes off by twelve sets,' I suggest, realising he wants to go for a jog.

'But what's an on? And what's an off?' Pete asks.

Oh God, this is getting complicated.

'Look, why don't you get Eamonn to coach you for this marathon?' I propose out of desperation. I need to get Pete off my back. 'He'll tell you what to do, and answer all your questions.'

Miraculously, Pete agrees to my suggestion.

Eamonn in turn gives Pete a training plan from hell. It is full of long runs at high heart rates, combined with really arduous efforts. If I were in Pete's shoes, I would devise intricate excuses for skipping half the sessions.

But despite the plan's difficulty, Pete actually completes all the sessions as stipulated. I am amazed to see Pete train so diligently for his marathon, when any training I've seen him do thus far has been haphazard to say the least.

'You're looking well,' I say to Pete one day before he heads out the door for his run. He is already a month into his plan. He has actually lost considerable weight over the last couple of weeks, and looks far more toned than before.

'I think those efforts really make a difference,' Pete says, proud of his new slim-line self. Any time I've told Pete to do efforts rather than long slow runs, he has ignored my suggestion outright. But now that Eamonn is the one instructing him, Pete is totally compliant.

'Just knowing that Eamonn is going to check my data and give feedback means I feel I have to do as he says,' Pete remarks. It is interesting to see someone else training under Eamonn, and the motivational effects that it has. It also makes me realise how lenient Eamonn has been with the training he gives me while I've been pregnant or breastfeeding.

A month before Belfast Marathon, Pete enters a local ten-mile race. It starts in the coastal town of Ballyliffin in County Donegal, on the Wild Atlantic Way. It is a stunning course, circumventing the peninsula just south of Malin Head, Ireland's most northerly point. Because it is so close to home, Aran and I decide to go along and spectate. Instead of waiting at the finish line on windswept Pollan Beach, I bring along my mountain bike and decide to ride the course to see the race pan out.

I hoist Aran up into his carrier, and strap him to my back. I am twenty weeks gone, still small enough to secure the waist strap safely under my emerging bump. When the gun goes, off Aran and I cycle, weaving through the crowds. Two miles in, and the runners have strung out sufficiently to allow us to bike alongside Pete. Though he is jogging along well, I decide to accelerate up the next incline, and wait for him at the top.

When we reach the crest of the hill, I take Aran off my back and place him on the ground so he can watch out for his dad. All of a sudden, Aran starts to clap every runner that comes past.

'No, that's not Daddy,' I tell him, hinting he can hold off on the applause for a bit. But Aran is getting so many smiles and cheers from the runners he's clapping, that he's encouraged to keep it up. When Pete does finally pass us by, Aran is ecstatic. He giggles and stamps his feet with all his might, making Pete wave and beam back proudly at the sight of his cheerleading son.

Once Pete has passed, I lift Aran back on to my back,

and pedal off towards the finish. All this clapping has, however, proven a little tiring for Aran. He soon falls fast asleep as I ride my mountain bike. I have to concentrate hard to balance bump on my front and Aran on my back without falling off myself.

A mere week later, Pete and I set off to hospital for the mid-pregnancy scan. Though we're both easy about the gender of this baby, I'm secretly hoping for another boy.

My desire is totally short-sighted. The mere thought of having to go out and look for girls' clothes tires me out, when we already have all the boys' clothes we need from Aran's hand-me-downs.

There's a more pertinent question I need to ask first, however, as soon as the sonographer starts the scan. 'Is there just one in there?' I say, fearing the imminent announcement that we're expecting twins. My mate Peter Cromie got two for the price of one, but I'm happy to forgo that special offer. When I find out that we're expecting one baby, and it's a boy, my Christmases come all at once. As soon as the sonographer has a good look around and sees the baby is in perfect health, then I'm practically skipping out the door, down the corridor doing the hula-hoop. It is only when I hear the midwife calling me to one side that my skipping stops with a jolt.

'Is it okay if we take your blood again for a test?' the midwife enquires.

'Sure,' I say, though I don't remember this happening the last time with Aran. 'What's it for?'

'Well, your file says that there were antibodies present in your last sample,' she explains. 'So the doctor wants them checked again.'

'Antibodies?' I say. 'What does that mean?'

The midwife tells me not to worry, that it's just a

follow-up check. But when I press her for more details, she says to ask my doctor the next time I see her.

I leave the hospital elated with the scan results, but confused by the extra blood test. Pete, at my side, is trying to reassure me. 'If it was serious, I'm sure they'd tell you,' he says, holding my hand, squeezing it tightly.

I wonder if he is concerned too, though doesn't want to say it. I nod in agreement, but I still can't help being distracted by what has just transpired. With the standard of care I've received thus far, I'm sure the doctors and midwives would sort it out if there was anything up with the pregnancy. But still, I can't stop wondering if something serious is wrong.

I continue to count down the weeks to my final due date. It is May and I've still over three months to go before this baby's birthday.

I haul myself on to Bike and start to slowly pedal. It's a Friday, and I have a one-hour bike session to do on my indoor rollers. I derive little enjoyment from Bike these days, as my bump is starting to get in my way, just like it did with Aran. But now that I have a power metre installed, I can see the exact effects of its growth. I try to keep a steady heart rate of around one hundred and twenty beats per minute but, by keeping this steady state, my power just drops and drops. My average power hits below one hundred watts. Aran's granny could pedal harder than this. And even with this reduced power, I get an annoying stitch.

I look down at Bike's crossbar and see stickers from last year's races that I've lazily left in place. The stickers have my race numbers on them and the names of the events. I see the stickers from Dingle, Killarney and Gaelforce West, and feel a surge of pride. If I'm going to stay motivated to keep fit through this pregnancy, these stickers will help serve as a constant reminder of future competitions.

I am lost in the world of racing when my mobile phone rings. I had left it on the sideboard beside me just in case I needed to call for help during my bike spin. I stop pedalling and pick up the phone. The saved number flashes up that it's from Altnagelvin Hospital.

'Hello,' the man on the line says. 'This is Doctor Glackin.'

I am so puffed from pedalling my bike that I just nod as I hear the name.

'We need you to come into the Fetal Assessment Unit at the Hospital as soon as you can,' he says. 'Your antibody levels have risen.'

'Well, I'm on my bike, so ... ' I stop myself. Normally nothing comes between me and my session, but this sounds serious. 'I can be there in thirty minutes.'

Nervous sweat drips from my hands. I nearly drop my phone as I hang up. I was right, something must be wrong. 'Pete, Pete!' I shout, shaking as I try to dismount Bike without falling. 'I gotta go.'

I hear Pete emerging from the office and rushing towards my training spot.

'I need to go to the hospital,' I say, bending down to unstrap my bike shoes.

'Oh my God, are you okay?' he says, grabbing hold of my arm.

'No, no, I'm fine,' I say, straightening up right away so to not raise any undue alarm. 'It's just ... ' A wave of emotion sweeps through me and I suddenly lose my words. Oh God, there's something wrong with the baby.

Pete holds me tight and leads me to the nearest chair. 'It's okay,' he says. 'Just tell me slowly.'

'The doctor just called,' I say. 'It's about those antibody levels. He wants me to go see him immediately.'

Pete offers to give me a lift to the hospital, but I politely decline. I can only deal with one person being stressed right now. Instead, I pull on the bravest face I can manage, and march straight out to the car. I can deal with facts, but not emotion. I need to suppress every feeling that is bombarding me at this moment in time.

It will be okay. The doctor will know what to do. He will make everything better again.

19

Blood

Half an hour later, I am stumbling around the hospital's maternity unit, trying to find the Fetal Assessment Unit and the consultant doctor who just called. I am sure there are signs around the building to show me the way, but I am in such a blind panic, I fail to notice a single one. Finally, a midwife takes pity on me, and leads me straight to his door.

'Moire?' he says, as soon as I enter his office.

I have to think a moment. 'Ah, yes. That's me.'

'Good,' Doctor Glackin says. 'Thanks for coming so quickly.'

I could have come sooner but I had to put my bike and rollers away, out of Aran's potential reach. I had to also strip off all my sweaty bike gear and change into respectable maternity wear. I skipped showering to save me a couple of minutes because there was no way I was delaying any further. I need to know what's wrong with my baby, and how this doctor can intervene.

'Your blood tests have come back and your antibody levels have risen considerably,' Doctor Glackin says.

'You said that on the phone. But what does that mean?'

'Well, I see from your notes that your blood group is O

227

negative,' he says. 'You must have been exposed to rhesus positive blood in the past, potentially from a previous pregnancy.'

'But, hold on,' I say. 'My husband has O positive blood and my first child has O positive blood as well. But I was given anti-D injections during my first pregnancy to stop antibodies from forming against their different blood type.'

'It is rare for it to happen, but sometimes the anti-D injections don't work,' Doctor Glackin says. 'It is something called Rhesus Disease. I think I see around two cases of this per year.'

Now I know why my own mother was so glad that all her children were the same blood group as herself. She had children before the anti-D injection was available, and what with my father having a positive blood group, getting pregnant with us was risky to say the least.

'Now we don't know for sure, but it is likely that this new baby is also O positive,' Doctor Glackin explains. 'That would explain the rise in antibody levels in your blood. Your body is detecting the baby's foreign blood cells in your system and is trying to destroy them.'

My body is attacking my own baby. That's what making this doctor so alarmed.

'But is the baby okay?' I say. There is real urgency in my voice. 'The twenty-week scan said he was completely fine.'

'Yes, everything looks fine thus far,' Doctor Glackin says reassuringly. 'But it's important that we keep a close eye on the baby from now until his birth.'

I nod silently. I hate the idea of additional medical checks. But I've got to remember that this isn't about my own health, but the health of my unborn child.

228

'We'll do an ultrasound scan every fortnight to check the blood flow in the baby's brain,' Doctor Glackin says. 'This will help tell us if your baby is becoming anaemic or not.'

'And if he does become anaemic?' I ask.

'Well, if that happens, then we might have to give him a blood transfusion while he's still in the womb.'

I recoil at the mere idea.

'But don't worry,' the doctor continues. 'We'll cross that bridge if we get to it.'

He instructs me to lie down on the raised, hard, narrow bench, and he squirts ultrasound jelly on my stomach. He switches on the ultrasound machine and, using the wand, finds the specific artery he's looking for in my baby's brain. He takes a series of measurements.

'It all looks fine,' Doctor Glackin says as soon as he knows the prognosis. 'Blood flow is normal, so no signs of anaemia thus far.'

I breathe a huge sigh of relief. 'So why the rise in my own antibody levels?' I ask, assuming the two would correlate.

'It's a bit of a mystery all right,' Doctor Glackin says. 'I once treated a patient whose antibody levels were sky-high, but the baby didn't seem to suffer any ill effects.'

I wipe the jelly off and slide off the couch. Good job I didn't shower before I came: this jelly is sticky and leaves an unpleasant residue no matter how hard I rub.

'I will make an appointment for you to return in two weeks' time,' Doctor Glackin says, typing today's results into his desktop. 'You'll have to give bloods again to check your antibody levels, and we'll do the same scan as we did today.'

'That's fine,' I say. I hate the idea of coming to the

hospital every fortnight from now on, but thankful for all the attention my baby is receiving. 'So we'll keep going with these checks until the baby's due date?'

'Well, yes, the checks will continue,' he says. 'The only thing is that it is best we don't leave the baby in there any longer than necessary, and risk further exposure to your antibodies.'

Did I hear the doctor right? Is there a silver lining to having Rhesus Disease?

'We'll probably induce you three weeks early, so when you're around week thirty-seven,' Doctor Glackin says.

That means I'll give birth at the start of August instead of at the very end. I so hate being pregnant that I can't help but be pleased that I'll have three weeks less to suffer this horrific state.

'The only thing is, we'll have to admit you to the normal wards for your labour instead of the midwifery unit,' he explains. 'We need to be able to monitor the baby's heart throughout the delivery, and that's not possible if you're having a water birth.'

Though I'm disappointed that he's just ruled out the birthing pool, I'm relieved that this condition has been caught before any damage is done, and that I'll be closely monitored going forward.

'I see this is your second child,' Doctor Glackin says, just as I am about to get up to leave.

I nod in confirmation.

'Just so that you're aware, you'll always have these antibodies present in your blood.'

I sit still and listen very carefully.

'It means that, if you do decide to have another child, and if that child is also O positive, your antibodies will probably rise even more,' Doctor Glackin explains. 'Any subsequent pregnancies will need to be monitored even more closely, as there could be a greater risk with each one.'

Is the doctor trying to tell me it's best I stop now at two children?

I could jump up and kiss this consultant, and thank him for this get-out-of-jail card. Instead, I sincerely thank Doctor Glackin for all his help, and go home to tell Pete all about my unscheduled hospital visit.

Pete greets me at the door and hugs me tightly. He looks relieved to see I am still in one piece.

'How did it go?' he says. 'Will everything be all right?'

The short car ride home has given me enough time to gather up my own thoughts and feelings.

'Yes,' I reply with conviction. 'There's no need to worry. Everything will be fine.'

I explain to Pete what these antibody levels mean, and how additional blood tests and scans that will be necessary from now until the birth. I reassure Pete that Doctor Glackin has everything under control, and that I have full confidence in him.

'There's just one more thing,' I say, hoping Pete can cope with the onslaught of information I've given him thus far. 'The doctor says it's risky for us to have more children after this one.'

I look up at Pete to see his reaction. His blank expression divulges nothing.

'The risk would be minimal if another baby had the same blood type as me,' I say, trying to explain further. 'But if they had your blood type, then this antibody issue could be even worse than now.'

'That's okay. Two is enough,' Pete says unexpectedly.

I raise my eyebrows. Where has this sudden change of heart come from?

'I've been thinking about how knackered I feel these days,' he explains. 'I'm too old to be running after a horde of young children, when I am barely able to cope with Aran's current antics.'

'So, two it is?' I say, making sure we are both okay with this plan.

'Agreed,' Pete says.

'Agreed.' We shake on it.

All I can think is, 'Whoopee!'

I don't dare suggest that maybe his tiredness stems not from Aran, but from the arduous training he is doing for the upcoming Belfast marathon. Pete is pounding out such high mileage with gruelling efforts that I'm amazed he's not injured yet. His Garmin data shows, however, that he is getting significantly fitter and faster. We both know he could potentially run a personal best come race day.

Pete, Aran and I travel to Belfast the day before the event. We stay in a hotel close to the city centre, so that we can all walk to the marathon start the next day.

We wake up early and Pete goes through his pre-race routine. He has a sausage roll and a coffee for breakfast, despite my protests on nutritional grounds. While Pete's digesting his fat-laden meal, I put Aran in the Bob buggy for the short walk to the start at City Hall. My bump is too big, and Aran is too heavy for me to carry him around these days.

'So where will I see you out on the course?' Pete asks as soon as we reach the starting line. I look at the map that was provided in Pete's race pack.

'We'll try to catch you on the bridge near Ann Street, around mile six,' I say. There's a nice shortcut we can take from the start to the bridge, that will mean we'll get there in time to see Pete. Then I note that Pete will head north and way out of the city. Then around mile twenty he will pass close by our hotel.

'Hopefully Aran and I will see you here,' I say, pointing to mile twenty on the map. 'If not, we'll catch you at the finish.'

Pete seems happy enough with that plan and heads off for his warm-up jog. As I watch him go, various advertisers hand Aran branded balloons and shaky things to keep him entertained.

As soon as the marathon starts, I push Aran over to the pre-determined rendezvous point to cheer Pete on. It is mild summer's day, so I sit on the kerbside while Aran cheers on random runners with his assortment of flags and toys. I'm not sure whether it is the day's heat or the waiting around that tires me out so much. Maybe it's the fact that I'm nearly six months pregnant. But when Pete finally passes us on the bridge at mile six, looking good and on target pace, I struggle to stand up.

'Let's go back to the hotel for a bit,' I say to Aran as I strap him back into his buggy. I think a little lie-down would help me out immensely.

By the time I get back to the hotel, I feel like I've run the entire marathon myself. Aran has been a model child all morning and has not tired me out in the slightest. It is his brother, who I'm forced to cart around inside me, who has drained me of all my energy. Though I had agreed with Pete that we would cheer him at mile twenty, I figure it wouldn't matter much if we changed the plan slightly, that Pete would understand. Aran and I take a quick nap, and wake up refreshed enough to walk towards the finish. We arrive there just as the three-hour-thirty runners cross the line.

Pete was hoping to do three hours forty-five. But when the race clock shows that time, there's still no sign of Pete. Aran and I wait. And wait.

Still no Pete. Aran's branded balloon slowly begins to deflate.

Finally, I see the four-hour pacer's flag rounding the last corner. And there is Pete, sprinting with all his might, trying to overtake him. He manages to edge just in front of the pacer before reaching the inflatable finishing arch. Pete throws himself across the line, and collapses in a heap.

'Well done, Pete!' I shout as soon as he resurrects himself and finds his way out of the enclosed finishing area.

'Where were you guys?' Pete says to me. 'I couldn't see you anywhere.'

I'm a little confused. We were at the bridge, and now we're here at the finish.

'I was looking for you at mile twenty,' Pete says.

'Oh,' I reply. 'Had a bit of a low-energy pregnancy moment. Sorry about that.'

'You had a low-energy moment?' Pete says, spitting out his words. 'I was the one doing the marathon!'

I feel like I'm in trouble, but I'm unsure what I've done.

'I hit the wall, and I was looking for you guys to give me a boost,' Pete says. 'And when I didn't see you, I ended up walking for miles.'

Pete drops to the ground again, grimacing in pain and disappointment.

'But you've finished,' I say. 'And that's the fourth fastest marathon time you've ever done.'

'That's not the point,' Pete says. 'I've supported all the races you did last year. And the first time I try to do something challenging, you let me down.'

I'm about to launch into a tirade about how it's not my fault that my husband can't overcome the marathon wall. Anyway, seeing I'm nearly six months pregnant, he can't count on me to be always there for him when he's feeling a little tired. And another thing: I've never asked him to support me on my events. It's just that he has had to come along so that he can look after the child *he* wanted me to have in the first place.

Fortunately, Aran sums up my frustration, without me having to say a word. Aran takes his battered balloon and starts beating up his daddy, who is lying lifeless on the ground. His actions lighten the mood a little and are surprisingly well timed: having a full-blown argument with my husband, who has just run a full marathon, could be considered inappropriate right now.

Pete eventually resurrects himself and finds enough energy to hobble back to the hotel. We don't mention the "mile-twenty incident" to each other ever again.

The whole experience painfully illustrates that Pete and I can't risk being simultaneously worn out. If we are, we end up having ridiculous rows that have the real potential to spiral rapidly out of control. From now on, we have to make sure that only one of us is tired at any given time. And, seeing that I'm on the cusp of my third trimester, Pete better make sure he's constantly in flying form.

Four weeks later, my third trimester arrives, and I can barely cope with the endless exhaustion. I've already given up running, unable to bear the resultant fatigue or the caustic heartburn it gives me. Bike and I are still just about soldiering on with easy indoor sessions. Eamonn continues to give me thirty minutes of strength and conditioning to do on alternate days. Most of these I skip, however, as they leave me breathless and shattered.

I am so depressed by my body's inabilities that I regularly come close to tears on my weekly calls with Eamonn. I feel fat. I feel unfit. I can barely even breathe these days, what with the baby taking up so much internal space. Even Eamonn's suggestions that I 'do what I can' make me want to cry. What I can do now is so below par compared to what I was capable of before getting pregnant. Eamonn listens to my pregnancy woes and reassures me that it will soon be over. I struggle to believe him, even though I know I've less than three months of this ordeal to go.

Eventually, I resign myself to going for the odd swim and giving the dog his daily walk. I convince myself that pushing Aran in his buggy, with Tom tied to its handle, is my new tailor-made strength session. But even this is soon curtailed when Aran decides he no longer wants to be pushed. Instead, he wants to walk Tom all by himself. He kicks and screams when I try to place him inside the buggy. I don't have the energy to fight him any more, so I let him toddle off, pulling Tom behind him. I soon realise this is a bad idea, as I struggle to keep up with Aran who wanders off at speed. But when I do catch up, Aran decides he wants to stop and sniff every wild flower and pick up every stone strewn across the trail's rocky path. If only Aran would learn to walk at one single consistent pace.

To make matters worse, Pete is immensely worried by Aran's new independent streak. During one of Aran's particularly bad temper tantrums, all this comes to a head. Pete tries to pick up his son, who is writhing around on the ground. But despite Pete's kind intentions, Aran wants nothing of his daddy.

'Go-way,' Aran shouts. 'Go-way, Da-de.'

'Go away, Daddy' is the first complete sentence that

Aran has ever said. Pete is visibly shocked by this grammatically correct outburst. I am amazed how such a small child can make a grown adult so upset.

Aran gets to his feet and makes a direct beeline for my legs. He wraps his arms around them both. 'Mama,' he says, gazing up at me with unending adoration.

'How am I going to cope with Aran when you're in hospital?' Pete says.

I am going to be admitted to hospital in a matter of weeks to have my baby induced. Pete has this pleading look in his eye, like he is begging me not to leave. It is true that we have not yet rehearsed this impending scenario; I have not left Aran alone for a single night ever since his birth.

'I'm sure you and Aran will get along just fine,' I say.

I'm lying. I'm not sure at all. I feel slightly responsible for this Oedipus complex of Aran's, but I really don't know how to crack it. Maybe making Aran go cold turkey, by me disappearing from our home, will break this Mummy attachment and allow Daddy some space on the parenting scene.

The weekend before I am admitted, the European Adventure Racing Championship is held in Ireland. It is a non-stop three-day event, where teams of four are running, biking and kayaking from Westport all the way down the Atlantic Coastline to Killarney. For the first time ever, I am thankful I am not competing. The weather is woeful, with gale force winds and sideways rain, the worst that Ireland can muster up mid-summer.

I follow the race online, watching each team's dot travel further and further south. It is riveting stuff, as I see teams do battle on the mountains and seas, with some taking wrong turns and other teams falling apart as team-members drop out along the way. I see photos of bedraggled competitors conking out on mountain summits, as exhaustion and sleep deprivation hit. I, on the other hand, watch all of this from the comfort of my own sofa, knowing I am about to undergo my very own special endurance test soon.

I am truly relieved when my induction date arrives. The veins in my arms look like pincushions, I've contributed so much blood for antibody tests. My maternity file is bulging with pictures of every brain scan taken of the baby's head. The baby, in turn, has fought valiantly against the onslaught of my antibodies and has not needed the blood transfusion that was threatened if he had developed severe anaemia in utero.

I am also relieved that, within days, I will get my body back. I have really suffered from being too tired to exercise over the last couple of weeks. And though I've known all along that this pregnancy will end one day, rational thoughts aren't always forthcoming when all you feel are worried and exhausted and fat.

Pete drops me to the hospital on Monday afternoon for my prearranged induction. The consultant has warned me that inductions are unpredictable. I could go into labour today, tomorrow, or even the day after. There is therefore no point in Pete hanging around the hospital waiting for his new son to arrive. It's best he goes home and begins his own bonding process with Aran.

I am straightaway admitted to the antenatal ward. It is crammed full of other women whose babies are also undergoing early evictions. One lady is waddling along the ward, clutching her back with both hands to support her enormous belly. She sees me watching her closely as she paces up and down the floor.

'Good luck,' she says to me, as I try to make myself comfortable on my hospital bed. 'I've been here three days already, and still not gone into labour.'

Oh dear. My adventure-racing friends have travelled halfway down the country in the time it's taken for her and her baby to go nowhere.

A midwife arrives to carry out some checks, and to start the dreaded induction process. Though I'm told to stay in bed for an hour to let the medication work, I'm allowed to wander the corridors after that.

Three hours after the midwife's visit, I start to feel a twinge while on a short walk. I was told that the medicine can cause false contractions and not to worry about them. However, the twinges start to repeat themselves thick and fast. This can't be labour, I tell myself. It's meant to take a day or two, not a couple of hours.

By 7 pm, I'm convinced these contractions are for real. I ask a midwife to check if I'm in labour, and within minutes I'm bundled off to the birthing ward. I pass the same lady who was pacing the ward earlier, her jaw dropping as she sees me being whisked away to give birth.

'Sorry,' is all I can say to her as I shuffle past at speed.

I can see her muttering something under her breath, something like 'I can't believe it.'

I'm welcomed into a birthing room by two midwives, a young lady and a more senior one. They show me my bed, but I have to stop mid-stride as I approach it, as another contraction arrives.

'I need to phone my husband,' I finally manage to say. I grab my mobile from my bag, and instruct Pete to get to the hospital immediately. He makes it to my bedside within thirty minutes of my call, but I don't have much time to fill him in on the birthing process thus far. My first labour took five and a half hours. I am less than an hour into this one, and there is absolutely no let-up. One contraction has barely finished before another one begins. I scream in agony. I find the louder I scream, the more I dull the pain. The young midwife seems shocked, however, by the primordial sounds I'm making.

'Do you want some pethidine?' she asks, out of desperation.

'No, no,' I whisper, before I let out another blood-curdling wail. I had forgotten to fill in the section in my maternity notes instructing the midwives how I'd like my birth to proceed. During my first labour, there was plenty of time to communicate such wishes between contractions. But this time around, I have no energy to explain my preferred pain control method is just gas and air. Every part of my being is instead focused solely on yelling.

I close my eyes, and an image from the weekend's adventure-racing championships flashes across my mind; I see a racer asleep on Galtymore Mountain, a stone wall holding his head up as an impromptu pillow. His body is splayed across the cold, wet bog, so exhausted is he from the endless racing. I feel just like that poor adventure racer, too shattered to get up. The only difference is the racer in the picture is finally getting some sort of rest.

I have been in labour for an hour and a half when the midwives tell me to push. I've heard some women saying that a short labour is best. But this is way too short to be even remotely pleasant. I am in such pain, however, I'll do anything to get this over and done with. I'm not going to keep this baby in any longer than needs be.

Our son bursts out on to the scene at 8.30 pm that evening. Pete hasn't even had time to yawn like he did during Aran's birth. The midwives put the baby into my arms so he can have a quick cuddle and breastfeed. But as soon as we've made our acquaintance, they whisk him away from my side.

The consultant had warned that the baby's birth would not mark the end of my Rhesus Disease complications. Once free from my body, the baby would suffer something different, called Haemolytic Disease of the Newborn. Some of my antibodies have passed into the baby's system during pregnancy and birth. These will now proceed to attack the baby's blood cells and cause a build-up of bilirubin. High levels of bilirubin could irrevocably damage his nerves, especially those involved in hearing and movement.

He needs immediate treatment.

As my baby is bundled off to intensive care, I bid him a brief farewell. I hope that he'll be able to fight the good fight, and that we'll be able to leave the hospital together in the coming days or weeks.

20

Home

I down the traditional hospital post-natal tea and toast before shuffling slowly over to the Intensive Care Unit. Pete says goodbye, then goes home to relieve Granny and take charge of Aran. In the meantime, I turn my attention to Baby. Pete and I still have no idea what name we will give our latest child. We figured we'd wait until he's born to see what kind of name suits him best. Baby is his title in the meantime.

I tentatively enter intensive care and look around for Baby. Inside the room, all I can see are high-tech machines with flashing numbers and blinking lights connected to transparent plastic boxes. The bleeps and alarms remind me of how serious Baby's condition is.

I am shown to an incubator near the door, and informed that this is my newborn. I peer inside, trying to recognise him from the countless ultrasound pictures that were taken throughout the pregnancy. Only the bracelet around his ankle confirms that he is indeed mine. 'Baby O'Sullivan' is scrawled upon the tiny plastic ring.

An Intensive Care nurse comes over and suggests I pick him up. I look up at her helplessly.

'But how do I get him out?'

I can't find the catches that undo the incubator's lid. And even if I do gain access, Baby has so many tubes and wires attached to him, I'm afraid I might accidentally disconnect him.

She helps me free Baby and places him in my arms. He is so small and fragile, what with being only a few hours old, even before considering the condition he's now fighting.

'Do you want to give him a feed?' the nurse asks me. I look down at Baby, and see that he is half awake and looking a bit hungry. Though I breastfed Aran for over a year, it takes a while for me to successfully guide Baby to latch on. It looks like both of us are in need of a bit more practice.

'Best we put him back into the incubator again,' the midwife says, when she sees Baby has had his fill. 'We need to keep him under the UV lights to help him get well.'

The consultant had already explained to me the treatment that Baby will need. He is now undergoing phototherapy, which helps break down the by-product bilirubin that is accumulating in his body. Aran in fact had the exact same treatment two years ago. The medical staff will start measuring every few hours the bilirubin levels in Baby's blood. If he can't clear the substance quickly enough, he may need to undergo a blood transfusion. I can't imagine how they'd go about pumping blood into this tiny being when his veins are so faint and thin.

I stand up to go to the post-natal ward and get a bit of rest. I struggle, however, to make it to my feet, and need to sit down again. What with all the concern over Baby, I nearly forgot I've just given birth and my own body isn't in great shape. But even when I do get back to my hospital bed on the post-natal ward, I have difficulty falling asleep. My head is buzzing with so many thoughts and fears that sleep is impossible to find.

My insomnia proves somewhat advantageous, however, as Baby needs feeding every couple of hours. So in the dead of night, I return to the ICU to give him some more milk. The nurse had informed me that breastfeeding Baby also helps his condition. The breast milk somehow binds with the bilirubin and helps remove it from his system.

I sit down in front of Baby's incubator, and start fiddling with its door. A nurse sees me trying to break in, and comes over to help.

'Would you like a screen around you while you're breastfeeding?' she asks once we're seated comfortably and about to begin.

I chuckle to myself. I fed Aran in Cambodia, balanced on street curbs as motorbikes cruised past. I gave him top-ups at adventure-racing start lines in Ireland with hundreds of competitors milling round. I think enough people have seen me breastfeeding that a screen is probably not necessary at this point.

Baby soon gets used to this mode of feeding. And, with regular doses of breast milk, he starts to fight the bilirubin onslaught. Within two days, he is moved next door to the less critical Special Care Unit. He is still under constant UV lights, but he is out of the incubator, and the tubes and wires are now gone.

At the same time, I am also discharged from the post-natal ward. Fortunately there is space for me to stay within the same unit as Baby, so that I can continue breastfeeding on demand. Pete continues to visit us every day, with updates on how he and Aran are getting on.

By the end of the week, Baby is sturdy enough for

Aran to also come and pay a visit. Pete and I have both spoken to Aran about his impending brother, but there is only so much a two-year-old can comprehend. When we introduce them to each other, Baby seems oblivious to it all, but Aran is not amused to say the least. He takes one look at Baby, his sullen expression seeming to say, 'And what exactly is *this*?'

Friends had warned us that Aran might not welcome a smaller rival. One friend has gone to the extent of buying a toy Thomas the Tank Engine to give to Aran. Our friend tells us to pretend to Aran that it's a present from his younger brother. Aran develops a strong attachment to this toy train, and insists on taking it everywhere. Unfortunately, similar positive sentiments towards his younger brother are painfully slow to appear.

Though warm fuzzy feelings towards his new brother aren't particularly forthcoming, in my absence Aran has finally started to enjoy the company of his father. Perhaps it's Pete's different pace of life that Aran appreciates. They take long walks together on the local beach with Tom, longer than I would ever go. Pete tries to teach Aran the art of rugby, though all Aran wants to do is run away with the ball. They go to the supermarket and wander the aisles, with Aran sitting in the shopping trolley and putting in whatever food he likes. Pete lets Aran wear his pyjamas until midday and stay up as late as he likes. And Pete allows him hours of screen time, as long as Aran stays quiet.

When Pete tells me the antics the two of them are getting up to, I don't mind a bit. As long as the two of them are alive and well when I get out of hospital, they can do whatever they like. However, when exactly Baby and I will be allowed out of hospital remains still a mystery.

Soon, Baby is one week old and still under UV lights. His bilirubin levels have hovered just below the danger line that, if crossed, would mean a blood transfusion. The doctors want his levels to drop further before he can be discharged, so I wait painfully each day for Baby's bilirubin result, to see if and when we can get out.

While Baby and I exist in limbo within the Special Care Unit, life continues on as normal outside the hospital's confines. I speak with Eamonn about how I'm doing, a week after giving birth. I've healed remarkably well, all things considered. He says he'll put a training timetable together for me to start once Baby and I are discharged. And though it seems premature, the thought of training again gives me something to focus on instead of bilirubin, which is all I seem to think of and speak about these days.

Friday arrives, eleven days since Baby's induced appearance. If we don't get out today, we'll be stuck here for the entire weekend. And though the doctors and nurses have been wonderful and have provided incredible medical attention, I can't help missing home and wanting my own food and bed.

When I see the doctors doing their rounds, I nearly tackle them to the ground to find out Baby's bilirubin result. Fortunately, they see my anxiety and come to Baby's bedside first.

'Well, the good news is that your baby's bilirubin levels have stabilised,' the lead consultant says. I look down at my poor baby in his cot, his hands and feet covered in red dots from where they've inserted microscopic needles on a daily basis. 'However, they've not dropped as much as we would have liked.'

My throat thickens. I blink hard. I fight back an angry tear.

'We do think he's on the right trajectory,' the consultant continues, ignoring my inner turmoil. 'If you agree to bring your baby back to the hospital next week for some additional tests, we're okay to discharge him today.'

I can't hold back the floodgates any more. I start to sob uncontrollably. My baby blues hit just when I get the best news I've heard all week.

The doctor smiles sympathetically and waits for me to calm down.

'You might be interested to know we went back and tested the bloods from your first child,' she says. 'It seems like his jaundice was caused by antibodies as well, so you must have developed them during your first pregnancy.'

With that mystery solved, I call Pete and ask him to collect Baby and I from the hospital at lunchtime.

After two weeks of uninterrupted observation, I feel I know Baby pretty well. And given that he needs a birth certificate, and hence a name, Pete and I resolve to come to some sort of agreement. After much deliberation, we settle on the name Cahal, an old traditional Gaelic name that means valiant warrior. It seems pretty descriptive of his life to date. Plus, Cahal is easy to say and spell, and marks the child out as Irish. It fits the bill perfectly.

Aran, our independent two-year-old, decides, however, to totally ignore our well-thought-out name choice. His brother has thus far been known as Baby, and that's what Aran insists on calling him.

As soon as I get home, I finally get to enjoy the fact that I am no longer pregnant. And with zero pressure to produce any more children, I can get down to business and try to get my body back in shape again. Eamonn's plan clicks into action, and I have ten minutes of strength and conditioning exercises to do on my first day of freedom. It is all very short and sedate, but I have to take things slowly seeing that I've no idea how my post-natal body will cope under this unusual stress. The next day I have a thirty-minute walk to do, with short little jogs in the middle. Though I'm dubious about my ability to run, the session proves easier than expected. Eamonn gradually increases the intensity week by week, but he keeps me away from Bike until four weeks after the birth. Unlike after Aran, when I got back on after a fortnight, my coach prefers to make sure my hips aren't an issue before allowing me to get back into the saddle.

While I am preoccupied with nursing Baby and getting fit again, there are bigger issues to deal with in our household. Pete has been offered a job in Myanmar, the country formerly known as Burma, setting up a new microfinance venture. He is wondering if he should take the position, and if we would move with him.

'I think we need to think bigger picture than this,' I say, trying not to betray my true feelings that I've no desire whatsoever to move back to South East Asia. I like living in Ireland, and want to stay right here for the foreseeable future. 'Like, where do you want the children to grow up?' I ask my wanderlust husband. 'Where do you want them to go to school?'

I can't believe I'm asking such things. I was the one who never wanted kids in the first place and now, here am I, wanting to plan our entire lives around them.

'I am sure there are international schools in Burma,' Pete says. 'And we could always get a nanny, like we had during our Cambodia trip.'

'You know I'd feel inadequate if I got full-time help,' I say, already feeling guilty about this hang-up. 'And if you are working in a start-up venture, you'll never be home to see your own children.'

Pete can get very focused on his job and will work long hours to succeed, just like he did in Greystones. Though this was understandable when we didn't have young children, I feel our focus needs to shift towards what is best for Aran and Cahal.

'But being overseas will expose them to different cultures and places,' Pete says. 'They could even learn Chinese.'

'They can travel over the summer holidays,' I retort. 'And they can learn languages here in Ireland.'

We go back and forth over the issues, both of us presenting valid points. It is only when Pete goes on a scoping mission to Burma that he realises how hot the weather is there, how expensive expat costs are, and how bad traffic is in Yangon. These three things are enough to swing the argument my way.

I feel, however, we need to make a final, clear-cut decision on where we are going to live. If not, Pete will continue to throw overseas curveballs at me whenever he gets offered another exciting job in an exotic far-flung location.

'If we were to be based in Ireland, where do you think we should live?' Pete says when he returns from yet another overseas assignment. He must have had a draining, disappointing trip if he is even posing this question. I am relieved though to hear him bring the subject up. We need to talk these things through so we can come to some sort of resolution.

Though Pete has no problem flying for days across the globe, he has struggled with the commute from Derry to Dublin, a four-hour, one-way journey. It means he has to overnight in the capital on a regular basis for at least two or three nights a week.

'Well, if I'm going to move again,' I say, 'we have to go some place mountainous.' The lack of altitude was one of the main reasons I begged to leave Cambodia and its never-endingly flat paddy-field land.

'We tried Wicklow, with all its mountains, and that didn't work,' Pete points out. 'I also struggled with the commute to Dublin from Greystones, which is only just down the road.'

'Why don't we head towards the Mourne Mountains?' I say, chancing my luck. The Mournes are on the eastern side of Ireland, equidistant between Dublin and Belfast in terms of travel time. They are also halfway between Waterford and Derry, where our respective parents live.

Regardless of their location, the Mournes are my favourite set of mountains. I have spent many a happy day running around their jagged peaks and scaling their dizzy heights. Once we stayed for a weekend in a place on the southern side of the Mournes called Rostrevor, over-looking Carlingford Lough and the Cooley Mountains. The place is a mountain biker's mecca, as well a friendly village with lots of restaurants and pubs. Even Pete seemed to like Rostrevor when we visited. I'm hoping he'd like to live there as well.

Pete says nothing for a while. I am hoping this is a good sign.

'We could rent a furnished holiday cottage for a couple of months, and see if we like the place,' Pete says. Typically, he is reluctant to commit long-term but seems open to at least checking the place out.

'We could see if the boys like the area,' I say. 'And if it's a good place for them to grow up.'

'And I'll see what the commute is like to Dublin,' Pete says. 'And whether I can work from home.'

Yes! It looks like I'm on a winning streak.

With this short-term plan in place, we complete Cahal's schedule of hospital checks until he's given a clean bill of health. We then move to Rostrevor when Cahal is still only a few months old. If we are going to live in Rostrevor, we want to find out as soon as possible if it will suit our nascent family.

The first thing I do when we arrive is look for some decent childcare. I need someone to look after the kids for a couple of hours each day so that I can fit my training in. When I just had Aran to mind, three times a week in a crèche was plenty. I could easily train together with Aran on the other days. However, I soon discover that minding two young children while trying to train is practically impossible.

I try turbo training with Aran and Cahal both in the same room. I manage to get Aran to stay quiet by plonking him in front of the TV. But the sound of *Paw Patrol* soon wakes Cahal up, forcing me to dismount Bike to calm Baby. Once Cahal is finally asleep, Aran gets bored of watching *Paw Patrol* repeats. He comes over to my rollers, which are spinning at high speed, and tries to play with them. I have to get off Bike for safety reasons, and end up abandoning the entire session.

I then consider buying a double-stroller so that I can instead run with both of them, but I fail to find any paths or trails wide enough to accommodate such a vehicle.

Faced with such difficulties, I search for someone to look after both kids five times a week. I'm embarrassed to need so much support, but I find I need a little break from the children every day so I don't totally crack up.

If I found looking after just one child hard, two proves overwhelming. It turns out that, if one is happy, the other is kicking and screaming. Once I've successfully soothed one, the other seems to kick off on cue. I come close to having a nervous breakdown whenever both of them flip out simultaneously, a scene that seems to occur with amazing regularity.

Fortunately, a local Rostrevor lady, Julie McGinn, comes to my aid. She looks after primary-school children before and after school, so is free every morning to look after my two in her home. I bring Aran and Cahal along on their first day in Rostrevor to meet their potential minder.

Aran is so used to childcare that he tears away from me within seconds and runs straight into Julie's sitting room. Her home is brimming with colourful games and toys, which Aran starts to play with straight away. Immediately I apologise for the mess he's making, as he upends boxes and clears entire shelves.

'Oh God, don't worry about that at all,' Julie says. 'I'm well used to it by now.' Julie is younger than me and seems very chill around children. If I had random kids tearing my home apart, I'm not sure I'd be as relaxed as her.

I take the time to explain to Julie where Aran is developmentally. Though he is sturdy on his feet, he seems to be all walk and no talk these days. His vocabulary is still limited for a child who's just turned two.

Julie assures me that every child is different; that the vast majority catch up before starting school. It is good to know that someone experienced like Julie is going to keep an eye on Aran. As a first-time mum watching her eldest grow, I don't know if Aran is completely normal or if his speech issues are something that should raise concern.

'And this is Cahal,' I say, presenting my two-month-old baby. 'He wears cloth nappies and is breastfed,' I explain, almost apologetically. 'I'll only leave him with you for a max of two hours anyway, so you shouldn't need to change or feed him.'

I know cloth nappies are still an enigma for many, and I'm dreading a repeat of Aran's bottle-feeding protest. Aran's refusal was hellacious for anyone who looked after him, up until the time he started eating solid foods at six months old.

'Sure, that's no problem changing cloth nappies, as long as you show me how,' Julie says. 'And you can leave a bottle with breast milk in it, and we'll see if Cahal takes it.'

I feel so relieved. I don't know how anyone can mind my baby with all these added idiosyncrasies, but Julie seems remarkably calm about it all. In Julie's care, within days, Cahal drinks from a bottle no problem. Maybe, in some regards, second time round can be easier, and I needn't have worried at all.

In the afternoons, the kids and I start to explore the neighbourhood. We discover the expansive grasslands of Rostrevor's Kilbroney Park, where Aran can run freely around. We wander up and down the banks of Yellow River, into which Aran chucks thousands of stones. Aran also takes to his balance bike and hits the mountain bike trails. It means I can carry Cahal and walk Tom in the forest, while Aran speeds along on his own two wheels.

We drive further afield to Castlewellan Forest Park, home to Northern Ireland's stunning national arboretum, a mere thirty-minute journey from Rostrevor. At the heart of the park is an expansive lake, overlooked by a formidable Victorian Castle. Twenty-seven kilometres of mountain bike trails wind their way through the park's woods. And at the trails' entrance, Aran discovers a mini jump track.

253

Aran does lap after lap on the track, competing against older kids who struggle to pedal up and over the bumps. When he tires of his bike, Aran runs off towards the Animal Wood playground. Deep in the forest, there are carved animals for him to clamber over, a scary spider spinning a gigantic web; a cautious badger emerging from its lair; and a red squirrel protecting his high-up den. It is a veritable outdoor paradise for a youngster like Aran.

When we tire of outdoor play, we retreat to the seaside town of Newcastle. There, Aran drinks mugs of sweet hot chocolate and I indulge in coffee and cake in one of the many cafes on the promenade. Cahal too seems happy enough as he sleeps soundly on my lap. Maybe Rostrevor and its surroundings will suit us, a young family starting to grow up.

21

Fit

Aran loves living in Rostrevor, with its veritable paradise of parks, forests, and playgrounds. I too need to discover whether this place can become my new home.

Two months have passed since I gave birth to Cahal, and I am faced with the uphill task of getting fit again. When I first gave birth to Aran, I had no idea whether this was even feasible. I doubted if I would ever shift the weight I had gained during pregnancy. I didn't know if my post-natal body would get injured while training. I wasn't sure if I would be able to juggle babysitting with biking and running. Second time round, I have the advantage of knowing everything will be fine, that it is indeed possible to get race-ready again.

Though this knowledge makes this endeavour mentally easier, it doesn't make it any less physically painful. Fortunately, what with Eamonn coaching me for the last two years, I know I've done as much as I can to maintain my strength and fitness over the latest pregnancy.

It is October, so a good time to start the long, hard slog of winter training for next year's racing season. If I want to do this groundwork, I need to find a gym near Rostrevor to do weights and some rowing sessions. I also want a swimming pool attached to the gym to do some cool-down laps. I find a sports complex in the neighbouring town of Kilkeel, a twenty-minute drive from Rostrevor. So when Eamonn gives me a thirty-minute rowing session to do one day, I go there to sign up to the gym and check the place out.

Driving into Kilkeel town fills me with trepidation. I have ten sets of thirty-second sprints to do on the rowing machine when I get there. I arrive at the sports complex and present myself at reception.

'Can I use your gym?' I say to the lady behind the desk.

'No problem at all,' she replies, handing me a form. 'Just fill in your details and we can make you a member.'

I write down my name and address, and other contact details. I then get to a section asking about previous medical history. When it asks whether I've been pregnant recently, I come clean and tick the box affirmatively.

I hand the form back to the receptionist, who takes a quick look at my answers.

'Just hold on a moment,' she says to me, as she picks up the phone, and makes a covert call.

A manager appears at the desk from out of nowhere. He looks at the receptionist, who silently hands him my completed questionnaire. He takes a moment and scans through my answers.

'Recently pregnant?' he says.

'Ah, yes,' I reply, catching my breath. 'But I've passed my six-week medical with my doctor. And I have a coach, and he says it's okay to train.'

I'm just about to give him the name and number of everyone who can vouch for my gym suitability. But just as I reach for my phone's contact list, I see him signing my form and approving my membership.

'Just had to check, love,' the receptionist says to me kindly, once the manager has gone on his way. 'Couldn't sign you up myself if any of those boxes are ticked with a yes.'

I nod, and tell her it's totally understandably. I then sneak into the gym and do my training. I proceed to nearly die from the half an hour rowing session. I develop blisters on my hands from pulling on the handlebar. I get friction burns on my ass from straining too hard on the seat. The next day my quads and core scream blue murder for the duress I put them under with each stroke.

I soon begin to have a love-hate relationship with my training timetable. I dread opening it up every morning to see if Eamonn will give me a nice or evil session that day. Admittedly, some weeks are easy, like on one Monday that starts off with a simple one-hour slow jog. Tuesday sees fifty minutes of strength and conditioning exercises, with an hour's easy bike afterwards. Then there's a bit of a step up by Wednesday, with a repeat of my dreaded thirty-minute rowing session. Thursday sees a repeat of Tuesday's session, with Friday concluding with another sixty-minute easy run.

Such a week's training shows Eamonn is still being careful. He wants to make sure I can cope with the load he suggests. It is perfectly understandable. I gave birth less than three months ago; I am breastfeeding Cahal, who still wakes up two or three times a night; and I now have two young children to run after and round up by the end of each day.

Eamonn also knows he can't let me off the hook forever. He has the task of getting me fit again. The week after, he starts to put efforts into a seventy-minute run, with twelve one-minute sprints, with three minutes recovery between each one of them. He increases my bike times to ninety minutes, and throws in twelve more thirty-second efforts at over two hundred watts each time.

Just when I feel like I'm starting to cope, Eamonn steps up the intensity again. I only notice he has slipped it into my timetable during our weekly call.

'You want me to race?' I say. 'Already?'

'Just a 10k,' Eamonn replies, before moving swiftly on to the next subject.

But he is not getting away with it so lightly. I have begun to purposely note in my timetable each week, as a subtle reminder, exactly how old Cahal is. I want to remind Eamonn that Cahal is still just a baby, and that I'm still getting used to being un-pregnant.

'Cahal will only be twelve weeks by then,' I say.

'It'll be a great way to mark the occasion,' Eamonn replies, a bit too casually for my liking. 'And it'll help you get used to racing again.'

I know I could point-blank refuse Eamonn's suggestion, and Eamonn would accept my stance. But ultimately, I know Eamonn is probably right, yet again, and I might as well follow his advice.

I find a ten-kilometre race up and down a local hill called Slieve Gullion, a mere thirty-minute drive from Rostrevor. When I arrive, I see Spiderman, Batman, and Wonder Woman milling around the car park. I didn't know it was a fancy-dress hill run in aid of the local hospice. Admittedly, I feel a bit like the Michelin Man these days with additional post-pregnancy fat rolls. I suppose this roly-poly outfit will have to suffice as my fancy-dress costume for today's fundraising event.

I have no idea how fast or slow I can go, having not raced in over a year. So when the starting gun goes, I take off at my normal pace, wondering how well I'll fare. Unfortunately, within a hundred metres, I realise I'm not faring very well. My body refuses to comply with how fast my head wants it to go. Instead, my lungs are self-combusting under my abnormal load. My legs are dissolving beneath me, with no air to fuel them forward.

Within seconds, I can't breathe or run. I start to walk, and I've not even emerged from the flat forest trail and reached the uphill bit yet.

The route is very short and simple compared to the adventure races I'm accustomed to. But this knowledge is little comfort to my post-natal body, which I barely recognise now. And as I take longer and longer to complete the race, my boobs run out of room to accommodate my growing supply of breast milk. I dive over the finish after an hour, oblivious to my placing. All I can think about is feeding Cahal, and avoiding a repeat bout of mastitis.

Fortunately, Pete is standing right there at the line, with Cahal in his arms. With Cahal violently wriggling and crying, the need to feed and be fed is undeniably mutual. We make a hasty dash to the car, where I give Cahal an emergency drink. I sit in the passenger seat, sore and sweaty from the race that I've just completed. I concede to the depressing fact that I am nowhere near competitive, but that it was definitely good to be racing again.

They say motivation follows action, and the ten-kilometre race has given me renewed enthusiasm to train. But just as I think I can get stuck back in to running and biking, Cahal gets horribly sick. It starts as a bad cough, and then he starts to throw up. I have to keep him at home with me instead of dropping him off at our child-minder where he would surely infect the other children. Unfortunately, I can't even leave Cahal with Pete and nip off for a quick one-hour jog. The very day Cahal gets sick, Pete has to fly off to Cambodia for work.

I bring Cahal to the doctor later that day and he is prescribed antibiotics. However, the medication does nothing to cure Cahal's illness. Instead, he seems to get even worse. So there I am, home alone, with a baby puking up all of his feeds. At the same time, Aran is having a terrible-two day and throwing strategically violent tantrums. I don't know whether to hold the baby or restrain the toddler. This is the exactly the scenario I feared happening before getting pregnant in the first place.

That night, I worry so much that I barely sleep a wink. I imagine my baby is going to vomit in his sleep and suffocate to death. I call the doctor the next morning and beg for an appointment, then leave Aran to Julie as soon as she can take him. I can barely cope with Aran and his current mood swings in addition to a sick baby.

I then hightail it to the surgery with Cahal. A different doctor sees Cahal this time and examines my son extensively. When he is unable to detect the oxygen levels in his blood, he tells me to go straight to the nearby hospital. I slip into autopilot as I speed down the road to Newry's Daisy Hill Hospital. I dump the car and rush to the children's ward. The medical staff do an assortment of tests and inform me Cahal has contracted bronchiolitis. The illness causes inflammation and congestion in the lungs' small airways, making it difficult to breathe. It is a common illness amongst the under-twos. Only a minority of children with this condition need to be hospitalized, and Cahal is unfortunately one of them.

I descend into sheer panic.

Is Cahal really that sick? Can I not care for him at home?

I nearly didn't bring him to the doctor. Am I a bad mother?

How did he even manage to contract this infection?

Did I put him in danger by bringing him to Rostrevor so soon after he was initially discharged from hospital?

What am I going to tell Pete? Should I even tell him, when there's nothing he can do for us now?

And who is going to look after Aran if I have to stay overnight in hospital with Cahal?

I pick up my phone to call someone, but have no idea who to talk to.

First things first. Aran. I need to call Julie and ask her to look after him for a bit longer than normal today. I am sure she will understand.

I then call my mother. She lives three hours' drive away from Newry and I doubt she can help me out of this mess. But in the absence of my husband, who is in the skies somewhere above the Middle East, at least she is someone I can talk to.

My voice resonates with deep shock as I speak to my own mum. Amazingly, she seems to understand my predicament, and volunteers to come over and look after Aran. I think she is probably just excited by the prospect of hanging out with her eldest grandson.

I then take a deep breath, and dial Pete's number. Surprisingly, he picks up.

'Where are you?' I say, dispensing with pleasantries.

'Bangkok,' he says. 'Why? Where are you?'

'Daisy Hill Hospital,' I say. 'Cahal's been admitted.'

'What? But, what? Why? Is he okay?'

I feel an explanation is required.

'Cahal has bronchiolitis,' I tell Pete. 'He'll be fine. They just want to monitor him for a couple of days to make sure he can breathe and feed properly again.'

'Oh God,' Pete says. 'Do you want me to come home?'

Yes, of course I want Pete to come home, to save me from this insanity. But I know that, if he turns around now, he'll likely arrive just as Cahal is discharged. It will look like I'm an over-reactive mother, or worse, that I made the whole thing up just to make Pete return.

'No, everything is under control,' I say, surprised by how convincing my voice sounds on the phone. 'Mum is coming over to look after Aran. And I'll stay with Cahal at the hospital until he's allowed go home.'

Pete is speechless. I'm gobsmacked too, astonished by how one small child can cause so much disruption to so many lives.

'Honestly, Pete,' I say, 'Everything will be fine.'

Though it sounds like I'm trying to reassure Pete, it is I who need convincing.

I stay in hospital for four nights with Cahal, sleeping beside him on a sofa bed. Nothing exists beyond the beeps of the machines and the slightest cry from my child. And although his condition is not a serious one, I am consumed by the entire affair. This is what being a mother is all about: I will drop everything for my child in their time of need.

I find it difficult to express large quantities of breast milk for Cahal, so I cannot leave him for long. When I do get a chance, I race back to Rostrevor to check on Mum and Aran. They are having a blast, wrecking the house, surviving on milk and buttered toast, playing outside in the garden all day long. I am just glad they are having a good time. It lets me concentrate on staying with Cahal while he makes his slow recovery.

While Mum and Aran are on their extended holiday, I

also manage to get some rest by Cahal's bedside. I manage to miss two rowing sessions on my training timetable and a particularly gruelling bike session. And though, before children, I would have cursed having to sit out these sessions, I am stunned that I'm okay with this change of plan. I have already invested so much of my time and energy into this tiny human being that a couple of extra days caring exclusively for Cahal doesn't really matter.

What bothers me though, during this time in hospital, is what I see unfurling on my phone. Feelings of such extreme envy engulf me so much that I literally want to explode.

With nothing much else to do while Cahal is undergoing treatment, I spend hours surfing Facebook and Twitter. On Saturday evening, I chance upon photos and results from the Sea to Summit adventure race. I had completely forgotten that the event was taking place this weekend.

Though I never intended to compete, I feel ridiculously jealous as I see old friends battling it out over the Westport course. I ran this race when Aran was four months old and finished in third place.

I want, I need to adventure race again.

I tell Eamonn about this revelation when Cahal is finally released back home.

'I want to try and win the National Adventure Race Series again,' I say.

Up until now, I wasn't sure if it was even possible to vie for the title with two young kids at home. But after seeing the Sea to Summit race results, I don't care if it's feasible or not. I would see myself as a profound failure if I didn't at least try again.

Eamonn tells me he's happy to support me with whatever race plans I have. And though it seems a little boring to try to repeat the same season as I had two years ago, I have discovered that repetition is sometimes for the best. The training and racing suited me well when Aran was a baby. If it worked then, it should help me now, seeing that Cahal is of a similar age.

The only problem with such a plan is its implementation. Its execution hurts like hell. Within a week of agreeing with Eamonn to compete in the Series, he pencils in a one-hour hill rep session on Bike. Such a session entails going up and back down the same hill multiple times. It is generally known to be a ball-breaker.

The wind is howling as I pedal up to the base of the slope I intend to cycle up and down nine times. Sudden sideways gusts nearly knock me off my trusty steed. As soon as I turn a corner, the winds try to push me all the way back home again. I speak soothing words to calm both Bike and me.

'It's okay,' I whisper. 'We'll be okay. We can do this.' But I need more than calming words to stop the heavens from opening up and pouring down torrential rain, straight on to my helmet.

I start pedalling hard and fast up the hill to start my first one-minute interval. And if the effort isn't hard enough, the cold rain soaks me to the skin. I turn around at the top, and start my two-minute recovery. The glacial wind cuts through my raincoat as I speed downhill, freezing me to the bone. I'm relieved to turn around and start the second uphill effort just so that I can warm up again. I try to forget that I have to do this a total of nine times. I tell myself this is character-building, and that I'll appreciate it in the end. It is only when I bike down to Julie's to collect Aran and Cahal that I realise how awful the session was.

'Oh my God, what happened to you? Are you okay?'

Julie asks as I walk through her door. I catch a glimpse of myself in her kitchen mirror. I look like I've been dragged backwards through a jungle. My hair is a mess, my cheeks are bright red, and my clothes are dripping wet.

I explain to her my bike session, and apologise for the muddy puddle I've just left on her kitchen floor.

'Oh, don't worry about that,' Julie says. 'My husband Martin mountain bikes. He is always coming in here caked in dirt, and ready to keel over.'

It is always good when your childminder completely understands and can relate to your weird biking obsession.

Fortunately, my training isn't always as punishing as this uphill bike session in the wind and rain. Living in Rostrevor means I can use the whole of the Mourne Mountains as my personal playground. I revel in running up and down the Mourne Way trail that traces its way through forests and meanders around stunning peaks. I explore the local country roads together with Bike, grinding his gears as I head up the steep slopes towards Spelga Dam.

I even get to join like-minded mountain runners as I compete in the local Turkey Trot on Boxing Day, something I could never do while living far away in Derry. I find the race advertised on the Northern Ireland Mountain Running Association's website. It is billed as the best event to work off the excesses of Christmas dinner. The route crosses two cols between three of the Mournes' highest mountains, Slieve Bearnagh, Meelmore, and Meelbeg. It's a nine-kilometre race with over four hundred metres of climb.

Despite the cold, wintery conditions, and the prospect of snow on the passes, most of the participants turn up in shorts and singlets. I had heard the Northern Ireland mountain runners were a hardy lot, but this is taking the biscuit. But it is only when the race starts that I realise how invincible these northern athletes are. They take off at a gallop, not one of them slowed down by Christmas overindulgence. We cross cascading rivers, clamber up sodden bog, scramble over stones, climb over the towering Mourne Wall twice, then slip down a mist-drenched valley before returning to the start via more rivers, rocks, and bog.

While most of the populace are at home, tucking into leftover turkey sandwiches and watching *Home Alone*, I am out in the mountains running full kilter, freezing my ass off and falling flat on my face in ice-caked mud.

I absolutely love it. Rostrevor is perfect. I think I have finally found my home.

22

Quest

The 2016 adventure-racing calendar is published in late January. I go online to see what events are included this time round. This year's race series is made up of a total of nine events. My five best race results would go towards my final score.

I scroll through the list to see which events would suit me most. Like in 2014, Dingle and Killarney adventure races are both included in this year's line-up. I make a mental note to enter both of these, seeing that I already know and enjoy their routes. I also feel compelled to do Sea to Summit this time, given my envious online encounter with the race while Cahal and I were confined to hospital.

A new company called Quest Ireland has also made it on to the series. They promise new adventures, firstly in the heart of the Wicklow Mountains out of the early medieval village of Glendalough, and then on the remote island of Achill on the western Atlantic-beaten coast of Ireland. Tempted by these destinations and landscapes, I add Quest Achill and Quest Glendalough to my final event wish list.

Quest Glendalough is earmarked to take place in mid-April. It is only January, so there are still three months of

267

hard training to do before I can turn up at the race start. And though three months seem like forever, it is a very short time considering the crude fitness base I am coming from.

Eamonn knows that time is of the essence as we embark on my training plan. He gives me short, sharp sessions day after day to build my strength and stamina. One day he gives me a two-hour bike to do, with twenty one-minute efforts, and a ten-minute run afterwards. The next day, it's seventy minutes of strength and conditioning exercises, followed by an hour's bike. The day after that, it's a ninety-minute run with twelve one-minute efforts.

I do the sessions, tick them off, and then move on to the next one. Granted, I grumble to Eamonn about how hard the training is whenever I get the chance. But when he advises I skip a session if I'm too tired, I'm the first one to take exception, insisting I can complete them all.

Despite how difficult the sessions are, or how much I dread doing them, I know this training is my lifeline. It is the one thing in the day that I have complete control over, an antidote to all the baby mayhem strewn around me at home. And admittedly, without exercise, my temper is shorter and my mood is terrible. Without training, I become a monster mum.

What with Aran becoming an increasingly independent child, I need to be in tip-top form to deal with whatever he throws my way. I need to be firm yet calm when he flings his dinner to the floor. I need to keep my cool when I discover he's scribbled in ballpoint pen all over the white wall. If I've not slept enough, or had an unforeseen break in training, such coolness and calmness can quickly elude me, and I'm the one throwing the temper tantrum.

Though my children can bring out the very worst in

me, I'm surprised sometimes by how they can also drag out the very best. I'm surprised how patient I can be when Aran wants *Fireman Sam* books read to him for the umpteenth time. I'm astonished that I listen to Aran's mispronounced words so carefully, and try to make him feel heard and understood. I'm amazed that I automatically kneel down and hug Aran tightly whenever he is hurt or tearful.

While I'm having my own ups and downs with the children, they seem oblivious to it all. They are too busy forging their own bonds with each other to be concerned by my ongoing parental woes. Cahal is now seven months old, and Aran is two and a half. And though Aran's initial encounter with his newborn brother was one of sheer disdain, he is now starting to realise that Cahal could be a possibly useful playmate.

Cahal can now sit upright on the floor, and enjoys the jumperoo as much as Aran did. However, unlike his older brother, Cahal shows zero interest in crawling. I resurrect Aran's old walker to see if Cahal would appreciate moving around with this alternate mode of transportation. But even when I place him in it, he just sits there and dangles his feet while sucking absentmindedly on his thumb.

Aran seems to understand my dilemma, and decides to help me out. He positions himself behind Cahal and the walker, and gives the two a firm push. The walker, with Cahal in it, trundles across the kitchen floor. Aran runs after it and pushes it again, only harder, as it starts to slowly dawn on him the potential fun this game could have. Soon Aran, Cahal, and the walker are careering around the house, with Aran pulling handbrake turns around corners and scraping long skid marks along the corridor floors. Cahal thinks it's great craic altogether

269

and giggles endlessly, as he sustains repeated whiplash from Aran's erratic turns.

Maybe Aran and Cahal will be good friends after all.

The days pass in a blur as I watch the boys grow up side by side. And before I know it, my own training plan tapers and Quest Glendalough arrives. I soon realise I need to travel with the entire family if I want to compete in the event. Just like with Aran, I am still breastfeeding Cahal who is eight months old by now. And if I travel with Cahal, Pete has to come along as well to mind him while I race. And if Pete and Cahal are with me, there is no leaving Aran behind alone in the house. Everyone has to come along if Mummy wants to compete.

Shifting a whole household for a weekend away is easier said than done. There are more bags to pack and more things to forget. I need to bring double the nappies and double the snacks. There are specific toys that need to be brought if Aran is going to sleep. And then I have to carry all my racing gear, and last but not least, I mustn't forget Bike.

Despite the dreadful logistical tasks, I'm really looking forward to Quest Glendalough. First of all, the course sounds incredible. The route starts off on bikes, with a short and sharp uphill cycle out of Glendalough Valley to the top of Shay Elliot pass. From there, it's a quick six-kilometre hill run to two summits, returning to the transition via mountain forests. Back on to the bikes, the route throws competitors down to the base of neighbouring Glenmalure Valley. From there, you can only emerge again via a steep climb up Slieve Maan to Drumgoff Gap. It's then another hill run, this time a five-kilometre loop up and over the rocky slopes of Croaghmoira Mountain. And then, back on the bikes for the final time, to cycle all the way back to Glendalough Valley.

Despite this long arduous loop, the route is not done with its participants yet. Yet another hill run beckons, this time up through the forest via zigzag trails, providing athletes with spectacular views of Glendalough itself. Far below, its imposing round tower and monastic settlement provide a welcome distraction, but these views are short-lived, as you follow the route back down to the glacial valley's floor, where the upper lake plays host to a short kayak section. You may have wet feet as you disembark from your boat, but there's still a two-kilometre sprint before you finally cross the finish line.

It's a brand-new course on the racing circuit, so it's anyone's guess what the winning time will be. And what with the sheer number of changes from bike to run and back again, no one knows who will cope best with all these transitions.

The entry list is released three days before the race, and I eagerly scan through it to see the competition. I note the names of athletes who performed well last year, but against whom I have yet to compete due to my enforced maternity absence. I don't see Emma Donlon or Fiona Meade on the list, the two women I had epic tussles with in 2014. This means I have no idea how I will fare in this opening race of the season, against unknown competitors on an unknown course. It makes the race an exciting, yet daunting, prospect.

I hit the road with my family entourage early on Friday morning. I need to do the customary registration on Friday afternoon in Glendalough before the race starts bright and early at 8 am the next day. Though the drive is a mere three hours from home, it is not without its issues. Cahal sleeps for part of it, but then wakes up when we are forced to stop at some traffic lights. He is soon upset with his car seat confinement, and objects to it loudly and ferociously. I try to distract him by talking to him, then singing, and finally by tickling his feet and toes. All these strategies fail royally. At last, a bread stick works its magic, and he chomps quietly on it for thirty seconds, before demanding another one, then another.

Aran meanwhile sits quite happily in his own seat, too old to nod off on the journey. But when he sees his brother getting an unending supply of bread sticks, he too wants part of the action. He screams at me to give him his share. My stomach sinks. I've only one left. And Cahal is demanding this last one.

Pete and I endure our two young children's screams all the way to Glendalough. My attempts at entertaining them for the trip's duration are totally exhausting. I have practically no energy left to race. But if I think I am tired now, there is far worse yet to come.

Our roadshow rocks up to the place we are staying for the night. We plan to sleep all in one room, with a bunk bed for the kids. Aran is delirious with the arrangement. He clambers straight up the ladder, and claims the top bunk for himself. Though I'm terrified he will fall out of it at night, I dare not move him less he puts up an almighty fight.

Cahal is too young to sleep in a single bed, however, so we've brought along a travel cot. But, for some reason, Cahal takes fright as soon as I put him inside this netted cage. He grabs hold of its sides and pulls himself up. Then he stands there bawling until I relent and lift him out.

'He's going to have to sleep with us,' I say to Pete apologetically.

'Whatever keeps him quiet,' Pete says with a yawn. He looks wrecked from a week's hard work and from having to drive all the way down to Wicklow today with two screaming kids in the back.

I put Cahal in my arms and lie down with him to get some rest. Cahal falls soundly asleep within minutes, confirming my change in strategy. But his heavy head and motionless body prevent me from getting comfortable. I really can't sleep together with him in my bed. I go to put Cahal back in his cot, but he wakes as soon as he hits the cold, hard mattress. I resign myself to bringing him back into my bed so at least he won't wake the others. Then I spend the rest of the night starring at the ceiling. It is less than ideal race preparation.

'I'm so wrecked,' I say to Pete as I fall out of bed at 6 am.

'Me too,' he says. 'You were wriggling around all night.'

'Sorry,' I say. I suppose I need to apologise to Pete on multiple levels. I'm sorry I disturbed his night's sleep. I'm sorry I've dragged him all the way to Wicklow for the weekend, when he really needed to stay at home and rest. I'm sorry I'm making him look after the kids all morning so that I can go off and race. I wish I wasn't the way I am, and didn't have this restlessness to compete. If only I could be content as a full-time stay-at-home mum, it would make our lives a whole lot easier.

I go down to the kitchen and drink copious amounts of coffee to wake me up for the race. I don't want to start cycling, then drop off to sleep on my bike.

Fortunately, when I do get to the start, I miraculously click into race mode.

Just do your own thing. Get around the course. Collect some points for the series.

Before I know it, we're off.

The first bike section is the remedy I need to shake me awake. The relentless road climb to Shay Elliot is a brutal shock to the system. And aided by all the caffeine I've consumed this morning, I reach the transition in first position.

It remains to be seen, however, how long I can hold on to the lead. I take off on foot, following the winding forest trails to the foot of the first two hills. I'm hoping my mountain running prowess will stand me in good stead as I hop, skip, and jump between the two boggy summits, then back on to Bike in just over half an hour. I power on down the hill towards Drumgoff village, pulling hard on my brakes as the road steepens dangerously. I can't help remembering that, once this race is over, I've still two young children to look after. I can't fall off at high speed and end up in hospital when they need me to return to them still in one piece.

It's on the long drag up to the top of Drumgoff Gap that I'm thankful for all the hard winter training I've done. The section is painful, but definitely not as bad as when I had to do hill reps in the Mourne Mountains in the freezing wind and rain. As I crest the hill, Pete pops up out of nowhere, cheering me on. He is standing by the roadside, holding Cahal in one arm. Aran is balanced on his shoulders clapping for all he's worth.

'I've timed you as three minutes ahead of the next woman,' Pete says. 'Go, Mummy!'

I glance up from Bike to see Aran bouncing up and down manically. How did I manage to end up with such a crazy team of fans?

Much to my surprise, I find myself still in the lead as I arrive at the next transition. The race is, however, taking a massive toll. As I begin this second run section, a marshal asks me to present a piece of mandatory kit before allowing me on to the mountain.

'Where's your rain jacket?' she says.

I look at her vacantly for a split second. Rain jacket. Now where did I put that damn thing? I start to search around in the back of my cycle jersey, and find everything but my coat. Finally, I locate it in a random side pocket. I pull it out proudly and present it to the marshal to gain access to Croghanmoira Mountain.

The mental energy I use finding my jacket means I can't work out how to put it away again. The easiest thing is to wear it, I think. But then, within a minute of donning it, I realise I'm too warm. I pull it off and stuff it away again. In my confusion, I'm losing precious seconds to the second-placed lady who's surely chasing me down.

When I finally complete the five-kilometre mountain run section, I'm about to keel over. I'm still not as fit as I thought I'd be, and I have obviously pushed too hard too early on. And though my body is feeling worse for wear, my mind has completely deserted me.

I arrive back to the transition realising I've no idea where I left Bike. Mislaying my jacket was one thing. Losing Bike is sheer stupidity. I look around for him, then start frantically running up and down the racks as if searching for a lost child. I'm about to confront a marshal and ask them where they've hidden him when, on a far-distance rack, I see Bike's saddle poking up all forlorn.

My heart is pounding as I mount Bike for my final cycle back to Glendalough. The idea of being separated permanently from Bike is too much for me to handle. This distressing thought helps distract me, however, from the cramp that suddenly seizes up my quads. I yelp from the pain, then shift down some gears so I can pedal softly and safely back to Glendalough.

Pete catches up with me in the car and starts shouting out the passenger window the latest update.

'You're six minutes ahead now,' he says. 'Keep going!'

I look up to see Aran and Cahal wedged into their respective car seats. I can't begin to imagine what they're thinking, as they see their daddy conduct a high-speed chase after Mummy across the Wicklow Mountains.

I have run and biked for over three hours but still have not finished the race. The final hill run to the kayak section drags on forever. And though the route description larked on about the stupendous views on this section, all I can see is a bird's-eye view of how far I have to go before I can finally cross the finish line.

I eventually drop down into the valley floor and run towards the kayaks. I grab an unsuspecting man to paddle with me in the double sit-on tops provided. As soon as we hit the water, I'm bowled over by the lake's tranquillity. Though I have visited Glendalough's lakes many times, I have never kayaked on them before. Those who manage them have granted the race organisers special permission to use the waters today. We are a privileged lot.

'Isn't it beautiful?' I say to my impromptu kayak partner, suddenly forgetting about the race.

'Amazing,' he says between heavy breaths, as he paddles frantically to the first buoy.

'Your first adventure race?' I say.

'Yes,' he says. 'You too?'

'Well, it's been a while.'

It's such a beautiful day that I would love to be out on the waters for a while longer. There are no crazy waves or wind to contend with like in Dingle or at Gaelforce

West, just lovely soothing lake waters. Unfortunately, we paddle too quickly and complete the circuit in under ten minutes. I try to jump heroically out of the boat, but end up hobbling to the shore as my cramps re-appear.

'Nice paddling with you!' I shout, as I shuffle off with soggy feet along the final strait. I duck and dive through the mass of tourists that lie between me and the finish. Little did they know they would have to contend with a horde of adventure racers trying to bowl them over on their day's excursion. I narrowly miss taking out a bunch of Germans before finally crossing the line. I'm the first lady home in three hours forty-one minutes, and I take home the maximum number of series points.

Pete and the kids are hanging out at the finish, busy sampling the free food on offer. Aran has already drunk a pint of alcohol-free beer, and is now running up and down a banking like a crazy man. And though Aran is full of beans after his comfortable ten-hour bunk-bed sleep, I collapse on the grass with Cahal, jaded from sleep deprivation and racing.

Though I'm proud to win Quest Glendalough, I don't have much time to bask in this achievement. No sooner am I home, than I'm back to the daily routine of child-minding, training, and house cleaning. It sounds like a terribly boring, monotonous lifestyle, something I would have fled from before having children. But somehow this routine seems to suit Pete, the kids, and I just fine, at least for the foreseeable future.

Six weeks later, I'm in Dingle once more, again with my entire entourage. It's billed as a rematch between Emma and I, Emma the clear victor from 2014. We battle it out from the get-go as soon as we start biking up and over Conor Pass. Dropping the bikes in Cloghane, this time around, I reach the summit of Mount Brandon just ahead of Emma. But I know I can't relax at any moment on this course. And true to form, as soon as I reach the ten-kilometre road run back to Dingle, Pete tells me Emma is closing in.

I pound the tarmac section, too scared to glance back over my shoulder. I just about hold on, reaching the kayaks before Emma. I paddle furiously around Dingle harbour, and then sprint towards the finish. Both Emma and I improve our previous times considerably. And, in the end, I manage to swap my 2014 runner-up spot with the 2016 first place prize.

With two wins out of two, my season is off to a flying start.

Cahal soon follows suit. He is nearly a year old, but still refrains from crawling. He is happy enough sitting on the ground observing everything from afar. But then, one day, Cahal pulls himself up to a standing position and takes not one step, not two steps, but three. The next day, he takes a total of ten steps on his own. The following day, he is walking.

Now the trouble really begins.

23

Family

With two children walking, and one of them talking, my work is really cut out. However, having lived with Aran as a mobile one-year-old, I already know the drill for Cahal. Kitchen cupboards are locked and doors are kept closed. Toilet tissue is taken off the dispenser so it can't be unravelled Andrex-puppy style. Dangerous items like knives and bleach are placed on shelves six foot high. I surprise myself at how efficiently I childproof the house this time around. And, just like Aran, Cahal gets frustrated as I foil every one of his destructive plans.

Friends had warned me how different a second-born child can be, but both Pete and I are surprised how similar Cahal and Aran are in many regards. Cahal has pretty much the same sleeping and feeding patterns as Aran had at this age. By the age of one, they were both walking but not really talking. They like the same toys. They enjoy comparable foods. They rebel over similar things.

If anything, it is Pete and I who are different now. When we only had Aran, we ran to hold him when he tried to walk, and freaked out if he got the slightest bump. Though Cahal has exactly the same behaviours and reactions, we are much more relaxed this time in our approach.

Slowly but surely, over these last three years, Pete and I have learned to become parents. And though we have struggled to adapt to the children's varied and changing behaviours, they are finally starting to knock us into pretty decent shape.

July and August come and go, with Aran and Cahal both celebrating their respective birthdays. And though the summer months promised warm, sunny weather, both the kids come down with nasty winter-like colds. I don't think much of it as I wipe their runny noses and tell them to cover their mouths when they cough. It is only when I end up contracting their illness myself that I realise how serious their condition is.

It is three weeks until my third adventure race of the season, Quest Achill. I am meant to be doing a week of heavy training in preparation. But as soon as I inform Eamonn that I'm coughing up phlegm, he cancels all the sessions, and prescribes Vitamin C and rest instead. He tells me my body can't heal itself properly if it's put under undue stress. And though I'm itching to keep training, I know my priority is getting better. I can't race in three weeks' time if I'm unwell.

Each morning I wake up feeling slightly better, only to later hack up mounds of green phlegm into the sink. I curse the children for making me sick, but they refuse to show me any sympathy. And though I want to go back to bed and try to get rid of this cold, they insist on making me stay awake to feed, clean, and entertain them.

It takes days for the sickly phlegm to subside and to morph into whiter tones. And when Eamonn finally allows me back on my bike, my heart rate is much higher than normal and my legs feel distinctly weak. But I've no choice. I must get back in the saddle and do what I can to be ready for Quest Achill.

At the start of September, Pete, Aran, Cahal and I all journey to Achill Island on Ireland's far western coast. It's pissing down rain as we leave the mainland and drive on to Achill itself. An Atlantic swirl whips up the sea's waves, battering the island's tall cliffs. The weather forecast looks surprisingly mild for tomorrow's race, but anything can happen on this exposed and barren outcrop. The race will be hard enough without having to contend with wind and rain as well.

Fiona Meade is making a late-season appearance at this event. I know it will suit her strengths perfectly, given the course's format. The race starts with a short sprint inland to Keel Lake for a quick kayak on its waters. Fiona is a stronger paddler, so I guess she will be looking to push hard here from the start. Then it's straight on to Keel Beach itself, for a fifteen-kilometre off-road run. This run route starts off on Keel's sweeping sandy shore, before ascending Minaun hill. It's a steep boggy descent back to the beach, to return to the start for the final bike section. This is where Fiona, one of Ireland's most formidable female cyclists, will certainly look to dominate. The bike route circumnavigates the southern part of the island, a forty-five-kilometre loop taking in rural windswept roads teetering above the Atlantic Ocean.

It's a relatively simple kayak, run, bike format, with only two transitions to make. Compared to other adventure-racing courses, it is also fairly short, flat and fast.

My husband Pete, as ever, is looking forward to the race far more than I. He enjoys driving around and pulling over in random places on the course, and watching the contest pan out. He is also convinced Aran and Cahal benefit from watching their mother compete. He thinks it will motivate his children to also take up sport one day.

And if that sport is competitive rugby, then all the better, according to him.

As I line up at the start, I know the only potential advantage I have over Fiona is a turn of flat running speed. I bolt out of the blocks on the starting gun, and try to get ahead of her for the kayak. And though I reach the boats first, I am not surprised when Fiona paddles right past me at the final buoy.

I leap out of the boat and push hard, too hard, on to the beach. I'm just so focused on passing Fiona, which I eventually do, that I run way past my limits. I ignore everything I've ever learned about endurance racing.

I'm breathless as I reach the base of the hill we must now run up. But at least I'm first, and I need to use the mountain run section to get as far ahead of Fiona before she tracks me down on her bike.

I am united with Bike an hour and forty into the race, and rush out of the transition. I see Pete in our car on the roadside, revving up the engine. He waves at me, unable to contain his excitement. He can't wait to watch this race unfurl.

I feel sorry for Bike as soon as I begin. My legs are already shot. I can barely push us both up the hill out of Keel village, having expended too much energy on the run. My legs are also trembling knowing that I am now bait, and that Fiona is starting to hunt me down.

As I round the southern peninsula, Pete drives up beside me.

'Who's that blonde girl behind you?' he asks out of his wound-down window. 'Is she in the race?'

Blonde girl? Fiona has brown hair. Pete is obviously mistaken.

I shake my head, and keep pedalling, annoyed by this

silly error that Pete's bothering me with mid-race.

I get to the bike turnaround point at the top of the island's western cliffs. Pete is already there, waiting with the kids.

'That blonde girl is getting closer,' he says. 'She's four minutes off your pace.'

I look at him and sigh from exasperation. I don't have the time or desire right now to start an argument with my husband.

I bike off, wondering what the hell is going on behind me. I push hard just in case Pete's got his story right for once. But even as I pedal hard, speed still eludes me. I seem to be going backwards.

The next thing I see is Pete zooming up in the car beside me.

'She's catching you!' he shouts. 'You've got to time trail it to the line.'

I'm so confused. What and who is he talking about?

Within a kilometre I find out that Pete wasn't lying after all. A girl with blonde hair, who is definitely not Fiona, sails past me up the last hill. And with her passing, my body gives up. My head sags from the weight of my effort.

I am so consumed by fatigue and confusion that I barely notice Fiona cruising past a minute later. It seems like I'm the least of her worries as she hones in on this mysterious blonde female.

Then out of nowhere, a third girl cycles past.

What? Where? Why? How?

I'm so close to giving up that I contemplate freewheeling up the hill.

This is ridiculous. I've not driven the width of the country just so that I can come home in fourth place. I grab on to this new girl's wheel, and ride with her to within a kilometre of the finish. Then I use every iota of power and pig-headedness within me to push past her with metres to spare.

I cross the line and immediately collapse on the grass. Pete comes running towards me with both boys in his arms.

'That was so exciting!' he says. 'That's the best race I've ever seen!'

I look up at him from the ground, drool hanging from my mouth. Aran jumps out of Pete's hold, and wraps his tiny arms around me. I am unable to return his hug.

'But I didn't win,' I say, when I regain my ability to speak.

'It was amazing though,' Pete explains. 'It's no fun if you lead from start to finish.'

It might not be fun for Pete, but the race scenario he's just described does make my life a lot easier.

I've fought so hard during the race that it takes me a while before I can get back on to my feet. My quads are screaming in so much agony that I have to cling on to Pete to make it back to our car.

At prize-giving that night I discover the amazing blonde girl is called Laura O' Driscoll, an Irish triathlete who has lived in Canada until recently. Her name hadn't featured on the original starting list, so she was an unknown entry to us all. Fiona closed in on her throughout the cycle, but was ultimately unable to bridge the gap Laura opened up on Fiona on the beach run.

I wake up the next morning, barely able to walk. I am totally drained from the race. I feel this way, not because I came third, as I know I was definitely beaten by better girls on the day, but because I left every part of me out on

284

the course yesterday, and now there's nothing left to give.

I shake Pete awake.

'I'm going to bring the kids to the beach,' I say. 'A dip in the sea might do me some good.'

Pete rolls over in bed.

'Great idea,' he mumbles. If it means I babysit the kids while he gets some extra kip, of course he's totally fine with it.

I drive Aran and Cahal to a beach close by, and get them changed into their wetsuits. Large waves roll in from the Atlantic, and both the boys run straight into them at full steam. I dip my own toe in and yelp from the cold. The boys don't mind a bit. They are too busy crashing and splashing into the sea to even notice its temperature.

They are having such fun that I can't help but be distracted from my own woes. The sun is shining, the sea is sparkling, the beach is soft and golden. On yesterday's race, I had forgotten to take a moment to look around me at this beautiful island. Sometimes it is Aran and Cahal who force me to stop and take in the bigger picture.

I return home to Rostrevor with four weeks to prepare for the Killarney Adventure Race. This race has also been re-branded, and now is known as Quest Killarney. It is September, and Aran has started going to a local play-group. And thanks to being surrounded by a new cohort of children at the start of a cool autumn, Aran succumbs to yet another cold. He duly passes it on to me, and to the rest of the family. I moan about being sick yet again and having to take more time off. Most athletes are plagued with injuries that force them to stop training abruptly. And though my joints and muscles have remained remarkably intact for the last three years, it seems like coughs and colds are the recurring injuries I must deal with.

I arrive in Killarney, having finally shaken off the illness. I am also equipped with all the lessons I learned from Quest Achill. So when the race starts, I run at my own pace and try to forget about the other female competitors. Knowing the course also helps a lot, so I know when to push hard and back off. This experience, combined with all the training I've done, allows me to come home in first position.

This means, out of four adventure races, I have three firsts and one third place to my name. I only have to finish a fifth race to regain the National Series title I won two years ago.

Getting to the last race in the series, Westport's Sea to Summit, is always easier said than done. Just before the event, Pete jets off to Papua New Guinea, an island off Australia, for ten days of work. He agrees to fly back to Dublin on Friday morning, the day before the race. The plan is, I am to pick him up from the airport at 7 am, and then we'll drive together cross-country to Westport in time for registration. It is our most ambitious rendezvous undertaking to date.

We are both pleasantly surprised when our crazy arrangement proceeds without major hitch. I arrive at the terminal just as Pete steps off the plane. Even Aran and Cahal are well behaved for the four-hour journey to Westport. I have enough games and breadsticks to keep them entertained for its entirety. Pete is also able to sleep off some of his jet lag in the front passenger seat. It looks like our family are becoming experts at relocating ourselves to remote places for adventure races.

The only thing we've yet to work out is how to make Cahal sleep soundly throughout the night when in a new place. But even this issue is quickly resolved when Cahal wakes up in our room at 3 am. Pete's system is still on Australia time. He gets up, grabs Cahal out of his cot, and heads downstairs to the hotel bar. This allows me to get some sort of pre-race slumber, while Cahal and Pete hang out with the Polish bartender, who supplies Cahal with free cookies and milk. Pete even meets some late-night drinkers originally from my birthplace of Derry. He swaps stories with them from back home while he waits for Cahal to nod off again.

But even with Pete's impromptu night-time babysitting, my pre-race nerves prevent me from settling. I've tried to give myself some realistic goals, like beating the time I did when Aran was four months old. The problem is, I've seen the race line-up, and there's some serious competition. Sea to Summit is one of Fiona Meade's favourites, and she wouldn't miss it for the world. Rachel Nolan, who was third last year, is also entered. Rachel is one of Ireland's best multi-day adventure racers, and is universally known to be tough as nails. Then there are a number of iron-women and triathletes who are testing the adventure-racing waters now that their own season calendars are over. Every athlete has their respective strength, and I'm not sure I stand a chance against them.

'Just finish the race,' I tell myself as I make my way to the starting line. It's cold and still dark on this early November morning. All I want to do is go back to the hotel, and snuggle up in bed with Pete, Aran and Cahal. The only thing that stops me is knowing I've dragged all three of them to Westport, so the least I can do is complete what I've come for.

As expected, the race starts at a furious pace, with everyone throwing down their own gauntlet. Girl after girl streams past me as we sprint towards the greenway for the initial five-kilometre run to our bikes. The lessons of Quest Achill reverberate in my mind.

Go at your own pace. Run your own race.

I have no idea where I'm placed when I reach Bike after seventeen minutes, but I don't have time to stop and work it out. I jump into the saddle, and pedal after a group of guys who are just ahead of me. I catch them as they begin to work together for the eight-kilometre section that leads to the base of Croagh Patrick Mountain.

Suddenly, I hear a dead whirring sound approaching from behind. I can't work out what this ghostly wail is until it pulls alongside. It's a girl, a very fast girl, decked out in a super tight-fitting triathlon suit with the name Aileen printed on the back. The sound I hear is her wheels cutting through the air as she powers at forty kilometres an hour past me. All I can think is, quick, draft her.

I edge into her slipstream, and immediately take advantage of her pull. But even though drafting saves thirty per cent of your energy, I struggle to keep up with her. She is a total bionic machine.

Croagh Patrick arrives quicker than expected, thanks to Aileen, and I drop Bike on my slot on the rack. I then turn and take a deep breath. I know this mountain ascent will hurt.

I pass a race marshal as I start on the stony trail.

'First lady,' he says. 'Well done.'

Now, I definitely didn't expect that. It must have been during the bike section that us female competitors switched up our places. The superwoman triathlete must have dragged me into second, and she is probably still with her bike now, changing into her trail shoes.

While I am doing this mental calculation, I lose this precious first place.

A blonde girl in a triathlete top bounces up the hill past me. I take a second look to see if it's Laura from Quest Achill, but quickly realise it's not her. There must be something about blonde female triathletes from Ireland that makes them all very speedy.

A couple of minutes later, Fiona Meade storms past me. Her biking strength stands her in good stead when power hiking up steep Croagh Patrick. We greet each other between laboured breaths. I now am in third position.

Reaching the top, I know these podium places could easily be swapped on the descent. I soon catch Fiona on the massive boulder section that covers the top third of the mountain.

'Poor Saint Patrick,' I mutter as I rock skid past her. 'How did he get up and down this by himself without the tourist track?'

I get on to the compacted trail section that leads back to our bikes. But as much as I throw myself down this rock-strewn path, I can't seem to close the gap with the blonde girl. Regardless, I continue to weave my way past other athletes who are still climbing up the mountain. I am struggling to find the best line down when suddenly I feel myself airborne. I land with a bang at the feet of a fellow competitor who is making her way to the summit.

'Are you okay?' she says, bending down to lift me up.

I panic.

'No, stop,' I shout. 'Don't touch me!'

The poor girl doesn't know what to do or say as I complete a quick scan of my body. My right knee has landed right on a rock edge and I'm not sure if I'll be able to stand on it. My left elbow is cut and bleeding from skidding along some loose gravel. My left toe hurts like hell. I must have whacked it against a stone and, what with the velocity I was descending, been projected into the air.

'I'm fine,' I say to the athlete standing over me, who has put her own race on hold to help me out.

I try to get up, but stagger with my first step. All I was meant to do was finish this race, and now I'm not even sure that's possible.

I don't know if it's the fact that Fiona's behind that makes me continue on. Or if I just want to prove to the girl, at whose feet I've just fallen, that I'm actually okay. In the end, I know that, if there is anything wrong with me, I have to get off the mountain anyway if I need emergency medical attention.

By the time I reach Bike, my knee has become sufficiently numb to cycle. I run past the ambulance and mount my ride, then start to pedal off towards the Maum hills. It's a long and lonely cycle along narrow, pot-holed roads. Soon enough, Fiona catches up with me.

'Did you fall on the mountain?' she immediately asks.

My left elbow is stinging sharply after its skin was grated off on Croagh Patrick. A large gaping hole in my clothing reveals the damage the fall has done.

'Ah, sure,' I say. ''Tis nothing. Keep her lit.'

Fiona wishes me good luck, then cycles off. I figure that's the last I'll see of her today.

All I need to do now is make it back to Westport intact, and hopefully defend this podium place. I nearly break my chain trying to get up the last steep incline on the bike course, and then work as hard as I can to get back into town.

I reach the quays where we're to drop our bikes before the final five-kilometre run back home. I look around to see Bike's slot, only to catch a glimpse of Fiona dropping her own bike off.

'No, that's not possible,' I think, before realising it's a total stroke of luck.

Before the race, I was dreading competing against Fiona again. She is such an amazing athlete who really pushes the pace. But, what with all the toing and froing between us this time around, I've actually really enjoyed this encounter. And because adventure racing has so many disciplines, with varied courses with each event, you are never too sure who is going to come home with the spoils on any given day. It makes it all the more exciting.

'Well done,' Fiona says to me as I pass her on the run in.

'Well done, *you*!' I say, willing the finish line closer with every step.

In the end, the triathlete Dena Hogan wins Sea to Summit. I am runner-up, and Fiona is third. All three of us have come home under the previous course record. It was quite a battle to finish this year's adventure-racing season.

Completing Sea to Summit has also allowed me to reclaim the Irish National Adventure Race Series title for 2016. There is nothing like setting a goal and achieving it to make the hard work and sacrifice all worthwhile.

As usual, Pete, Aran and Cahal are at the finish line complete with hugs and kisses.

'Didn't Mummy do well?' Pete says to the boys. They both look tired and bored.

'Come on,' I say. 'Let's go home.'

I take Aran by the hand, while Pete carries Cahal high up on his shoulders.

Maybe Pete's right. Maybe I have done well after all.

Acknowledgments

Where would I be without my husband, Pete? If it weren't for him, this book quite simply wouldn't exist. Thanks Pete for all your love, encouragement, support, and patience. You really are the best.

This book would have been an entirely different story if not for the unfaltering support of my coach, Eamonn Tilley. 'Happy days,' as he'd say.

My children wouldn't be in such good health if it hadn't been for the raft of doctors, midwifes, consultants, sonographers, nurses, and health workers that have cared for them both so well. To all of you, my family is totally grateful and forever indebted.

Thanks too to all the women who feature in these pages, women I admire profoundly and from whom I have learned so much. I want to particularly thank Niamh O'Ceallaigh for allowing me to go ahead and write whatever I like; Susie Mitchell for her inspirational words in her own book, *Pregnancy to Podium*; Bridgeen Kavanagh for assuring me that children, training, and breastfeeding can mix; and Julie McGinn for putting up with my crazy kids on a daily basis.

Thanks too to Fiona Meade, Emma Donlon, Laura

O'Driscoll, and all the other girls for our great battles out on the hills. Special word for all my adventure racing buddies, Paul Mahon and Peter Cromie, who have helped and encouraged me in so many ways. Also to Ollie, Noel, and Harold for putting on all these amazing events around our beautiful island.

Big shout out to Nathalie Houben and Cara McLoughlin who told and showed me that having children isn't so bad after all.

Thanks also to Beth McCluskey and Orla Baxter for lending us their lovely homes.

Huge thanks too to all at Sandstone Press, especially my editor Kay Farrell, for spotting this book's potential and for helping me to polish it up for publication. Thanks to Kate O'Mahony, Susie Mitchell, Avril Mahon, and Se Gorman for trawling through my first drafts and giving me loads of constructive feedback. Special mention also to Hilary Jenkinson and Margo Barry: it's amazing what a bottle of red wine in Glenmalure Lodge can lead to!

I want to also thank my own Mum and Dad for being wonderful grandparents, and for always being on call to babysit. Hope you enjoy the read.

Thanks too to the makers of CBeebies and RTE Junior. Without you, I would never have had the peace and quiet required to write this story down.

Finally, I would like to thank you the reader for getting to the end of this work. If you enjoyed it, I would really appreciate it if you spread the word: Tweet about it, post on Facebook, write a review on Amazon, or simply just tell your friends!